A History of Black Baptists

# A HISTORY OF BLACK BAPTISTS

## Leroy Fitts

**BROADMAN PRESS**
Nashville, Tennessee

4265-80
ISBN: 0-8054-6580-4


Dewey Decimal Classification: 286.09
Subject Heading: BLACK BAPTISTS - HISTORY

Library of Congress Catalog Card Number: 84-1851
Printed in the United States of America



**Library of Congress Cataloging in Publication Data**

Fitts, Leroy.
    A history of Black Baptists.

    Bibliography: p.
    Includes index.
    1. Afro-American Baptists—History.   I. Title.
BX6443.F57   1984       286'.173'08996073       84-1851
ISBN 0-8054-6580-4 (pbk. : alk. paper)

To my parents, Mr. and Mrs. Johnnie Fitts,
and my wife, Mrs. Alice L. Fitts,
whose love speaks volumes

# Preface

This book emerges out of my deep conviction that the black Baptist movement has contributed its insights and virtues to the common treasury of American ideas and values. Black Baptist tradition, significantly oral, has engaged itself dynamically and perhaps redemptively in dialogue with other traditions and movements, both religious and secular, in the advance of civilization.

Authentically, the tradition of black Baptists is auspiciously pregnant with wholesome instruction, principles, and precepts for lay church leaders, pastors, teachers, and students of Christian culture. Its many narratives of the lives and deeds of energetic, intelligent, Christian men and women are well calculated to impart useful knowledge, beget lofty aspirations, and direct the life of each serious-minded student of black religious culture to high, manly, womanly achievements.

My hope is that a careful perusal of this book will emit some rays of our black religious tradition and help Christendom to gradually discover how the truths of our respective traditions may be harmonized with that universal, growing truth in which all of us share. I believe that the study of black church history makes it possible for us to appropriate from the past that which is good, true, and holy, discarding the profane, the ugly, and hatefulness of racism and discrimination. Ideally, such a study will take the reader from the terrestrial concerns of civilization to the ethereal halls of faith and true humanity.

I am under deep obligation to many people. My debt to Mrs. Bertha Winston, Mr. Harlow Fullwood, Jr., Mr. Wardell T. Richardson, Rev. Sloan S. Hodges, executive secretary of the Progressive National Baptist Convention, Incorporated, and Dr. William J. Harvey, III, executive secretary of the Foreign Mission Board of the National Baptist Convention, U.S.A., Incorporated, Dr. Bob Boyd, Dr. Ronald Rogers, Dr. Ron Walters, chairman of the History Department of Johns Hopkins University, Mr. S. E. Grinstead, Sr., archivist of the Sunday School Publishing Board, Mrs. Brenda Berkins, director of The Southwest Research Center of Zale Library at Bishop College, Ms. Cynthia Mc Gee, library assistant of the Peabody Collection at Hampton Institute, and many other distinguished scholars and black church leaders is particularly great.

Several persons read the manuscript and made many helpful suggestions for revisions: Dr. Lynn E. May, Jr., executive director-treasurer of the Historical Commission of the Southern Baptist Convention; Dr. Sid Smith, Ethnic Liaison Unit of The Sunday School Board of the Southern Baptist Convention; and Dr. Emmanuel L. McCall, director of Black Church Relations Department of the Home Mission Board. Finally, the love and understanding of my family and my members of the First Baptist Church of Baltimore, Maryland, have made possible the preparation of this manuscript.

# Contents

# Introduction

The dramatic story of black Baptists in America needs to be told afresh in order for our generation and its posterity to understand and appreciate the vitality of such a tradition. Each one of us is born within a certain tradition, which stamps its peculiar seal on our basic drives to participate in the creative moments of our life. Our black Baptist story is a rich deposit of such tradition.

Strangely enough, the story of black Baptists in America has not been told from the standpoint of its tremendous spiritual momentum through the ages of American history. Of inestimable importance is the fact that black Baptists were distinctive and eminent in the development of American Christianity. This book will attempt to document objectively our tradition as a unique trend within that experience. I shall attempt more than an apology of black Baptists, exalting the denomination and praising its leaders; rather, my purpose is to tell the black Baptist story as a part of, though unique, the general history of American Christianity, noting social, economic, and political influences on the development of the tradition.

In chapter 1, I have attempted to relate the creative forces in historic black Baptist religion. It is evident that black Baptists share in the great spiritual heritage of the ages. However, they did not simply absorb the spiritual heritage. On the contrary, a creative momentum was developed to adjust that heritage to the unique psychological, sociological, and political needs of black Americans. Black Baptists appropriated from European and white American Baptist tradition many of the great doctrines of the black Baptist church and its organizational policy.

Chapter 2 deals with the exodus of black Baptists from white churches. The discrepancy between the ideal and actual of white Baptist tradition and practices led several black Baptists to follow the example of Richard Allen and the African Methodist Episcopal Church to withdraw from white churches and establish independent churches. Curiously enough, these churches evolved from plantation missions. This was particularly evident in the rural South. But, alas, out of these plantation missions grew independent churches which subsequently sought to establish cooperative relationships.

Furthermore, chapter 3 deals with the actual development of cooperative relationships among black Baptists particularly in the area of Christian missions. The antebellum period (roughly 1815-1860) was a time of intense missionary activity. We may note in passing that white Baptists sent missionaries to the American West and to foreign lands. By the 1840s, whites had even created what historians call a "Benevolent Empire" of missionary organizations. It is not surprising then that this missionary momentum should take hold in black Baptist churches. Against this background, a detailed account of the missionary enterprise of black Baptists is related to the evolution of associations and conventions.

Against the background of cooperative relationships, chapter 4 focuses on the role of black Baptists in Christian and secular education. Soon after the end of the Civil War, black Baptist leaders progressively experienced and reflected the genial rays of that light which came from Christian and secular education. To be sure, these liberated men and women were anxious to avail themselves to high ideas and ideals of Western civilization. This motivated them to enter journalism in greater numbers and to establish institutions of education with a distinctive philosophy for the education of black Americans.

Chapter 5 surveys the sociopolitical vitality of black Baptist tradition. Contrary to the supposition of some, black Baptists very early inherited, though unintentionally on the part of whites, a tradition of freedom in the development of American democracy. Out of this heritage, they readily developed a social and political momentum in their theology unparalleled in white American Christianity up until the time of Walter Rauschenbusch, the prophet of social Christianity. To discern the moral springs of social and political action in black Baptist churches, one must seek to understand the mystery of how black slave preachers were able to utilize simple biblical stories and Negro spirituals for the progressive liberation of an enslaved and oppressed people. Fundamental to the contemporary civil rights movement was the evolution of black social Christianity from slave preachers to those liberated black preachers of versatile genius and illustrious character—some acclaimed, others unhearalded—who saw clearly the meaning of Jesus in man's social and political life.

Finally, chapter 6 analyzes critically new trends in black Baptist life against the background of the tremendous changes in the religious, social, and political life of America. Special attention is given to the causative factors precipitating the new trends. Black Baptists are challenged to work out a new theology of participation in the evolution of a new ethos in the general southern life and the broader American experience. In the meantime, black theology must reflect the new ethos and provide the frame of reference for black Baptists to affirm new liberties in the American experience. Such theology must be seen, however, as a transitional theology. By transitional black theology is meant the process of doing theology that will allow black and whites Americans opportunities to cross the bridge between racism and an authentic anthropology based on Christian principles. The moral implications of such theology must be worked out in connection with the Moral Majority movement in America. To be sure, black Baptists are challenged to apply the faith experiences of their churches to the moral and spiritual life of the nation.

Following the Bibliography is a section entitled Historical Documents. The interviews in this section will help readers understand some of the significant elements in the religious and sociopolitical framework in which *A History of Black Baptists* developed. To be sure, we have moved beyond the settings described in these documents; however, we must not forget from whence we have come.

# 1
# Creative Forces in Historic Black Baptist Religion

Many of the possessions which we regard as most significant to our experiences come to us as a part of an accumulated inheritance from the past. All Christians share in the great spiritual heritage of the ages. This is especially true of black Baptists in America. We are a people with deep streams of early historic tradition, like a mighty river draining many hills and valleys, containing muddy trends as well as clear waters. Our task is therefore twofold: to promote the flow of the stream and to enhance the purity of waters.

Our black Baptist heritage will be more meaningful for us if we try to explore the riches of our spiritual inheritance from its European background, American slavery, and the great body of white American Baptist history. We must acknowledge our indebtedness to Baptists of European and early American history. Many of our doctrines, church organizations, and polity were borrowed from Baptists of all ages.

At one time, our images of the black religious experience before the Civil War were dominated by special tendencies of the institutions of slavery and the plantation. Currently, we have begun to realize that black Baptists, both slave and free, had a variety of experiences and that they managed, even under the harshest of conditions, to construct a vital cultural, religious, and institutional life. Again, this development has to be traced to the accumulated inheritance of Baptist tradition.

## The European Background

There has been considerable controversy over the origin of Baptists. Church historians of the nineteenth century and some thinkers of the twentieth century have held the theory that the Baptist's origin evolved from the remotest ages of antiquity. Such historians as Mosheim and Milner of the nineteenth century attempted to show that the sentiments of the Baptists were held by the primitive church, and not departed from until the year 253 when Cyprian, an African bishop, decided, "That those whose weak state did not permit them to be washed in water, were yet sufficiently baptized by being sprinkled."[1]

So viewed, church history would tend to suggest that, in every age since Christian origins, there have existed communities of Christians among whom were held most, and by some all, of the peculiar doctrines of the Baptists of today. Such were the Piedmontese, Waldenses, and the disciples of Gundulphus. Each of these "radical" groups shared tendencies of doctrines later identified as Baptist.

Specifically, the Baptists of Holland, France, Switzerland, and England were mainly descendants of the Waldenses. Some historians have held that the Waldenses go back to primitive Christianity. By 1120, their basic doctrines were well developed. The Waldenses maintained: "We acknowledge no sacrament as of divine appointment, but Baptism and the Lord's Supper. We consider these as visible emblems of invisible blessings."[2]

With reference to the primitive antecedents of Baptist polity, the conservative historian Mosheim claimed: "The churches in those early times were entirely independent, none of them subject to any foreign jurisdiction; but each one governed by its own rulers and laws."[3] Hence, the independent congregational polity of Baptist churches has been traced by such historians to some of the practices of the early church movement.

Black church historians, Miles Mark Fisher and E. M. Brawley, have more or less sided with early conservative historians relative to Baptist beginnings. Brawley wrote an article entitled "Contending for the Faith" which evidenced tendencies of support to the theory of Baptist origin in primitive Christianity. Brawley remarked: " 'Contend for the Faith' has been the inspiring battle-cry of Baptists all along the centuries, and with it they have conquered. It should be ours no less; for Christianity is powerless unless aggressive."[4]

Clearly, an apologetic motif underlies the interpretation of Baptist historical tradition on the part of these conservative historians. They tend to believe that Baptist tradition must maintain a certain vitality through linkage with primitive Christianity. They have also been very critical of historians who have a different viewpoint, suggesting that the latter fail to distinguish between the concept of the beginnings of Baptists and the crystallizing of what became the beginnings of the modern Baptist movement about 1643.

The rise of the scientific approach to the interpretation of biblical and other historical data ushered in a new era in church history. Much debate emerged over the nature and methodology of interpretation utilized by historians through the ages. Questions of accuracy and reliability of a wide variety of literature were raised by the more critical historians. Hence, this approach swept the air fresh in hermeneutics, apologetics, and the general interpretation of history. Out of this movement emerged a new school of church historians.

These historians began the tendency to identify Baptists as latecomers along with other early Protestants of the seventeenth century. Robert G. Torbert remarked: "The rootage of Baptists lies in the sect-type of Christianity as over against the church-type with its sacerdotal ministry and institutionalism."[5] The Anabaptists, a sectarian expression of Christianity, paralleled the Protestant Reformation. This movement emphasized believers baptism and the autonomy of each local congregation. So strong was the fervor of their beliefs that they rebaptized former members of the established churches.

Clearly then, in my judgment, Baptist origin must be

traced from the evolution of sectarian expressions of Christianity as expressed in the Protestant Reformation. Specifically, the Anabaptist movement was the antecedent movement of the Baptists. The emergence of the Anabaptist movement went severely against the grain of religious, social, and political opinion in Europe. In England, it posed a tremendous threat to the Church of England; and, in continental Europe, the Anabaptist movement was bitterly resisted by the established religious tradition and political authorities. Indeed, all of Europe was to be plunged into tremendous battles over the significance of Anabaptist opinion. The whole way of life of the Europeans was challenged by this new radical movement. The result was a severe era of persecution. Many Christians of Anabaptist persuasion were forced to leave Europe in search of a more congenial climate for their movement.

## The Genesis of Baptists in North America

When we recollect that most of the early emigrants to New England came from their fatherland in search of "freedom to Worship God," we are not surprised to hear Cotton Mather saying, "Many of the first settlers in Massachusetts were Baptists, and as holy and watchful and fruitful and heavenly a people as perhaps any in the world."[6] Specifically, Baptists of America trace their primary roots to the work of Roger Williams, the first who pleaded for liberty of conscience in America and who became the pioneer of religious liberty for the New World. The rise of Baptists in America has a strong claim to the status of indigenous denomination.

The tremendous influence of Roger Williams in the birth of Baptists in America is a matter of great significance to the subsequent development of the sociopolitical thought among black Baptists. Governor Hopkins once remarked: "Roger Williams justly claims the honor of having been the first legislator in the world, in its latter ages, that fully and effectively provided for and established a full, free and absolute liberty of conscience."[7] Having been a Puritan minister, Roger Williams was driven from England by those persecutions of opinion which, like the confusion of languages at Babel, drove men asunder and peopled the earth. When he arrived in Massachusetts, Williams proclaimed that the only business of the human legislator is with the actions of man as they affect his fellowman; but, as for the thoughts of his mind and the acts or omissions of his life as in respect to religious worship, the only lawgiver is God; and the only human tribunal is a man's own conscience.

Roger Williams's sociopolitical concepts of church and state relationships led to tremendous encounters with the principle leaders of the Massachusetts colony. He was exiled by the court because of opposition to church membership right of suffrage, all laws compelling attendance at church, and all taxed for the support of worship.

While exiled from Massachusetts colony, Roger Williams was able to lead a movement for the founding of Rhode Island colony. He obtained a charter from the king and stood in the high estimation of the civilized world. He ruled the colony on basic biblical principles. These principles of Williams were soon adopted by Ezekiel Holliman who applied them particularly to church life. In 1639, Ezekiel Holliman baptized Roger Williams, the first American to be baptized by immersion on a profession of faith, who then administered the same rite to Holliman and ten others.

At this time, Roger Williams became officially identified with the Baptist denomination. (He did not maintain this relationship and later became a Seeker.) The little group of newly baptized believers styled themselves Baptists and organized the first Baptist church on the continent of North America.

Subsequently, emigrants from England who were Baptists planted themselves in New England, Virginia, and in most of the principle towns of the colonies. Therefore, a number of Baptist churches were founded in the seventeenth century. The first Baptist church in New York was founded in 1762; but from 1669, Baptist worship and an irregular church arrangement had been maintained in that city. The revolutionary war led to an accelerated expansion of Baptist churches through the travels of many faithful soldiers.

## Baptists and Slavery

One great paradox of American religious history is the accommodation to slavery on the part of Baptists. The paradox stands out with brilliance when we remember the great humanitarian concerns of Roger Williams and other early Baptist leaders. How could a group so exposed to persecution in Europe support the oppression of black men and women from Africa? How could a people who supported the freedom of conscience issues fail to recognize the evils of an institution styled to enslave both body and conscience of a people? These are some of the agitating questions of consideration in Baptist history.

Initially, white Baptist involvement in the evangelization of slaves was minimal. There were scattered instances of black Baptists holding membership in white churches. As early as 1772, Robert Steven and eighteen other black Baptists held membership in the First Baptist Church of Providence, Rhode Island. By 1772, the First Baptist Church of Boston was receiving black Baptists in its membership. However, the southward advance of Baptists encountered attitudes which discouraged work among slaves. Here, as in other parts of the Baptist advance into new regions, the question of slavery began to trouble Baptist churches. In 1798, the Mill's Creek Church sent to the Kentucky Baptist

Association the query: "Has a black slave a right to a seat in the Association?" The prompt answer sent back was, "Yes, provided he be sent as a messenger from a church."[8] The decision of the Kentucky Baptist Association was not readily received by several local churches. In 1795, the Lick Creek Church split over the slavery question. Similarly, "A disaffection existing in the Rolling Fork Church, on the account of slavery, the whole church except three withdrew from the association."[9]

The initial decades following the American Revolution was a time of spiritual stresses and unremitting social tensions relative to the slavery question. In many cases, those black Baptists who had been admitted to the membership of white churches were limited in their privileges and responsibilities. An obvious allusion to this tendency was reflected in an 1802 report of the Dover Baptist Association in Virginia. Here it was said that some churches admitted to their church meetings all male members whether slave or free. Nevertheless, the report reflected a movement against this tendency.

> By experience this plan was found vastly inconvenient. The degraded state of the minds of the slaves, rendered them totally incompetent to the task of judging correctly respecting the business of the church, and in many churches there were a majority of slaves; in consequence of which great confusion often arose. The circular letter argued and advised, that although all members were entitled to the privilege, yet that none but free male members should exercise any authority in the Church. The Association after some debate, sanctioned the plan by a large majority.[10]

This action made unmistakenly clear that the slavery question was sufficient to cause many white Baptists in America to set aside basic principles of the denomination to accommodate slavery.

With a poignant sense of the extremity of their circumstance, some whites turned to violence as a means of restricting the freedom of black Baptists. In 1809, a Baptist church in Williamsburg, Virginia, principally composed, if not altogether of blacks, experienced some violence within its membership. Reverend Moses, a black preacher, was often whipped for holding meetings in connection with the church's ministry. One historian pointed out that "the Association had advised that no person of color should be allowed to preach, on the pain of excommunication; against this regulation many of the blacks were rebellious and continued to hold meetings."[11] Similar considerations give full warrant to the conclusion that slavery subjected white Baptists to great emotional stress especially in the South relative to the treatment of black Baptists. By the nineteenth century, white Baptists found themselves increasingly on the defensive, increasingly compelled to improvise, as the code by which their fathers had justified the holding of slaves became less and less intelligible. Accordingly, this sense of frustration was reflected in the treatment of whites toward Baptist slaves.

Strangely enough, the westward expansion of Baptists seems to reflect a diminishing emotional stress over the slavery issue. Active work for the black population was under way in Saint Louis, Missouri, as early as 1818; and in 1822 a separate church was organized for black Baptists, but still under the supervision of white Baptist leaders. Rev. J. M. Peck, an early Baptist missionary and pioneer, was for several years the white representative who regularly visited and gave guidance to this church. The same church was instrumental in helping several slaves to obtain their freedom. Rev. John Berry Meacham, "a free man of color" who had attained his freedom by industry, was their pastor. Meacham's father, a Baptist preacher and slave in Virginia, was purchased by the church.[12] Hence, the westward expansion was motivated by a missionary spirit manifesting itself in caring for "the regions beyond."

Of course, the general influence of the westward expansion was not sufficient to continue a diminishing tendency of emotional stress over the issue of slavery. But, in 1829, the issue of slavery gained new potency in the strides of white Baptists. This was the beginning of a trend destined to continue into the Civil War period.

Beginning with the New England Society in 1832, antislavery societies grew rapidly and soon demanded an attitudinal change on the part of the churches toward the challenge of slavery. The Rhode Island Anti-Slavery Convention at Providence in February 1836 claimed "that the people have a right to expect of the ministers of Christ that they will cheerfully engage in the work of abolition, and to call upon them to proclaim the truth on this subject, as those who are bound to declare the counsel of God."[13] They held, unreservedly, that "so far as moral means are concerned the system of American slavery is now sustained chiefly through the influence of the pulpit."[14]

To be sure, the southern clergy reacted sharply to this new offensive of antislavery Baptists. They readily developed a defense of slavery both in argumentation and in prevention of unfavorable action by the national religious bodies. A small number of northern conservative clergymen joined them in the defense of slavery from the Bible, holding it not a sin since the New Testament recognized its existence and did not forbid it to be practiced by Christians.[15] Rev. Richard Furman, a conservative Baptist and slaveholder, defended the right of holding slaves as "clearly established in the Holy Scriptures both by precept and example."[16]

Accordingly, the slavery controversy had become an explosive issue among Baptists in America. As expected, the controversy soon took on sectional characteristics, slaveholding versus nonslaveholding states. The Baptist Association of Hancock, Maine, adopted a report in 1836 declaring that in their opinion "of all the systems of iniquity that ever cursed the world, the slave system is the most abominable," and that the only remedy is immediate emancipation.[17] The next year the same association resolved, "That, we as the professed followers of Jesus Christ, have no fellowship or communion with those who under the character of Christians continue to hold their fellow-men in bondage."[18] Generally, the antislavery men, though not all abolitionists, followed a similar trend in speaking against the institution of slavery. On the other hand, the Savannah River Baptist Association considered the conduct of the abolitionists "considerable and meddlesome," and requested their state convention to instruct their delegates to the Triennial Convention of 1841 to demand of the northern brethren whether "they can acknowledge these fanatics as their co-workers," and to "inform them of the impossibility of further cooperation by the Georgia Baptists unless the Abolitionists are dismissed."[19]

The sharp sectional strife over the issue of slavery was the seed of the eventual separation between northern and southern Baptists prior to the Civil War. However, there were several attempts to preserve the union of the American Baptists. There were moderate white Baptists who sought to preserve the union by preventing any discussions of slavery in national meetings of Baptists. Among the most noted of the Baptists who opposed both slavery and agitation about slavery was Francis Wayland. In a letter to William Lloyd Garrison in 1831, he explained why he did not desire to have *The Liberator* sent to him. He believed slavery to be wicked and destructive of best interests of both master and slave; but immediate emancipation was neither wise nor just.[20] By 1845, his views had become progressively more radical. In a letter to Richard Fuller, a conservative Southern Baptist, Wayland argued:

> Jesus Christ has taught us that the hungry, the thirsty, the naked, the sick, the prisoner, the stranger, are his representatives on Earth, and that our love to him is to be measured by the universal sympathy which we extend to every form of human distress; and he adds, "Inasmuch as ye did it not to one of the least of these my brethren, ye did it not to me." The special representatives of Christ in this country seems to me to be the oppressed, and I fear I must add the frequently lacerated, Christian slave. How shall we stand before the Savior, if we make no effort to comfort and deliver this slave—much less if we count ourselves among the number of his oppressors?[21]

Rev. Francis Wayland further dismissed any sociopolitical arguments held by proslavery Baptists. He asserted: "But it will be said, the abolition of slavery will ruin the Southern States. Should it be so, as you have well remarked, if it be wrong, it ought to be abandoned."[22] Hence, certain Northern Baptists held that religious and political grounds favored the cessation of slavery.

The initial sign of the crisis, in the national body of the white Baptists, came when the Charleston Baptist Association called on associations and churches to consider the necessity of the formation of a Southern Board of Foreign Missions since their appeals to stop discussion on slavery had been disregarded at the Triennial Convention, and the Abolitionists seemed by no means disposed to change their course.

When the General Convention assembled in Baltimore in 1841, conditions looked unfavorable for a continuation of the peaceful union of Baptists, North and South. However, tremendous attempts were again made to preserve the union of Baptists in America.

In a secret caucus, consisting of Northern conservatives and Southerners, a compromise was worked out to minimize the influence of abolitionist Baptists in the convention. Many believed that slavery was a subject with which the convention had no right to interfere. Nevertheless, the abolitionist Baptists were not defeated at the convention in Baltimore, and antislavery sentiment grew. The best minds among Baptists in America were engaged to struggle against slavery. Also, the antislavery Baptists created a literature to give a deathblow to the peculiar institution.

In 1844, the issue of slavery became so controversial that the unity of Baptists was hopelessly impaired. The question of whether a slaveholding Baptist could be appointed for missionary service was raised by the Alabama Baptist State Convention. The Baptist Board of Home Missions answered on December 17, 1844, saying that in thirty years in which the Board had existed, no slaveholder had applied for appointment. "If however anyone should offer himself as a missionary having slaves, and should insist on retaining them as his property we could not appoint him."[23] This position was the virtual end of the unity. American Baptists, North and South, deemed it expedient to work in separate missionary organizations both at home and abroad. Hence, in 1845, Baptists from the South organized a new movement called "The Southern Baptist Convention"; and in 1846, the Northern Baptists reorganized their mission society under the title "Baptist Missionary Union."

## The Evolution of Plantation Missions

Long before the clash between white Baptists over the issue of slavery, there were some black Baptist leaders who gradually became aware of the need of separate churches from whites. Such were the originators of plantation missions led by black preachers. It may be said, with reasonable certainty, that the evolution of plantation missions began as independent slave plantation owners were very reluctant to permit an evangelistic program with the utilization of black Baptist preachers. However, there were some exceptions to the general order of things on certain plantations.

For instance, there was one good example of a more liberal attitude, despite legal codes restricting congregations of blacks and the ministry of black preachers, on the part of a plantation owner in North Carolina. In that state, the first black preacher to receive permission to evangelize his race was "Uncle Harry Cowan," as he was known at that time. He was the servant of Thomas L. Cowan. His master being present at a funeral was so struck with his gift to preach God's Word that he granted him "privilege papers" to preach anywhere on his four plantations. His papers were prepared by a lawyer. Rev. Harry Cowan, the slave preacher, was extremely successful in the evangelization of black slaves on this plantation. Therefore, his owner, Thomas L. Cowan, soon extended Rev. Harry Cowan preaching privileges to other nearby plantations wherever he was promised protection. During the struggles of the Civil War, Rev. Harry Cowan was the body servant of General Joseph Johnson and preached every night when General Stonewall Jackson fell in battle.

There were many other black preachers who labored for God on plantations for the evangelization of slaves. Many of their names have been lost to historical research. Long before the organization of black churches and associations, these black plantation preachers labored ardently for the conversion of their race. Generally, black slaves were not permitted to have their own churches, pastors, and preachers. It was the common practice throughout the slave territory to permit them to attend preaching services in the white churches at the time designated under conditions prescribed by their masters. Nevertheless, the spirit of Christianity motivated black preachers to encourage the slaves to grow in grace and knowledge of Jesus Christ. Consequently, these blacks often stole off to the woods, canebrakes, and remote cabins to have preaching and prayer meetings of their own. To be sure, these movements were the antecedents to organized black Baptist churches.

It can be argued that the secret or underground prayer meetings served as the only forum wherein the slaves could vent their true religious feelings. The early sunrise prayer meeting was one in which blacks spent their happiest moments, no white person being present to molest, restrict, or make them afraid. It was an unusual coincidence that gave rise to these prayer meetings. The patrols would be on duty all night to see that no black persons walked or assembled with others without the written consent from their master. Early in the mornings the patrol would retire from duty and sleep during the day. Therefore, on Sunday mornings the black people would gather at the church and other places of worship and have these early prayer meetings, in their own way, while their mistresses and masters and the ever-dreaded patrols were asleep.

It is not surprising that pioneer black preachers continued similar methods for the evangelization of the race for several decades. To mention one example, for more than forty years such a preacher called "Uncle Jack" went from plantation to plantation in Virginia to preach to whites and blacks. It is not surprising that the rapid spread of such evangelistic methods soon led to the organization of independent black Baptist churches.

On some plantations, the laws restricting the open evangelistic strides of black preachers were gradually ignored by generous or kindhearted masters. The pulpit vitality of certain black preachers or "exhorters" was so potent that white Baptist churches were no longer able to contain them. Hence, the emergence of independent black Baptist churches gradually appeared on the scene of American Christianity. The roots of black Baptist beginnings in South Carolina, Georgia, Canada, Africa, and the West Indies may be traced to an organized effort as early as the 1780s.

The pioneer black missionary and preacher who led indirectly to the establishment of independent black churches was Rev. George Liele. He preached powerfully on the plantations of South Carolina and Georgia. Many black slaves were converted by the preaching of this great pioneer. Among the two most prominent were David George and Andrew Bryan. These men established the earliest independent mission churches among black Baptists in America.

We may note in passing that historians have not agreed on the place of the first independent black Baptist church in America. Some have cited the First Colored Baptist Church, Savannah, Georgia, as the oldest black Baptist church. On the contrary, a few historians like M. M. Fisher have advanced the theory that the Silver Bluff Baptist Church, Aiken County, South Carolina, was the first such church.

For a necessary starting point, let us survey Baptist beginnings in Georgia. The First Colored Baptist Church, Savannah, Georgia, perhaps the oldest black Baptist church in America, was organized January 20, 1788, by Andrew Bryan along with a few slaves to whom he had preached the gospel. Bryan was the slave of Jonathan Bryan, esq., who indulged him to preach on his plantation. After a short while, Jonathan Bryan permitted Andrew Bryan along with a few other black Baptists to erect a rough building on his land at Yamacraw in the suburbs of Savannah, Georgia. This was designated as a house of worship for the little congregation inspired by Andrew Bryan.

It is not surprising, however, that Bryan's little mission or church encountered many interruptions from whites who opposed the idea of an independent black religious congre-

The First Colored Baptist Church, Savannah, Georgia, erected in 1794.

gation. Beyond a shadow of a doubt, however, this was a limited congregation in its independence. Nevertheless, there were certain whites in Savannah who held to the custom of not allowing the assembly of black people without the presence of a white person. Hence, many of the early members of this church were taken before magistrates, imprisoned, and whipped.

In every instance, the congregation was united in willingness to endure persecution for the continuation of the plantation church. Sampson Bryan, who was converted about a year after his brother Andrew Bryan, was very supportive of Andrew and the congregation during this intense period of persecution. Both Bryan brothers were twice severely whipped because of their persistence in the evolution of an independent black Baptist church movement. About fifty of the members were also severely whipped by outside white agitators.

With few exceptions, members of Bryan's entire congregation were persecuted for their faith and practices. Rev. James M. Simms has left us a succinct account of their sufferings.

> Frequent, then, became the whipping of individual members by patrol on the plea of not having proper tickets-of-leave, which finally culminated in the arrest and punishment of a large part of the members, all of whom were severly whipped; but Rev. Andrew Bryan, their pastor, and his brother, Sampson Bryan, one of the first deacons, were inhumanly cut, and their backs were so lacerated that their blood ran down to the earth, as they, with uplifted hands, cried unto the Lord; and this first negro Baptist pastor, while under this torture, declared to his persecutors that he rejoiced not only to be whipped, but will freely suffer death for the cause of Jesus Christ.[24]

Subsequently, the majority of the congregation were ac-

cused of plotting insurrection and placed in prison. Their
meetinghouse was also taken from them sometime about
1790.

Fortunately, Jonathan Bryan, the master of Andrew
and Sampson, interceded for these persecuted black Baptists
fully believing that they were martyrs to prejudice and
wickedness. They were examined by the justices of the
Inferior Court of Chatham County who found them inno-
cent and released them.[25] Chief Justice Henry Osbourne
also gave them liberty to continue their worship any time
between sunrising and sunset. Bryan informed the chief
justice that he would give them the liberty of his own house
or his barn at a place called Brampton to serve as a meetinghouse, not to be interrupted by anybody.

After about two years of worship at Brampton, Rev.
Thomas Burton, an elderly Baptist preacher, and Rev. Abraham Marshall visited this little slave church and gave them
two certificates. The first certificate constituted this little
plantation mission an official Christian church and read as
follows:

> This is to certify that upon examination into the experi-
> ences and characters of a number of the Ethiopians at and
> adjacent to Savannah, it appears that God has brought them
> out of Darkness into the light of the Gospel, and given them
> fellowship one with the other; believing that it is the will of
> Christ, we have constituted them a Church of Jesus Christ,
> to keep his worship and ordinances. January 19, 1788.
>
> A. MARSHALL, V. D. M.[26]

The second certificate gave Andrew Bryan the authority to do the work of a gospel minister including the right
to administer the ordinances of a Baptist church and read as
follows:

This is to certify that the Ethiopian Church of Jesus Christ at Savannah, have called their beloved brother Andrew Bryan to the work of the ministry. We have examined into his qualifications, and believing it to be the will of the great head of the Church, we have appointed him to preach the Gospel, and administer the ordinances as God, in his providence may call. January 20, 1788.

A. MARSHALL, V.D. M. [27]

These certificates gave to this plantation mission a new status and vitality. Strangely enough, an unprecedented degree of freedom was granted America's first slave pastor and congregation. Later, we shall see a drastic change in this policy throughout the nation, in general, and the South, in particular.

It will be remembered that Bryan's church became a member of the old Georgia Association in 1790 and so continued as the only black Baptist church in that body for several years. Later, the association was split into the Upper District Georgia Baptist Association and the Lower District Georgia Baptist Association. The black Baptists remained with the association of white churches in their particular district.

We may note in passing that Andrew Bryan purchased his freedom, bought a lot in Yamacraw, and later built a residence near the original Sampson mission. After another brief period of struggle, the First Colored Baptist Church of Savannah, Georgia, was well established and grew rapidly.

By 1800, the membership of First Colored Baptist Church numbered eight hundred. Such growth was too rapid to be accomodated in the church edifice. Hence, the First Church concluded, in consultation with the Georgia Baptist Association, to organize new churches from its overflow membership. On December 26, 1802, the Second African Baptist Church was organized near Savannah.

Not only does the year 1800 reflect a new development in church growth in Georgia, but it also reflects a growing freedom on the part of Andrew Bryan. The growing freedom of his ministry was related to Dr. Rippon in one of the letters addressed in the year of 1800.

> We enjoy the rights of conscience to a valuable extent, worshipping in our families, and preaching three times every Lord's Day, baptizing frequently from ten to twenty at a time in the Savannah, and administering the sacred supper, not only without molestation, but in the presence, and with the approbation and encouragement of many of the white people.[28]

As mentioned earlier, the black Baptists of South Carolina have also a claim to the distinction of being the first independent black Baptist movement. Dr. Miles Mark Fisher has advanced the primacy of South Carolina's black Baptists. He believed that the Silver Bluff Baptist Church, Aiken County, South Carolina, was the first plantation church in America for Baptist slaves.[29]

We observed earlier also that the Silver Bluff Baptist Church was organized by a convert of Rev. George Liele named David George. Initially, eight slaves were converted by George Liele, and David George was subsequently given the responsibility to manage and preach in this mission. This was about the year 1778. Strangely enough, these new converts later traveled to the Georgia plantation mission to worship.

Nevertheless, some of these slaves probably maintained an independent mission in South Carolina. Records show that the Silver Bluff Church lived again in Edgefield County after the revolutionary war. It was officially constituted in 1781 with Rev. Jesse Peters as its first pastor.

Accordingly, tradition in South Carolina has maintained that the Silver Bluff Mission had a continued existence at Strombrance and Seven Springs. Later, the Seven Springs Church was located on a still branch of the Savannah River, called the Dead River.

In the light of the foregoing, we may readily understand why there is some discrepancy among historians relative to the establishment of the first plantation mission for black Baptists. The oldest tradition, however, seems to substantiate the primacy of the Georgia plantation movement.

# 2

# The Exodus of
# Black Baptists

There were two principal factors which led ultimately to the exodus of black Baptists from white churches. One was the segregational and discriminatory policy of most white Baptists. The other may be expressed as the new theological awakening among black Baptist preachers. Each of these factors was pregnant with broader implications than most white Baptists realized.

It is not surprising that the very nature of the Baptist denomination made black Baptists gravely concerned over the faith and practice of white Baptists and led to a desired separation. Primary among Baptist beliefs were the church as a regenerate membership, baptism by immersion, the authority of the Scriptures with the New Testament as a guide of faith and practice, the autonomy of the local church, the separation of church and state, and the equality of believers.

To be sure, many white Baptists never sought to apply most of these basic principles to their black membership. In fact, such principles were at variance to the "peculiar institution" of slavery. Even in the North there were no significant challenges to slavery until the rise of the great abolitionist movement. Yet, the failure to apply basic Baptist principles led to the fertilization of the ovum for the birth of an independent or separate church movement among black Baptists. White churches across the country were pregnant with this new being long before they became aware of it. The birth of an independent or separate black Baptist movement was unthinkable to the vast majority of the slave masters. Strangely enough, even nonslave owners largely shared this view.

It follows from previous discussion that the embryonic stage in the development of independent black Baptist churches may be defined as plantation missions on the one hand and the restless Baptist slaves in the balconies of white churches on the other. So, alas, growing numbers of slave

43

preachers became increasingly aware of the fact that white Christian movements were forcing certain disabilities in the form of dehumanization upon the Christian slave population. They discovered in the "Fatherhood of God and brotherhood of man" a new anthropological concept of human freedom and dignity. Little did white masters realize that these slave preachers were discovering such an orientation to life from the simple Bible stories of the Old Testament.

The new awakening among slave preachers, a gradual process, led them to see their fellow slaves differently. They became closer to the slave community. Slave preachers were aware of the fact that they shared the "peculiar institution" in common with other sons and daughters of Africa. So, in a real sense, the common experiences that they shared in white churches formed the basis of a new unity, an in-group feeling in the balconies, a sense of belonging to a group distinct from the dominant group of Baptists.

From these strong psychological and spiritual motivations were early black Baptists anxious to be delivered— both slave and free blacks. Separate churches could not have been born during slavery if nobody had become dissatisfied with their religious experiences in white churches. The nature of this dissatisfaction may be seen in the necessary response of a Christian conscience to its own enslavement. Central to any independent movement is the prior emergence of free thought.

## Separate Black Baptist Churches of the Antebellum Period

Within a decade after the establishment of black Baptist churches in Georgia and South Carolina, slaves and free Baptists in other parts of the country began similar movements away from white churches and the establishment of their own churches. Virginia Baptists were next to gain momentum in the separate church movement. Here, they developed three types of black Baptist churches which became a pattern throughout the rest of the country: the mixed church, the separate church under white leadership, and the separate church under the leadership of black Baptist preachers. It should be remembered, however, that this same pattern persisted among other denominations; and all three types existed simultaneously, but the gradual tendency was toward the separate, all-black church.

In Virginia both the Gilfield and the Harrison churches claim priority. Miles Mark Fisher cites the year 1774 as the organizational year for these two Petersburg churches. He affirms that the Gilfield Church was the first church of black Baptists in Petersburg to continue the organization of free blacks and of race conscious slaves who had been connected with neighboring churches before 1760.[1] On the contrary, Dr. Carter G. Woodson, our most reputable historian of the black Church, differs with Fisher relative to the organizational date for the Harrison Street Baptist Church, citing 1776 as the correct date.[2]

The first black Baptist church in Williamsburg, Virginia, was organized in 1776. Four years later, the First Baptist Church of Richmond, Virginia, was organized in 1780 just one year after the removal of the capitol of Virginia from the city of Williamsburg to Richmond.[3] Initially, First Baptist Church constituted a mixed membership. It did not become an all-black Baptist church until 1841. That year 1,708 black members remained in the old location on Broad Street while the white members, numbering 387, moved to a new location.[4] Today, this church has the distinction of being the first to organize a black Baptist missionary society —the Richmond African Baptist Missionary Society—organized in 1815 by Rev. Lott Carey and Collin Teague. In 1846, two other black Baptist churches were organized in the City of Richmond—the First African Baptist Church and the Second African Baptist Church.

The story of the advancement of black Baptist churches moves from Virginia to Massachusetts where we find the organization of the Joy Baptist Church, originally called the African Meeting House of Boston which was constituted in 1805. On December 4, 1806, Rev. Thomas Paul was official-ly installed as pastor of the church, an association destined to endure for a full quarter century. From this humble be-ginning, the Baptists of Massachusetts spread throughout the state.

In 1808, the black Baptists of New York organized their first Baptist church. The Abyssinian Baptist Church of New York City was organized by a group of traders who came to the city from the country of Abyssinia, better known today as Ethiopia. According to tradition, these "Abyssinians" attended the First Baptist Church of New York where they were promptly ushered into the slave loft. They resented this expression of American church life and walked out in protest along with Rev. Thomas Paul, a liberal white preacher from Harvard University.

Adamant in purpose, the small group of protesters pooled their resources and in June 1808 bought property on Worth Street on which they established the Abyssinian Baptist Church. The organization of this church followed the style of other separate Baptist churches. That is, it was initially led by white ministers. Another point deserving consideration is the fact that Abyssinian Baptist Church was the first Baptist church in the entire North to establish a nonsegregated membership.

From the beginning, Abyssinian attracted people from all over New York. Many traveled by boats from nearby Brooklyn and northern New Jersey. The membership there-fore grew rapidly. It may be said that Abyssinian grew with the city of New York to be one of the greatest gathering of peoples in the world.

To be sure, the dramatic story of New York's mother church for black Baptists must be understood in the light of their advancement throughout the region. The leadership of Abyssinian observed with growing concern the large influx of members from Brooklyn, then separated from New York City by water without bridges, and decided to urge these blacks from nearby Brooklyn to organize their own church. Hence, the Abyssinian Baptist Church sent Rev. Samson White to organize a Baptist work in Brooklyn. The result was the organization of the Concord Baptist Church on May 18, 1847. This new church became the second independent black Baptist church to be organized in New York during the antebellum period.

One year after the founding of Abyssinian Baptist Church of New York, the black Baptists of Pennsylvania organized their first independent church. It should be noted that the independent black church movement began in Philadelphia with the organization of Bethel A.M.E. Church. So the Baptists of Pennsylvania had a good precedent for an independent movement. Just so, the First African Baptist Church of Philadelphia was organized on June 19, 1809.

The pioneer roots of the First African Baptist Church of Philadelphia go back to the eastern shore of Virginia and to Savannah, Georgia. During the closing years of the eighteenth century, a few black people migrated to Philadelphia from Virginia to escape the cruel treatment of slave masters. Soon after their arrival, some of them united with the white First Baptist Church of Philadelphia. Subsequently, about thirteen black Baptists decided to organize an independent church and were granted letters of dismission upon their own request "for the purpose of establishing a Church of the same faith and order," under the care and protection of the white First Baptist Church.[5] Beyond Virginia, the pioneer roots extended to Savannah, Georgia, where Rev. Henry Cunningham was being prepared for a fruitful ministry in a distant city. He became the first pastor of First African Baptist Church.

In passing, a brief resumé of Rev. Henry Cunningham may reflect some light on how the independent church movement advanced during the antebellum period. Nothing is known of Cunningham's early years. In 1802, he appeared in church records as a deacon of the First African Baptist Church of Savannah. Later, he requested a letter from this church to join the white Savannah Baptist Church due to a problem in the independent black Baptist church in Savannah. He became the pastor of this new church in Savannah with a membership consisting mostly of "intelligent domestic servants and some mechanics."[6] After a brief pastorate in Georgia, Rev. Henry Cunningham was influenced by Rev. Henry Holcombe to come to Philadelphia and accept the pastorate of the First African Baptist Church in the city.

In harmony with the foregoing, we may contend that white Baptists played a significant role in the organization of most separate black Baptist churches. The style and faith of these separate churches tended to reflect the white churches from which the founders left. Yet, we must also maintain that these black Baptists adopted their style of religion to their own unique psychological and sociological needs.

Again, with certain patterns now well established, the independent or separate black Baptist church movement extended southward to Louisiana. The extension of Baptist faith and practice to this region was connected with the great frontier movement of the Protestant church. During the colonial period, the primary religious work in this area was carried on by the Roman Catholic Church. However, with the coming of Joseph Willis (1762-1864), a free black

from South Carolina, a new religious dimension was introduced to the territory of Louisiana prior to its political ties
with the United States. Willis initially migrated to Mississippi with other migrants in 1798. From the southwestern
part of that territory Joseph Willis went forth as an apostle
to the Opelousa Indians in the year of 1804. The territory
of this Indian nation was Louisiana at Bayou Chicot.

Interestingly enough, the planting of the first black
Baptist church in Louisiana took place just one year after
the great debate over Louisiana's stride for statehood. When
Jefferson purchased Louisiana, in the interests of the slaveholding states and the West, his critics from the North
forsaw the day when Westerners would rule the nation and
New Englanders would have no influence in Washington.
So strong had been the opposition to Louisiana that when
the territory applied for statehood Josiah Quincy declared:
"It is my deliberate opinion that, if this bill passes, the
bonds of this Union are virtually dissolved, that the states
are free from their moral obligations, and it will be the right
of all . . . to prepare for a separation, amicable if they can,
violently if they must."[7] Hence, Rev. Joseph Willis successfully planted a separate black Baptist church in Louisiana at
a time when the first idea of secession was ever debated in
the United States Congress. From this time onward, political
issues effected, positively at times and negatively at others,
the exodus of black Baptists from white churches.

About the same time of Rev. Joseph Willis's work in
the territory of Louisiana, the black Baptists of New Jersey
commenced their stride to establish a separate movement in
that state. In 1812, they organized the First African Baptist
Church at Trenton. The same year another separate church
was organized at Salem, New Jersey.

The early planting of a separate church movement
among the black Baptists of New Jersey has been called into
question by a significant historian. James A. Pawley asserts

that "The first Negro Churches in New Jersey were organized at Trenton and at Salem in 1812." Another tradition,
according to Pawley, "claims that the first Negro Baptist
Church in New Jersey was organized in Burlington, under
the influence of the early Dutch, it is exceedingly difficult
to establish these beliefs on historical facts."[8]

Nevertheless, the black Baptists of New Jersey still
favor the early 1812 date for the emergence of the separate
church movement in the state. The movement progressed
slowly until the mid 1850s. In 1856, the black Baptists of
Camden, New Jersey, organized the Kaighn Avenue Baptist
Church at the home of Mrs. Marry Colding, then living at
736 Chestnut Street. The church began initially as a house
prayer-meeting movement under the leadership of Rev.
Sampson White. In 1857, the first public services of this
church were held in a blacksmith shop at Sixth and Kaighn
Avenues. From this date, the separate movement gained
momentum in the state of New Jersey.

Southward again, the black Baptists of Kentucky began
organizing churches at an early date. The first black Baptist
to preach in Kentucky was a slave of Lewis Craig, formerly
from Spotsylvania County, Virginia, named "Brother Captain" or "Old Captain."[9] He had been dispatched by Craig
in 1780 to raise a crop in Kentucky for his master. The
Indians destroyed the crop, and Brother Captain returned to
Virginia. He later returned to Kentucky and settled at Lexington. Here, Captain began to exhort or preach the gospel
to blacks in his own rude cabin and in the houses of other
blacks from about 1790-1797. Prior to his ordination,
Brother Captain baptized several converts who, in 1801,
erected a rude structure for worship on Maxwell Street,
Lexington, Kentucky. From this humble beginning the African Baptist Church of Lexington (1790) and the first black
church west of the Alleghenies took definite form. However, the separate movement did not really gain significance

in Kentucky until about 1829 when the followers of Brother Captain became known as Pleasant Green Church while the African Baptist Church remained in its original location with Rev. Loudon Ferril serving as pastor.

Northward into Ohio, the black Baptists of that region established their first church in 1822, named the Middlerun Baptist Church of Xenia, Ohio. The leadership of this church were the first missionary minded blacks of the westward movement. Reverends Godfrey Brown and F. S. Brown ordained Rev. Wallace Shelton of Cincinnati, Ohio, and sent him forth as a missionary to other areas of Ohio. Other antebellum churches in Ohio include: First Baptist Church of Chillicothe, organized in 1824; Baker Street Baptist Church of Cincinnati, organized in 1831; Second Baptist Church of Columbus, organized in 1835; Zion Baptist Church of Xenia, organized in 1839; Bush Creek Baptist Church in Brown County, organized in 1839; and Providence Baptist Church of Berlin Cross Road. The latter church played a significant role in the early abolitionist movement in Ohio.

To be sure, the black Baptists of Ohio were among the most progressive Baptists of the antebellum period. Not only did they begin the first missionary movement of the Northwestern United States, but they organized in 1834 the first Black Baptist Association in the United States, namely, the Providence Baptist Association. Hence, the separate church movement of Ohio experienced a rapid expansion.

In 1825, the separate church movement began in Saint Louis, Missouri. Northern American Baptists played a key role in black Baptist beginnings in Missouri. As early as 1818, Rev. John M. Peck, missionary of the Massachusetts Society to Saint Louis, baptized a black man who later served in Peck's "Negro Sabbath School" for the black communicants of the white First Baptist Church, organized in 1818.[10] In 1822, Rev. John M. Peck assisted the black Baptists in forming a branch of the white Baptist Church of Saint Louis. By 1825, this little movement had separated from the white church and constituted the First African Baptist Church of Saint Louis. That year, Rev. John Berry Meachum, a free black, was ordained to become the first pastor of the separate church.

About a decade later, the black Baptists of Maryland established their separate church movement in 1834. As early as 1818, an attempt was made to begin separating black Baptists from white churches but failed. J. F. Weishampel, Jr., an early historian on Maryland Baptist beginnings noted:

> In 1818, a colored Baptist preacher, whose name is forgotten but whose labors are remembered, came to Baltimore, and preached about a year to a few Baptists in a private house on Potter Street, near Fayette. But it does not appear that any Church was organized. There were a few Colored Baptists to be found, and occasionally a meeting was held in some private house, but the race was then in slavery, and both laws and public opinion were unfavorable to their separate organization. A number, however, were members of the First (white) Church.[11]

It was, however, not until the early 1830s that significant developments took place to pave the way for the establishment of a separate movement among black Baptists in Maryland.

Curiously enough, Deacon William Crane, a white leather merchant and member of First Baptist Church of Richmond, Virginia, led the way for the establishment of a separate church movement in Maryland. Before moving from Richmond to Baltimore in 1834, Crane organized in 1815 a school for blacks in the First African Baptist Church of Richmond where a slave named Moses C. Clayton attended. Soon after Crane arrived in Baltimore, he became quite concerned over the neglect of the white Baptists of Maryland to cultivate a serious missionary cause among the black population. He frequently confronted the white Baptists about this neglect. With determination to alter the situation, William Crane communicated with Moses C. Clayton, formerly a slave, but at that time he was a free black residing in Norfolk, Virginia. He succeeded in persuading Clayton to move to Baltimore and work among his race. Sometime in 1834, Moses C. Clayton arrived in Baltimore with a burning desire to establish a significant ministry among Baltimore's black Baptists. Initially, Crane aided Clayton in obtaining an old schoolhouse on the corner of Young and Thompson streets, owned by A. Stirling, to be used free of rent for a Sunday School.

Rev. Moses C. Clayton took on his new responsibilities with energy of purpose and strength of resolve. He worked as a carpenter during the week and on Sundays taught and preached in the newly organized Sunday School. A certain historian has forcibly remarked:

> Clayton had learned to read and write, could speak with some fluency, and began teaching and preaching at once. . . . He began a school with three children, two of them his own, and gradually gathered a few others. He often preached to an audience comprising his wife and two or three others, and strange as it may seem, spoke with as much ardor and enthusiasm as if he were addressing a thousand people.[12]

On February 20, 1836, Clayton's Sunday School was organized into a separate black Baptist church. His piety and earnestness had attracted some eight or ten persons to become founders of the new church. The formal organization of the First Colored Baptist Church of Baltimore took place with the assistance of the following American Baptist ministers: Rev. John Healy, of Second Baptist Church; Rev.

Rev. Moses C. Clayton, a slave preacher
from Norfolk, Virginia, was the founder of
the First Colored Peoples Baptist Church in
Baltimore in 1836.

S. P. Hill, of the First Baptist Church; and Rev. G. F. Adams of the Calvert Street Baptist Church. At first, this initial separate church movement progressed slowly.

One year later, Rev. Moses C. Clayton was able to obtain legal status for his separate church as an incorporated body. In 1841, the First Colored Baptist Church, a Maryland Corporation, joined the Maryland Baptist Union Association. At that time, the association began to supplement Clayton's salary as a missionary among blacks in Baltimore. Later in 1841, he led the congregation to begin an effort to build a small edifice on Lewis Street. The challenge of this building program was so strenuous that Rev. Clayton resigned the pastorate in 1849.

In 1849, Rev. John Carey succeeded Rev. Clayton in the pastorate of First Colored Baptist Church. Rev. John Carey had previously been employed by the American Baptist Home Missionary Society as a missionary in Maryland and Virginia. Soon after accepting the new pastorate, Rev. John Carey discovered that he had inherited an economic storm. The support of the Maryland Baptist Union Association had decreased, and the church was impoverished. The economic stress and upheavals within the church soon forced Rev. Carey to resign in 1852, resulting in the recall of Rev. Moses C. Clayton to the pastorate. Rev. Clayton retained this position until his death in 1861.

The next separate black Baptist church in Maryland was established again through the cooperative strides of the Maryland Baptist Union Association and Deacon William Crane. In the early 1840s, Crane and other leaders of the association again looked to Virginia for another black preacher to establish an additional church in Baltimore. This time, the hand of Providence was organizing events in the life of Noah Davis (a slave) to take on the new challenge. Noah Davis was born in Madison County, Virginia, March, 1804, to Mr. John Davis and Mrs. Jane Davis. The Davis family belonged to Robert Patten, a wealthy merchant, who lived in Fredericksburg, Virginia. Shortly after 1840, Noah Davis was able to purchase his freedom along with some other members of his family. In 1847, he responded to the call of the Maryland Baptist Union Association to come to Baltimore as a missionary.

Upon Noah Davis's arrival in Baltimore, Deacon William Crane and other officials of the association rented a room up a flight of stairs for Rev. Noah Davis, who had previously been ordained, to establish the Second Colored People's Baptist Church, Courtland Street, Baltimore, Maryland. After several years of persistent labor, the church began showing some signs of growth resulting in the erection of a larger and more commodious chapel in 1855 on the corner of Saratoga and Calvert Streets. Hence, the name of the Church was changed to the Saratoga Street African Baptist Church. By 1827, Rev. Noah Davis was able to report a membership of seventy-one to the Maryland Baptist Union Association. Unfortunately, however, this new church movement did not last very long. It experienced some serious economic difficulties and eventually went out of existence as a separate church for Maryland's black Baptists.

In 1852, the turmoil in the First Colored Baptist Church, as mentioned earlier, led to the founding of the third independent church movement in Baltimore. Rev. John Carey resigned the pastorate and along with a small nucleus of members from First Colored Baptist Church formed another church, the Union Baptist Church of Baltimore. Initially, Union Baptist Church met for worship in a small building on Lewis Street, near Mullikin Street. This property was attained as the result of a court litigation with the First Colored Baptist Church. In 1854, Rev. John Carey resigned the pastorate of Union Baptist Church.

Rev. Chancey Leonard succeeded Rev. John Carey as

pastor of Union Baptist Church in 1856. By this time, the church was well on its way to becoming one of the leading separate church movements in the state of Maryland.

In the deep South, the separate church movement began in Mobile, Alabama, as early as 1836. Mobile had the reputation of being the most liberal city toward blacks in the state. Hence, the first black Baptist church in the state was the Stone Street Baptist Church of Mobile. Prior to the Civil War, the congregation was led by Rev. J. B. Hawthorne. The progress of this church was substantial until an internal problem developed which led to a split within the congregation. This split led subsequently to the birth of another church, Saint Louis Street Baptist Church of Mobile. Significantly enough, the new church enjoyed the reputation of being more missionary minded than the "mother church." The missionary spirit of Saint Louis Street Baptist Church inspired several other antebellum preachers to participate in the Baptist witness in the State.[13]

There were several other antebellum black Baptist preachers in other parts of Alabama. Rev. Caesar Blackwell, a slave preacher, labored with a white Baptist preacher named Rev. James McLemore in Montgomery, Alabama. His rare ability as a preacher was recognized by the Alabama Baptist Association. This association purchased the freedom of Rev. Caesar Blackwell for the sum of $625 and ordained him to participate in preaching tours. He was able to gain the favor of many whites in Central Alabama and opened the way for the ministries of two other pioneer black Baptist preachers, Rev. Nathan Ashby and Rev. Jacob Belser.

In Tuscaloosa and Jefferson counties, Rev. Job Davis labored to spread the black Baptist witness in Alabama. In 1806, he was brought from Africa to Charleston, South Carolina. Soon, Davis was converted and licensed to preach in 1818. Subsequently, he moved to Alabama in 1822 and preached in the state for several years. Rev. Job Davis was ordained by the Rock Creek Baptist Church (white) in Tuscaloosa County. He was referred to an "an acceptable preacher, a man of deep thought, sound judgement, and was well skilled in the scriptures."[14]

Black Baptist work in Alabama grew slowly until the end of the Civil War. There were only one or two other separate black Baptist churches in the State. One was the First Colored Baptist Church of Selma, Alabama. Again, most of the separate work centered in Mobile. Nevertheless, a significant number of black Baptists worshiped in white churches with their masters. The "integrated" Baptist churches were in the vast majority of the organized witness of Baptists in Alabama.

The separate church movement in Mississippi began very early. A sizable number of slaves worshiped in separate churches with the written permission of their masters or overseers. Many of these were actually plantation missions. State laws prohibited black preachers from serving these "churches," and white preachers served them by appointment.[15] Subsequently, other state laws were passed which abridged the privilege to worship on the part of these slaves. The Pearl River Baptist Association (white) along with two other associations petitioned the state legislature to repeal "such part of said law as deprives our African churches of their religious privileges."[16]

In 1829, the white Baptists of Mississippi began to provide accommodations in their own churches for black Baptists. The old Salem church took the lead by constructing a "shed to her meeting house" separated from the auditorium of the whites by a tall partition.[17] Furthermore, the white Baptist associations entreated their member churches to take notice of any improper treatment of their members toward slaves, and to "deal with them (the overbearing masters) in brotherly love, according to the rules of the gospel."[18]

The influx of black Baptists into white churches result-ed in a decline in the initial momentum for separate church-es in Mississippi. Black Baptists often outnumbered whites in many churches of the state. For example, in 1846, the Natchez Church had a total membership of 442, only 62 of whom were whites; the Clear Creek Church at Washington had 154, with only 15 whites; and Grand Bluff near Port Gibson numbered 113, of whom only 8 were whites.[19] Hence, Mississippi was largely characterized by a tendency toward "integrated" churches until the emancipation of black slaves in the United States.

Similarly, the black Baptists of Tennessee made some attempts at an independent or separate church movement. Initially, they too worshiped largely in white Baptist churches. Seemingly, they were less inclined to follow the course of many blacks in other parts of the nation. Most of the state's black Baptists worshiped in "bush arbors," while others worshiped in white churches, either as members or holding "after services."[20]

In 1843, the black Baptists of Tennessee were able to organize a separate church in Middle Tennessee at Co-lumbia, the Mount Lebanon Baptist Church. Subsequently, those of West Tennessee organized the Beale Street Baptist Church at Memphis. Prior to the Civil War, the latter church was led by Rev. Morris Henderson and Rev. Scott Key. In 1846, a separate mission grew out of the First Baptist Church of Nashville. The mission conducted its work large-ly as an established church, subject to approval of the white mother church. It was not until 1865 that this mission was organized into the First Colored Baptist Church of Nash-ville. These churches were the earliest attempts at separate churches in the state. Again, the Civil War marked the turning point in Baptist relations in the state which resulted in the growth of separate churches based on race.

The westward expansion of black Baptists of the late antebellum and early years of freedom continued through the ministries of Rev. Zachariah Bassett and his two sons in Indiana. They were natives of Greene County, North Carolina. In 1844, the family moved from North Carolina and settled in a Quaker settlement in Park County, Indiana. It was here that Rev. Zachariah Bassett first began to preach in the West, having organized a little church out of the persons who followed him from North Carolina.

Rev. Miles Bassett, the eldest son, was ordained in 1865 to preach in Indiana. He served the Second Baptist Church of Shelbyville for nine years, and the congregation grew rapidly under Bassett's administration. Subsequently, Rev. Miles Bassett became pastor of the Second Baptist Church of Rising Sun, Indiana; and at the same time by unanimous consent of this church, he supplied alternately the churches of Carrollton, Kentucky, and Madison, Indiana. He later became the founder of the Eastern Indiana Baptist Association.

The youngest Bassett son, Rev. Richard Bassett, was ordained at New Albany, August 1867, and served the pastorate of the Shiloh Baptist Church of Rising Sun, Indiana. Subsequently, he was called to the pastorate of the Corinthian Baptist Church of Indianapolis.[21]

## Slave Rebellions and the Separate Church Movement

During the last decades of the antebellum period, the separate church movement among black Baptists was seriously hindered especially in the slaveholding states. One primary hindrance to the separate church movement was white political reaction to the unrest of slaves. During the decade of the 1830s, there was considerable slave unrest,

resulting in sporadic conspiracies and uprisings. Their exposure to the presence of free blacks and the changing levels
of consciousness within separate churches were significant
factors in the unrest of slaves.

In 1831, the general slave unrest exploded in a critical
rebellion in Virginia. That year, Rev. Nat Turner, "a slave
and a Baptist exhorter," organized and executed a rebellion
of far-reaching magnitude.[22] Inflamed by a new level of
awareness relative to the black man's plight in slavery and
in the light of biblical anthropology, Rev. Nat Turner gathered a band of followers in Southampton County, Virginia,
one summer night and fell upon the sleeping white community and massacred sixty-one persons. The white community initially responded violently by killing more than a
hundred blacks. Southerners everywhere felt a kindred terror of a potential enemy presence in their midst.

After the initial violent reaction of whites abated, most
political leaders throughout slaveholding states sought
ways and means to prevent future slave rebellions. One
strategy was to revise the slave codes so as to make them
more severe and in particular to prohibit blacks from
preaching or assembling for religious or any other purposes
unless white men were present. Beginning in 1832, slave
codes in Virginia provided that a free black or mulatto,
ordained or otherwise, was prohibited from preaching, ex-
horting, or conducting any meeting for religious or any
other purposes in the day or night. This provision was
merged in an Act of 1848, which provided further that any
assemblage of slaves, free blacks, or mulattos in the daytime
for religious worship conducted by a slave, free black,
mulatto, or such assemblage in the daytime for the purpose
of instruction in reading or writing, or such assemblage at
night for any purpose, constituted an unlawful assembly.[23]
This was a serious blow to the separate church movement
particularly under the leadership of black Baptist preachers.

The law required that all separate church movements must be led by white ministers. Black preachers were legally silenced in Virginia. This state of affairs continued until the Civil War.

Similarly, other slaveholding states passed codes to silence black preachers, in response to Rev. Nat Turner's slave rebellion. In 1831, almost immediately after the rebellion, blacks were banned from preaching in North Carolina. This accounts for a meager separate church movement in the state during the antebellum period. Likewise, the Maryland State Legislature followed North Carolina in passing stringent codes against blacks. The fine for an imported free black for remaining in the state after ten days was fifty dollars a week—half to the informer—on conviction before a justice, and sale in default. For harboring or employing the black, the fine was raised to twenty dollars a day after the expiration of four days—half to the informer—to be recovered before a justice, with the right to appeal to the court. And any black who might leave Maryland and remain away over thirty days would be deemed a nonresident and liable to the law, unless before leaving he should deposit with the county clerk a written statement of his plans or, on returning, could prove by certificate that he had been detained by sickness or force. In 1839, the regulation was enacted that no free black belonging in any other state could enter Maryland, except servants with their master, under penalty of twenty dollars for the first offense to be given as a reward to the "taker-up" and of five hundred dollars for a second offense. In default of payment to these fines and costs, the blacks would be sold as slaves to the highest bidder, whether a resident of Maryland or not.[24]

To be sure, most of the white churches were not in complete agreement to such regulations as they felt religion made slaves better men, hence better workers and more loyal rather than potential enemies. The white Baptists generally ignored Maryland's codes and imported Reverends Moses C. Clayton and Noah Davis to organize separate church movements in the state. There is no record of any attempt to stop these men from preaching in Maryland. Similarly, the Charleston Baptist Association passed a resolution in 1835 which provided:

> Resolved, that as Christians we feel a responsibility in regard to the religious instruction of this class of people [referring to Negroes]; that we hereby affectionately call upon the churches in this connection to use every consistent method, in accordance with the laws of the land, to give them the knowledge of salvation [through oral teaching, since it was unlawful to teach them to read] through Jesus Christ, and that in the discharge of their whole duties with respect to them, our brethren be urged to act, not as taunted and insulted by fanatics, but as ever remembering that they also have a master in Heaven.
>
> We moreover urge on the members of our state legislature, not to curtail or restrict the religious privileges of these people, except in cases where necessity, either as to some existing abuse or obvious danger.[25]

In harmony with the association's position, Rev. Richard Furman, a white Baptist pastor in Charleston, had previously delivered an address in 1823 to protest the laws restricting religious instruction for slaves. He argued that such instruction could not endanger the institution because the Bible supported the institution of slavery. This was perhaps the first apology for slavery given by a Baptist minister.[26] Curiously enough, even the proslavery church leaders favored generally the separate church movement among black Baptists. This was due to the rapidly developing ideology of racial segregation based on biblical hermeneutics, southern style. Nevertheless, the political climate in the slaveholding states still exerted a tremendous force of restraint on the separate church movement prior to the Civil War.

## The Rise and Growth of Cooperative Movements

At one time, our images of the black religious experience before the Civil War were dominated by slavery and the plantation. We have now begun to realize that blacks, both slave and free, had a variety of experiences and that they managed, even under the harshest of conditions, to construct a vital cultural, religious, and institutional life. Under slavery, black preachers were able to preach, although sometimes hindered, a unique gospel interpretation of the black experience and to organize separate churches. After emancipation, free blacks of the North and South were able to accelerate the organization of churches and develop a cooperative movement among the churches.

The roots of the cooperative movement among black Baptists go back into the antebellum period. In the early 1830s, the organizational consciousness of black Baptists gained momentum. A mixture of a missionary motif with a general desire for racial progress fostered a new development in the evolution of the black denominations. Such spirit led to the rapid organization and proliferation of cooperative programs across America. Distinguished black Baptist preachers found it necessary that their churches should affiliate and cooperate for the edification of all and the general spread of the gospel throughout the world. Consequently, general missionary societies and associations were soon organized.

The earliest associational movement developed out of the independent church movement of the Ohio black Baptists. Reminiscences of the early history of the Baptists of this state will show how a mixture of a missionary motif with a general desire for racial progress gave birth to the first

associations among black Baptists. To begin with, the evolution of cooperative movements among Ohio's black Baptists encountered great opposition. Blacks were not initially
welcomed in Ohio, and what few were there already were
Christians and holding membership in white churches.
Nevertheless, pioneer black preachers were able to begin a
cooperative movement among the churches and, subsequently, organize church associations.

In 1834, the Providence Baptist Association was organized at the Providence Baptist Church of Berlin Cross
Roads, Ohio. This was the first such association to be organized by black Baptists in America. The association was
named after the church in which it was organized. Among
the organizers of the Providence Baptist Association were:
Reverends William Bryant, Jonathan Cradic, T. W. Frye,
Benjamin Sales, Jeremiah Walker, Lewis Wright, J. B.
Steptoe, P. H. Williams, and Kendall Carter. These were the
pioneers of the associational movement among black Baptists. Not only did they concern themselves with the organization of an association for missionary and educational
purposes, but also the Providence, the Middlerun, and the
Union Anti-slavery Baptist associations thus merging a
missionary motif with the sociopolitical development of the
race.

The Union Anti-slavery Baptist Association was organized in 1843. Initially, it was composed of about 13 churches, having a total membership of about 1,000. By 1872, the
association had 68 churches with a membership of about
4,567.[27]

In 1856, a movement emerged with the design to divide
the Union Anti-slavery Baptist Association. However, it
was not until 1872 at a meeting held in Xenia, Ohio, that the
actual division was consumated, the dividing line being the
Little Miami Railroad from Cincinnati to Columbus and
from the locale to Cleveland by air line. All west of this line

was to constitute the Western Union Anti-slavery Baptist
Association, and all east was the Eastern Union Anti-slavery Baptist Association. The Eastern Union Anti-slavery
Baptist Association was organized by electing Rev. James
Poindexter, moderator; J. T. Ward, clerk; O. P. Wright, treasurer; and Rev. B. Harper, missionary. They decided to hold
their first annual meeting in Washington Court House on
Wednesday before the fourth Sunday in August, 1873.
Similarly, the Western Union Anti-slavery Baptist Association was organized by electing Rev. Wallace Shelton, moderator; Rev. J. M. Meek, clerk; and Samuel Troy, treasurer.
This group decided to meet at Yellow Springs, Ohio, Thursday before the first Sunday in September, 1873.[28]

At the time of the initial division of the original Union
Anti-slavery Baptist Association, an agreement was made
by the leadership of the new associations that every four
years a union meeting should be held. In 1878, the first
union meeting was held in Columbus, Ohio. The delegates
of this union meeting laid the groundwork for the subsequent organization of the Ohio Baptist State Convention in
1896.

Following the leadership of Ohio's black Baptists, the
black Baptists of Illinois organized in 1838 the Wood River
Baptist Association of Illinois. By this time, the associational movement gained new momentum. In 1865, the Baptists of Louisiana organized their first association, followed
in rapid succession by other states.

Against the background of the associational movement, black Baptist leaders soon sought even wider cooperative movements among their churches. They saw the
need for a unified program of cooperation even among the
various associations. Hence, the development of cooperative programs among associations led to the organization of
state conventions. The black Baptists of North Carolina
were the first to bring the vision of cooperative associational

programs to fruition with the organization of the General Baptist State Convention in 1866. Other states followed such as Alabama in 1866, Virginia in 1867, Arkansas in 1868, and Kentucky in 1869.

By the early 1870s, the organization of state conventions was well on the way. The black Baptists of Georgia organized in 1871 the Missionary Baptist Convention of Georgia at Central Baptist Church, Augusta, Georgia. Eighty-six delegates were present and Rev. Frank Quarles of Atlanta was elected president.[29] At this time, these associations and state conventions grew in sagacity. Some of the cooperative bodies adopted resolutions which provided for the spiritual and intellectual development of young men aspiring to the gospel ministry. Local pastors and churches were encouraged to pay more attention to these young preachers.

As early as 1840, the black Baptists of America sought to develop a cooperative movement beyond state lines. They were anxious to unite as many Baptists as possible to struggle for the advancement of the race and the spread of God's kingdom. Hence, The American Baptist Missionary Convention was organized in 1840. Black Baptists who lived in New England and the middle Atlantic states met at the Abyssianian Baptist Church of New York to organize this pioneer regional convention. Rev. John Livingston served as the moderator of the initial organizational meeting. A constitution was drawn up to reflect the nature and purpose of the new convention.

Unwittingly, the new convention met with stress very early in its existence. Many of the pastors and local churches became concerned over the apparent attempt of the convention's leaders to make missionaries out of too many pastors. To be sure, the foreign mission motif was the dominant reason for the organization of the American Baptist Missionary Convention. Hence, some of the most ambitious pastors in the convention resisted what they believed to be an over emphasis on missions, charging the leadership with "demoting the elders."[30]

To be sure, there were other factors, sociological in nature, which hindered the rapid growth of the American Baptist Missionary Convention. A prevailing agitation in the mind of whites was the antislavery proclivities of the convention's leading ministers. Hence, some of these ministers were prescribed in many instances. Nevertheless, the heroic among them still struggled courageously to advance the program of the American Baptist Missionary Convention.

The spirit of cooperative movements beyond state lines soon spread westward. In 1864, the black Baptists of the West and South met in Saint Louis, Missouri, to organize a cooperative movement to serve their regional needs. That year, they organized the Northwestern Baptist Convention and the Southern Baptist Convention. These two conventions continued in operation from 1864 to 1866. During those two years, the latter convention spread with unprecedented rapidity.

In 1866, the Northwestern Baptist Convention and the Southern Baptist Convention met in a special session with the American Baptist Convention. The meeting was held in Richmond, Virginia. At this meeting, the three conventions united to form the Consolidated American Baptist Convention. Subsequently, the new convention met annually in the following places: in 1867, Nashville, Tennessee; in 1868, Savannah, Georgia; in 1869, Paducah, Kentucky; in 1870, Wilmington, North Carolina; and in 1871, Brooklyn, New York.

The first president of the Consolidated American Baptist Convention was Rev. William Troy of Richmond, Virginia. Other officers included Rev. R. L. Perry of Brooklyn, New York, corresponding secretary; Rev. William T. Dixon of Brooklyn, recording secretary; and, Rev. Samuel Harris, also of Brooklyn, New York, treasurer.

In 1866, Rev. Edmund Kelley, a noted evangelist and church organizer in Tennessee, gave a detailed account of the organizational genesis of the Consolidated American Baptist Convention. He published an article in *The National Baptist,* September 13, 1866, which detailed the nature, object, and structure of the convention. Several interesting points were reflected in the article. First, the Consolidated American Baptist Convention was an attempt to unite and discourage sectionalism among the black Baptists. The Baptist leadership readily recognized the danger inherent in sectionalism of destroying the national spirit of a cooperative movement among black Baptist churches. Hence, these leaders structured a convention designed to unite black Baptists from Maine to the Gulf of Mexico. Second, the organizers of the Consolidated American Baptist Convention provided for the practical operation of four district auxiliary conventions, state conventions, and associations. However, these groups were to function as vital parts of the whole, the focal point of all work being the Consolidated American Baptist Convention.[31]

The original motion to organize district associations was offered by Rev. William Troy in 1867. At that time, Rev. William Troy was pastor of the Second Baptist Church in Richmond, Virginia. The motion prevailed, but its execution was delayed. It was not until 1872 that the motion gained attention within the report of the Executive Board of the convention explaining:

> That our work may be more efficient, and more thoroughly done, your Board would respectfully recommend a division of the Southern States into district, with local district secretaries.
> 1. South-Eastern District

That there be a South-Eastern District, embracing Maryland, the District of Columbia, Virginia, and North Carolina. That Rev. Henry Williams be the Secretary of this District, and paid a salary, such as he and Board may fix.

2. Southern District

That there be a Southern District, embracing South Carolina, Georgia, Florida, Alabama, Mississippi, and Louisiana, and that Elder J. F. Boulden, or Elder J. L. Simpson, be the Secretary thereof, under a salary of $800, without a pastorate, or such salary as may be agreed upon, with a pastorate charge.

3. South-Western District

That there be a South-Western District, embracing Missouri, Kansas, Arkansas, and Texas, with a Secretary to be nominated by the Convention, and confirmed with salary by the Board.

4. Middle District

That there be a Middle District, embracing Tennessee and Kentucky, with a salaried Secretary.[32]

Apparently, the convention desired a more detailed study of the proposal for the district auxiliary conventions. The report was referred to a special committee chaired by J. H. Magee. A glance at the report of this committee reflects a broader program for the district auxiliary conventions. The committee recommended:

1. Southern District—Embracing Maryland, the District of Columbia, Virginia, West Virginia, and North Carolina, with board and secretary at Richmond, Va.

2. Southern District—Embracing South Carolina, Georgia, Florida, Alabama, Mississippi, and Louisiana, with local board and district secretary at Savannah, Ga.

3. Southwestern District—Embracing Missouri, Arkansas, and Texas, with local board and district secretary at St. Louis, Mo.

4. Middle District—Embracing Tennessee and Kentucky, with local board and district secretary at Louisville, Ky.

5. Western District—Embracing all the territory north of the Ohio River and west of the chain of lakes, with a local board and district secretary in the City of Chicago; with W. C. Phillips recommended to the general board as such district secretary.

6. Eastern District—Embracing all the New England and Middle States, with a local board in the City of Philadelphia: all subject to the general board, to which all reports must be made for combined publication.[33]

Subsequently, in 1873 the black Baptists of the West organized the General Association of the Western States and Territories; and in 1874 the East organized the New England Baptist Missionary Convention. Strangely enough, the subsequent growth of state conventions and district associations soon overshadowed the other four district conventions of the Consolidated American Baptist Convention and even the convention itself. A persistent spirit of independence and sectionalism on the part of the General Association of Western States and Territories and the New England Baptist Missionary Convention caused the gradual decline of the Consolidated American Baptist Convention, resulting in the termination of its activities at the last meeting in Lexington, Kentucky, in 1878.

Yet another factor to be considered in the failure of the Consolidated American Baptist Convention was the tendency to hold triennial meetings. The Executive Board was of the opinion that such meetings "would be more largely attended, and would prove more impressive and influential, and the hundreds of dollars spent annually in railroad transportation or fare of delegates, might be put into the treasury of the Lord, to be used in the work of Mission."[34] This, of course, would tend to strengthen the local boards which met annually.

## The New England Baptist Missionary Convention

The greater challenge to the old Consolidated Convention came as the result of rapid growth and vitality of the New England Baptist Missionary Convention. Most of the larger churches and ablest leaders among black Baptists were members of the new convention in New England. Hence, this district convention was able to live on as a separate convention after the decline of the Consolidated American Baptist Convention.

In August 1874, the call was issued to the Baptist leadership of New England, New York, New Jersey, and Pennsylvania to meet in Providence, Rhode Island, on the ninth, for the purpose of organizing the New England Missionary Baptist Convention. The initial meeting was held in the Congdon Street Baptist Church, Providence, Rhode Island. Rev. William Jackson, an exchaplain of the 64th Massachusetts Regional Division (Civil War), was the pastor of the Congdon Street Baptist Church. At this meeting, the convention elected the following officers: Rev. William Jackson, president; Rev. Spencer Harris of New York, vice-president; Rev. William A. Burch of New Bedford, Massachusetts, recording secretary; Rev. Edmond Kelley, corresponding secretary; and, William M. Green of Providence, Rhode Island, treasurer. These men were to carry on the administrative affairs of the convention in counsel with the board of managers which consisted of Reverends William Jackson, Edmond Kelley, William Ferguson, William Thomas, and Ebenezer Bird.

For about two decades the principal black Baptist leadership hailed from the rank and file of the New England Baptist Missionary Convention. This convention experienced a rapid growth in membership. Many independent churches were organized by the pioneer leaders of the New England Baptist Missionary Convention.

To be sure, the developers of the New England Baptist Missionary Convention's constitution were careful to reflect a broad and progressive scope of ministry. Provisions were made for the convention to foster and maintain home and foreign missionary work, establish and maintain educational institutions, and to establish other agencies necessary for the development of the convention.

In 1892, the leadership of the New England Baptist Missionary Convention decided to organize the Women's Auxiliary to the Convention. This was done to give the women of the local churches a greater opportunity for participation in the growth of the convention. Baptist women were ascending to new heights in local and foreign missions.

That same year, the convention's leadership sought legal status for the civil and ecclesiastical basis of the convention. They were able to obtain a Certificate of Incorporation for the convention issued by the state of New York. The principal office of the convention was established in the city of Brooklyn, New York.

Perhaps the greatest contributions of the New England Baptist Missionary Convention have been its strides in the organization and support of new churches and the support of missionaries on the foreign fields. It has also given substantial support to educational institutions for black Baptists across America. The convention remains today as the oldest regional convention among black Baptists.

## The Baptist Foreign Mission Convention

As previously mentioned, the growth and vitality of the New England Baptist Missionary Convention precipitated the demise of the Consolidated American Baptist Convention. Subsequently, a vacuum in the missionary movement was created in the cooperative movement of a national scope among black Baptists. The apparent failures of the movement affected the primary work of the African mission. Black Baptist leaders soon realized that a new evaluation of the cooperative movement was necessary in order to sustain the African mission. To be sure, the African mission had been a primary cause of the cooperative movement extending back into the antebellum period. Any setback in this mission would have repercussions in the local churches.

In response to the critical situation, Rev. William W. Colley, a missionary to Africa appointed by the Foreign Mission Board of the Southern Baptist Convention, returned to the United States with a strong determination to arouse his black brethren to the urgent need for missionary work in Africa. When Colley arrived in America, the black Baptists of Virginia employed him to canvass the United States to organize a general denominational convention among black Baptists. He wrote letters and traveled extensively, urging black Baptist leaders to meet in Montgomery, Alabama, on November 24-26, 1880, for the purpose of organizing a national convention to fill the vacuum created by the disintegration of the old Consolidated American Baptist Missionary Convention. Rev. Colley was particularly interested in the organizational movement to do extensive foreign mission work.

On November 24, 1880, at Montgomery, Alabama, about 150 Baptist leaders, principally pastors, responded to the call of Rev. W. W. Colley for the noble purpose of organizing a new convention. He met with these leaders in the First Baptist Church of Montgomery to organize the Baptist Foreign Mission Convention. At this initial meeting, Rev. W. H. McAlpine of Alabama was elected president of the Baptist Foreign Mission Convention. Eleven vice-presidents were elected, one from each state represented. A Foreign Mission Board was set up, and the convention elected

Rev. A. Binga, Jr., of South Richmond as its first Chairman along with Rev. W. W. Colley, corresponding secretary.

Now, alas, the organization of the Baptist Foreign Mission Convention gave black Baptists across America a new sense of pride, national power, and responsibility. The founders of this great cooperative movement were anxious to define the essential principles. First, they were impelled by a sense of duty to extend the influence of the black Baptists in the general movements of American Christianity to advance the mission of Jesus Christ in the world. The missionary strides of the white American Baptists and Southern Baptists were especially attractive to black Baptist leaders. Black Baptists were not nearsighted in the evangelistic ministry, despite limited geographical exposure resulting from the recent peculiar institution of slavery, but telescoped into distant areas for the planting of churches and the building of lives on the foreign field in the name of Jesus Christ.

Second, the leadership of the Baptist Foreign Mission Convention, like earlier cooperative movements, were influenced to continue and advance the African mission in particular. To be sure, they believed that the African mission claimed their most profound attention. However, they were also divinely inspired to do work in other parts of the world.

The developmental years (1880-1895) of the Baptist Foreign Mission Convention were characterized by growing pains. Its initial progress was somewhat slow. However, the brilliant missionary mind of Rev. W. W. Colley was sufficient to unite the majority of the black Baptists of America in the cause of foreign missions. The fact that various groups all over the country fell in line with W. W. Colley's movement attested that brilliance. Only two major organizations of black Baptists declined to unite with the movement, namely, the New England Baptist Missionary

Convention and the Baptist African Mission Convention. Nevertheless, the Baptist Foreign Mission Convention was still able to advance a significant foreign mission program.

## The American National Baptist Convention

Like earlier cooperative movements among black Baptists, the Baptist Foreign Mission Convention experienced some initial problems. One significant problem was the developing attitude on the part of some strong pastors against cooperation with white Baptists in the advancement of foreign missions. A strong spirit of complete independence from other Baptist bodies was a cause of controversy in the Baptist Foreign Mission Convention.

Rev. W. J. Simmons, the first black Baptist preacher from Kentucky to graduate from a standard college, strongly opposed the new tendency within the Baptist Foreign Mission Convention. He thought that there ought to be a convention that would cooperate with white American Baptists in the advancement of foreign missions. Hence, Rev. W. J. Simmons issued a call on April 9, 1886, for those of the clergy and laymen who were interested in his idea to meet in a special session with him. On August 25, 1886, black Baptist representatives from twenty-six states and the District of Columbia met with Rev. W. J. Simmons in Saint Louis, Missouri, and organized the American National Baptist Convention. The delegation was comprised of leaders in thought and training among black Baptists of the nation.[35] The organizational meeting was held in the First Baptist Church of Saint Louis.

The first officers of the American National Baptist Convention were W. J. Simmons, president; J. R. Young and T. L. Johnson, vice-presidents; T. S. Clanton and W. H. Steward, recording secretary; D. A. Gaddie, treasurer; and Miss L. W. Smith, historian. One of the motivating drives of this convention was its hope for the unification of all black Baptists of America for the cause of Christian missions. In 1886, Rev. T. L. Johnson, vice-president of the convention, declared at the first meeting: "Knox lifted Scotland, Luther lifted Germany, and it remains for us to lift up the heathen in the land of our fathers—Africa."[36]

The Baptist Foreign Mission Convention, through its Board in Richmond, Virginia, continued to do the foreign mission work for the American National Baptist Convention. However, the initial hope for the unification of all black Baptists of the United States remained unrealized. This lack of unity continued to hamper the foreign mission enterprise of black Baptists.

## The National Baptist Educational Convention

In 1893, another organization proposing to be national in scope was founded in Washington, D.C. The new convention was named the National Baptist Educational Convention. The main objective of this convention was to provide for an educated ministry in the leadership of black Baptist churches. This was the first attempt of black Baptists to direct, in a unified way, the educational policy for all churches of the denomination.

The leading person in the organization of the National Baptist Educational Convention was Rev. W. Bishop Johnson, pastor of the Second Baptist Church, Washington, D.C. The idea for such a convention grew out of Rev. W. Bishop Johnson's earlier strides in Christian education. He had (in 1885) organized the Sunday School Lyceum movement in the United States. With the organization of the National Baptist Educational Convention, Rev. W. Bishop Johnson along with Rev. P. F. Morris of Virginia, federated all schools owned, controlled, and managed by black Baptists making them a part of the educational machinery of the denomination. He gathered educational data and statistics from these institutions and showed their number, location, and property value. This afforded the local churches information on the relative strength of the denomination. The convention also raised large sums of money for the support of these educational institutions among black Baptists.

## The Tripartite Union

The decade-old stride for national unity among black Baptists continued into the 1890s. In a meeting at Washington, D.C., several leading preachers raised again the question concerning a united Baptist organization with national scope and purpose. It was suggested that what was called the Tripartite Union be formed to consist of the New England Baptist Missionary Convention, the African Foreign Mission Convention, and the Foreign Mission Convention of America. Regretfully, the consolidation effort failed.

However, the spirit of the Tripartite Union lived on in the minds and hearts of several prominent black Baptist pastors. Reverends S. E. Griggs, L. M. Luke, and A. W. Pegues, a graduate of Bucknell University, led a movement at the meeting of the Tripartite Union at Montgomery, Alabama, in 1894 to unite the black Baptists all over the nation. They developed the form, structure, and machinery of an organization to serve the said objective. A committee was appointed to report to the next session in Atlanta, Georgia. Hence, the three bodies adjourned to meet in Atlanta, September 28, 1895, at which time the Committee on Plans, Constitution, and so forth, would make its report.

On September 24, 1895, in Friendship Baptist Church of Atlanta, Georgia, the committee made its report to the Tripartite Union. The report was adopted. Subsequently, in 1895 at Atlanta, Georgia, the Foreign Mission Convention, the National Baptist Educational Convention, and the

American National Baptist Convention consolidated to
form a new national convention with Rev. E. C. Morris of
Helena, Arkansas, president, and Mr. W. H. Steward, secretary. The new consolidated convention was organized by
black Baptist leaders of great genius. They were careful to
lay the structure of a viable and durable Baptist organization. These leaders were also determined to structure the
new convention broad enough in scope to facilitate a Tripartite Union. It was hoped that such an organization could
withstand any devisable tendency on the part of the various
regions of the nation. The result of this organizational meeting was the National Baptist Convention of the United
States of America. Finally, the dream of national unity was
realized.

## The Formative Period of
## the National Baptist Convention

As previously mentioned, the organizers of the National Baptist Convention of the United States of America
were careful to develop comprehensive plans for a convention structure of tremendous viability. This effort was reflected in the constitutional development of the convention.

Whereas, It is the sense of the colored Baptists of the
United States of America, convened in the city of Atlanta,
Ga., September 28, 1895, in the general organizations known
as "The Baptist Foreign Missions Convention of the United
States of America," which had been engaged in mission
work on the West coast of Africa; "The American National
Baptist Convention," which has sought to look after the
educational interest, that the interest of the Kingdom of God
requires that the several bodies above named should unite
in one body.[37]

Again, the primary concern of the new national convention was to facilitate an aggressive home and foreign missionary program. While the African mission was still very much a concern of the leaders, the convention also advanced a lively interest in missionary work in America and throughout the world of oppressed people. Provisions were also made for the cause of education and the publication and circulation of religious literature designed to meet the special needs of black Americans. In order to facilitate a practical structure for these objectives, the organizers of the convention decided to work through specialized Boards. Hence, they organized a Foreign Mission Board, a Home Mission Board, an Educational Board, a B.Y.P.U. Board, and a Publishing Board.

In the early 1900s, the constitution was revised for the first time to reflect the extensive growth and development of the National Baptist Convention of the United States of America. In a special report issued in 1906 by the Department of Commerce and Labor, Bureau of the Census on "Religious Bodies," a significant growth in the convention was reported: in 1890 there were 1,348,989 members in the continental United States; and in 1906 the number had increased to 2,261,607 members. A large percent of all black Christians were by 1906 united with the National Baptist Convention of the United States of America. Hence, certain constitutional provisions were made for this great growth in the black Baptist denomination.

Some of the essential revisions in the constitution were as follows: first, the representation fees of messengers, district associations, or conventions were increased to reflect the new economic needs of the growing denomination; second, new regulations were established for life membership; and, third, positions and eligibility requirements were established for new officers with the convention reserving the right to try such officers, particularly officers of the Executive Board, and dismiss them. The Executive Board was given power to create from its own body an executive committee consisting of nine members. Also, provisions were made for the organization and government of subsidiary bodies to the convention.

The constitutional history of the National Baptist Convention of the United States of America reflects its program development. A careful and in-depth study of the program development of the convention also reflects the broad and informed views of its founding fathers.

Specifically, the first leaders of the convention left their marks upon the advance of the new connectional movement. Most influential among the first leaders was Rev. Elias Camp Morris, the new organization's first president. On May 7, 1855, near Springplace on the Connesauga in the hills of North Georgia, was born Elias Camp Morris of slave parentage. His early education was through the common school, but practically from nature and necessity. At age ten, he moved with his parents to Stevenson, Alabama. Here Morris learned the shoemaker's trade. While still a youth, he felt a call to the gospel ministry. This call led Morris on a journey of tremendous importance for the progress of black Baptists in America.

In 1879, Rev. Elias Camp Morris accepted a call to the pastorate of the Centennial Baptist Church of Helena, Arkansas. His ability to organize was fully recognized among the Baptists of Arkansas. In 1884, he organized the Arkansas Baptist College and for sixteen years served as chairman of its board of trustees. In 1894, Rev. Elias Camp Morris was elected president of the National Baptist Convention of the United States of America. Initially, he inspired the black Baptists to begin publishing interests of their own. It was his active mind that conceived the idea of the National Baptist Young People's Union Board.

To be sure, Rev. Elias Camp Morris was the guiding figure throughout the formative years of the convention. He led the National Convention through many growth pains to a position of respect throughout the Christian world. He served as president of the convention for twenty-seven years.

The greatest growth pain that the National Baptist Convention of the United States of America experienced developed into a crisis over the various boards. A succinct summary of the actual organizational dates of the boards of the convention will set the background for the later conflicts. Really, the oldest Board was the National Baptist Foreign Mission Board organized in 1895 and located in Louisville, Kentucky. By and large, the new Board was a continuation of the old Foreign Mission Convention of America. The initial officers were Rev. John H. Frank, chairman; and Rev. L. M. Luke, corresponding secretary. By 1911, the Board members had changed to include additional leaders such as Rev. C. H. Parrish, president of Eckstein Norton University, Cane Springs, Kentucky, chairman; and Rev. H. A. Gaddie, of Green Street Baptist Church, Louisville, Kentucky, recording secretary.

The next board to be organized was the National Baptist Publishing Board. In 1896, the convention made plans for the organization of this Board. Rev. R. H. Boyd, who had played a significant part in the development of the concept, was subsequently appointed general secretary of the National Baptist Publishing Board with Rev. C. H. Clark serving as chairman. By 1898, this Board had been in operation and located at Nashville, Tennessee. It was the largest black publishing enterprise in the world. The Board was given the exclusive right of publishing all church and Sunday School literature for the National Baptist Convention of the United States of America. By 1911, the Board had property, machinery, and stock estimated at $350,000 and employed about 150 clerks, stenographers, and skilled workers. As early as 1909, the Board had installed a Scott's all-size Rotary Book Printing Press, the first of its kind south of the Ohio River at a cost of $18,000. For the year September 1, 1908, to August 31, 1909, the Board published 11,717,876 copies of Sunday School literature, besides its songbooks and Bibles. It raised $159,652.27 and reported a balance in hand of $3,008.92 in 1909.[38]

In 1908, the Board began the manufacturing of church and school furniture; and in 1909, it inaugurated the National Baptist Teacher-Training Service with Rev. N. H. Pius, superintendent.

Correspondingly, the Educational Board of the National Baptist Convention of the United States of America was organized about the same time as the Publishing Board. In 1895, the Educational Board was organized and located in Washington, D.C., with Rev. W. Bishop Johnson serving as corresponding secretary. Actually, this Board was a continuation of the old National Baptist Educational Convention previously led by Rev. W. Bishop Johnson. By 1911, the Board had moved its headquarters to Nashville and elected Rev. T. J. Searcy, chairman, and Rev. A. N. McEwen, corresponding secretary. This Board was designed to federate all black Baptist Schools in the United States, except the eight owned by the American Baptist Home Mission Society, and to establish and operate a National Theological Seminary at Nashville, Tennessee. In 1911, the Board made plans for the erection of a $50,000 building for the theological seminary. That same year, Rev. Sutton E. Griggs was elected corresponding secretary of the Educational Board.

In 1899, the National B.Y.P.U. Board was organized with Rev. N. H. Pius, chairman, and Rev. E. W. D. Isaac, secretary. The Board was also located at Nashville, Tennessee. By 1911, the Board had elected Rev. P. James Bryant, chairman. Over a ten-year period, the Board had led in the organization of 7,600 local B.Y.P.U. societies and thirty-eight state societies, plus three hundred and twenty B.Y.P.U. district conventions.

The last Board to be organized during the formative period of the convention was the National Baptist Benefit Association Board. It was organized in 1903 and located at Helena, Arkansas. The initial officers were Rev. C. B. Brown, chairman, and Rev. W. A. Homes, corresponding secretary. On the death of Reverend Homes, Rev. A. A. Casey became corresponding secretary. The purpose of the Board was to pay death claims to Baptist ministers and laymen who became members of the association. In 1911, the Board projected plans to establish a home for aged and disabled ministers. With the organization of these Boards, the National Baptist Convention of the United States of America was well on the way to becoming a vital and progressive convention in the black Christian world. However, trouble soon developed in two of its Boards which subsequently led to two splits of the convention.

## The Lott Carey Baptist Foreign Mission Convention

By 1897, a significant amount of internal disturbance within the National Baptist Convention, U.S.A., had developed with the potential for destroying the unity of its constituency. Several clergymen of national prominence prepared statements designed to sway the sentiment of the delegates of the forthcoming session to their unique persuasion on the convention's program. In September 1897, the National Baptist Convention, U.S.A., met with the Ebenezer Baptist Church of Boston, Massachusetts. The initial business session began with a debate among the clergymen. The debate centered around several key and somewhat emotional issues: (1) the advisability of the removal of the Foreign Mission Board from Richmond to Louisville; (2) the use of American Baptist literature and cooperation with white

Baptists in general; and (3) the primacy of foreign missions as a greater emphasis for the convention.

Most, if not all, of these issues grew out of the original consolidation of the various black conventions, each with unique objectives or emphases. The issues of the primacy of foreign missions and cooperation with white Baptists were debated with strong emotions by some of the convention's most competent leaders.

Obviously, the majority of the delegates to the convention favored an independent spirit from white Baptist bodies. The original dynamics of the exodus movement was still very real to the majority leadership of the National Baptist Convention, U.S.A. Accordingly, they wanted to chart their own course in the areas of missions, education, and the publication of literature responsive to the black experience. Furthermore, the majority leadership believed that a separate and independent black Baptist denomination was necessary for the progress of the race.

Conversely, several clergymen from Virginia and North Carolina opposed unremittingly the majority opinion of the National Baptist Convention, U.S.A. In the meantime, they held firmly to their contention for the primacy of a foreign mission emphasis and cooperation with white Baptists. The issue of cooperation with white Baptists was particularly sensitive to the delegates from North Carolina. The black and white Baptists of that state had developed an amenable relationship for a significant period of time.

In harmony with the foregoing, J. A. Whitted, a noted black church historian, alluded to the spirit of cooperation among black and white Baptists in North Carolina. He observed:

> From the beginning the negro Baptists of North Carolina have felt that their white brethren, with superior advantages, could be of substantial aid to them in their religious

and moral development, and they invited representatives to
meet with them even in their organization of the Convention (The Baptist Educational and Missionary Convention of
North Carolina, organized in Goldsboro, N.C., in the year
1867). In the annual meeting of the white Baptists at Wilmington in 1867 the request was granted; the brethren were
present and rendered valuable service, bidding Godspeed to
their colored brethren.[39]

Hence, several decades of cooperation had served to win a
sustained desire to continue a working relationship between
black and white Baptists in North Carolina.

By and large, the cooperative relationship between
black and white Baptists in North Carolina was envied by
certain other states. With respect to outside reaction, J. A.
Whitted also observed:

The American Baptist Home Mission Society did so much
for the colored Baptists of North Carolina and in so many
ways it was thought by some of the Baptists of other States
that the society was partial to North Carolina Baptists, and
to an extent the charge was doubtless true, for it was claimed
by certain leading Home Mission Society representatives
that the Negro Baptists of North Carolina were the most
grateful and loyal people with whom they were associated
in Christian and educational work, and hence they were
necessarily inclined to do more for North Carolina.[40]

So when the debate transpired in the National Baptist
Convention, U.S.A., over cooperation with white Baptists,
the delegation from North Carolina took the lead in an
effort to dissuade the majority opinion of the convention.
This faction of clergymen held a caucus session at Boston
to evaluate the relative strength of their idea and to plan a
strategy for the realization of their goal. There was enough
enthusiasm generated at this minisession to motivate the
disengaged National Baptist brethren to call a subsequent

meeting at Shiloh Baptist Church in Washington, D.C., on December 16, 1897, for the purpose of developing a new conventional strategy.

Accordingly, the Lott Carey Baptist Home and Foreign Mission Convention was organized in Shiloh Baptist Church, Washington, D.C., in 1897. Rev. J. A. Taylor, pastor of Shiloh Baptist Church, cordially welcomed the delegates, and his good people entertained them. This was the preliminary organization formed December 16, 1897, at which meeting Rev. J. A. Whitted presided. The convention was subsequently confirmed September 8 and 9, 1898, by large delegations from North Carolina, Virginia, the District of Columbia, Maryland, Pennsylvania, New Jersey, New York, and the New England states. The relative strength of this new convention surprised the National Baptist Convention, U.S.A., and angered its leadership.

Nevertheless, the leadership of the new convention persisted. In 1899, the annual meeting of the Lott Carey Home and Foreign Mission Convention was held at the First Baptist Church, Baltimore, Maryland. Rev. J. C. Allen was then the pastor. He, along with several other Baltimore churches, entertained the new convention. At this meeting, the first idea of a women's auxiliary was conceived. The following year, the Lott Carey Home and Foreign Mission Convention formally organized such an auxiliary to the parent body. President C. S. Brown led several women of high esteem to formulate a nominating committee to recommend women of great leadership ability to develop a viable women's auxiliary.

Several decades later, the convention in 1943 organized the Baptist laymen of the parent body. That year, Deacon R. L. Hollomon of the First Baptist Church, Norfolk, Virginia, led a movement within the convention for the organization of the Lott Carey Laymen's League. His plans were received warmly by the convention. The convention's lead-

ership was quick to recognize the vast potential of black
Baptist laymen.

The formative years of the convention witnessed the
evolution of the basic organizational structure which
proved formidable in the advancement of a missionary enterprise. Black preachers and lay leaders were united in a
missionary objective.

There were several early attempts to bring the leadership of the Lott Carey Home and Foreign Mission Convention back into organic relationships with the National
Baptist Convention, U.S.A. A proposal for cooperation with
the National Baptist Convention was presented to the fifth
annual session of the Lott Carey movement. This proposal
touched some sensitive nerves in both conventions. Rev. W.
M. Alexander reported to the Lott Carey constituency that
the time was ripe to bring the two bodies into an organic
relationship. He noted the changing mood of several National Baptist leaders.

President C. S. Brown received this proposal for organic
relations with cautious optimism. He cited several important conditions that must be met by the National Baptist
brethren before a workable relationship could be developed
between the two black Baptist bodies. He maintained that
the National Baptist brethren must make concessions on
several points before the Lott Carey brethren could be reu-
nited. He offered a list of things that must be done:

1. A readjustment of our foreign mission work so as to
heal the breach that produced our separation and a compromise of minor matters.

2. An agreement to refrain from unwarranted attacks
on the officers of the American Baptist Home Mission Society and their work, and the adoption of a cooperation policy
with the same when such action would strengthen the work
among us.

3. An agreement to permit our Sunday Schools to use

the literature of either publishing house without considering them loyal or disloyal, and also to permit the agents and
representatives of either house or both houses to appear in
our convention, associations, and other meetings, and be
courteously received and entertained.

4. A decision to demand the officers of our general
organization to refrain from slanderous assaults on brethren
who dare to differ with them.

5. By conceding the supremacy of state bodies in all
matters appertaining to the work within the respective ju-
risdictions.

Within two years, many of these points of difference
between the two black Baptist conventions were settled. In
1905, they entered into an organic relationship. Rev. C. S.
Brown negotiated the new relationship and actually served
as a member of the Executive Board of the National Baptist
Convention, U.S.A., until 1922. The cooperation was restricted primarily to the foreign mission program of the two
conventions. Specifically, the Lott Carey Convention enrolled as the First District Convention of the National Baptist Convention, U.S.A. The compact between the two
organizations remained undisturbed until internal discord
came to a head in a crisis over the ownership and management of the National Baptist Publishing Board. The crisis
developed into some significant changes in cooperative
strides among black Baptists.

## The National Baptist Convention of America

To be sure, the greatest cleavage within the National
Baptist Convention, U.S.A., during its formative years came
in 1915. All efforts to maintain unity and harmony within
the convention had previously posed vexing challenges to
the officials. Unlike the crisis which led to the birth of the
Lott Carey Convention movement, the severe crisis of 1915

was primarily a legal problem with reference to the ownership and management of the National Baptist Publishing
Board. Signs of the crisis were apparent for almost a decade
before the actual separation of 1915.

Documents, reflecting the great cleavage of 1915 within
the National Baptist Convention, U.S.A., tend to give conflicting evidence relative to the real issues involved. It is
therefore important for understanding to evaluate the more
significant documents from the period to get a coherent
account of the controversy.

Rev. R. H. Boyd, a powerful leader in the convention,
published a lengthy document stating his views relative
to the cleavage within the National Baptist Convention,
U.S.A. He claimed that the original constitution of the convention did not contain a clear provision for the establishment of the National Baptist Publishing Board. Rev. Boyd
further argued that the Board was organized with little or
no help from President Elias Camp Morris and other officials of the convention. The leadership of the parent body
seemed more interested in other matters of Baptist work at
home and abroad. The fact that the convention played little
or no attention to the organization of the Board was cited
as a justification for the claim of an independent legal status
for it from the National Baptist Convention's official structure.

Presumably, Rev. R. H. Boyd had developed at the turn
of the century a specific strategy for the organization of the
National Baptist Publishing Board which gave it the independence so claimed. Initially, he consulted with President
Elias Camp Morris, but detected a difference of view about
the proposed Board. Hence, Rev. Boyd developed his own
strategy for the purposes of the Board.

The strategy of Rev. R. H. Boyd prevailed at the National Baptist Convention, U.S.A. Boyd held the secrecy of
his strategy for the operation of the Publishing Board until

the second day's session of the convention being held in the First Baptist Church, Saint Louis, Missouri, September 1896. While the session was chaired by Rev. A. N. McEwen, of Mobile, Alabama, Rev. Boyd offered a resolution for the establishment of a publishing board independent of the American Baptist Publication Society which was owned and operated by white Baptists. Obviously, the resolution met with some opposition because many of the leaders had become dependent on a cooperative arrangement with the American Baptist Publication Society. Hence, the resolution was referred to a committee consisting of Rev. E. K. Love, of Georgia; Rev. C. H. Parrish, of Kentucky; Rev. R. H. Boyd, and several other influential clergymen. This committee met and referred the matter to a subcommittee consisting of Rev. R. H. Boyd, Rev. E. K. Love, and Rev. C. H. Parrish.

To be sure, Rev. R. H. Boyd was able to control the committee in support of his original proposal for the independence of the Publishing Board. The committee members reported to the convention that the Boyd resolution was, in their judgment, feasible, possible, and profitable, and recommended its adoption. Again, a tremendous controversy developed in the convention. On a motion by Rev. I. Toliver, of Texas, the matter was referred to the Home Mission Board of the National Baptist Convention, U.S.A. This seemed to have calmed the troubled waters, and peace was restored among the delegation throughout the remainder of the session.

After a very lengthy period of rather intense negotiation, the idea of a publishing board was finally approved. Rev. R. H. Boyd suggested that the new Board, initially called the "printing Committee," should have a place in the constitution as other boards separate from the Home Mission Board. Accordingly, he suggested that it should be called the National Baptist Publishing Board.

Under President Elias Camp Morris's directives, the

Home Mission Board and the Publishing Board worked jointly together as one Board until 1904. Later, he recommended the separation of the two Boards. When the convention met in Chicago in 1905, the convention ordered that the management of the Home Mission Board and the Publishing Board be separated in a way that each would have a separate and distinct corresponding secretary. Conversely, the two Boards did not obey the orders and stood in open rebellion against the command of the convention in 1914. A whole decade prior to the actual split of the convention was characterized by intervals of strong agitations concerning the popular policy of conventional control of all boards.

During the decade of controversy, there were discussions, arguments, and investigations made as to the rightful ownership and control of the National Baptist Publishing Board. The failure of the Publishing Board to obey the orders of the convention led ultimately to the question: Does the Publishing Board belong to the convention? This question gave birth to the "Popular Policy of Convention Control of Boards."[41]

At the annual session in Chicago in 1915, a tremendous legal battle took place within the National Baptist Convention, U.S.A., over the issue of the Publishing Board. A lawsuit was filed to decide between those who followed Rev. R. H. Boyd's claim of independency for the Publishing Board and the popular policy of conventional ownership of all Boards. In 1915, Judge Smith of Chicago, Illinois, in open court, pronounced the Boyd group a "rump" convention and dissolved an injunction which they had taken out against President Elias Camp Morris and other officers of the National Baptist Convention, U.S.A.[42]

Initially, the Boyd group did not leave the courtroom as a separate conventional body, but from the judge's decision they scattered about the city of Chicago. Shortly, however, they rallied themselves together at Salem Baptist

Church and organized the National Baptist Convention of America. Initially, they called the new body the National Baptist Convention, Unincorporated, organized on Thursday night September 9, 1915.

In 1916, the new convention published a document entitled "The Rightful and Lawful Ownership of the National Baptist Publishing House," establishing:

> Of late there has been a great deal of controversy, first, about the ownership of the National Baptist Publishing House, its management and control; second, about the rights of the Publishing Board to make a choice of what faction it will affiliate with. Let us here and now make a clear statement that no messenger attending this body may go away from here deceived or disappointed: The National Baptist Publishing Board is a legal entity; it was created by the state of Tennessee on the 15th day of August, 1898, under the acts of legislature of 1875, chapter 142.[43]

Accordingly, the National Baptist Convention, Unincorporated, held that the Publishing Board did not belong to any convention; hence, it had the right to affiliate with any convention it so desired. This was done to counter the opinion of a few delegates to the new convention who were still a little doubtful of the ethics of the Publishing Board's leadership.

Hard feelings between the two National Baptist conventions prevailed for several years after the split in 1915. One severe area of contention centered around the attempt of both conventions to claim the same original date of the founding of the National Baptist Convention. As late as 1933, Rev. L. G. Jordan, historian and general missionary of the National Convention, U.S.A., Inc., made a critical report on the new convention. He referred to the new convention as the "Boyd National Convention" and rejected its claim to an organizational date earlier than 1915. None of the officers of the original National Baptist Convention joined or took part in the so-called "rump" convention, but the National Baptist Convention continued to meet Friday, Saturday, Sunday, and adjourned Monday, unmolested at the 18th Street Armory.[44]

Strangely enough, neither of the two national conventions was organized in 1880. The black Baptist convention that was organized in Montgomery, Alabama, in 1880, as mentioned earlier in this book, was named the Baptist Foreign Mission Convention. However, black Baptist leaders, from the outset of the cooperative movements of a national scope, developed the habit of claiming the organizational date of antecedent black Baptist conventions.

Another issue of significance was the question of the legal status of the National Baptist Convention. The convention had adopted a policy of doing its "secular" business through the various boards. Actually, the boards were first to be incorporated legally. The National Baptist Publishing Board was chartered by the state of Tennessee, August 15, 1898, and recorded in the Corporation Record Book 00, Page 276. In 1928, President L. K. Williams reported in his address that the following had been incorporated: the Foreign Mission Board; the B.Y.U.P. Board; the Sunday School Publishing Board; the American Baptist Theological Seminary; and, the National Training School for Women and Girls, Washington, D.C. The actual convention was not incorporated until sometime in the early 1930s. However, the constitution of the convention was amended in the annual session in Savannah, Georgia, September 1916, and adopted September 1917. Apparently, many of the National Baptist brethren believed this was an act of incorporation. After the constitutional revision, they commonly referred the members of the National Baptist Convention of America as the "Unincorporated Convention." This designation was to find itself in much of the literature of the period relative to the relationship between the two bodies.

After 1915, the National Baptist Convention, U.S.A., was confronted with the existence of two major black Baptist conventional splits. Many of the convention's leaders were deeply troubled by the division within the black Baptist denomination which evidenced something of a regression to the early states of conventional development. Several attempts were made for unity. However, each attempt failed to unite the National Baptist Convention, U.S.A., and the National Baptist Convention of America.

Some progress was made between the National Baptist Convention of America and the Lott Carey Baptist Foreign Mission Convention to promote a cooperative program. Inasmuch as the former convention did not have a foreign mission board initially, it negotiated for several years with the latter to channel a combined foreign mission program. Subsequently, the Lott Carey Baptist Foreign Mission Convention acquiesced, and in 1924, a formal compact was agreed upon by the two bodies. President C. S. Brown of the Lott Carey Convention applauded the compact in his annual address of September 1925. He expressed the confidence of the Lott Carey administration that the new compact with the National Baptist Convention of America was more in keeping with the original philosophy of the convention than the earlier one with the National Baptist Convention, U.S.A.

Again, there was an attempt to form a triparte union between the three black Baptist conventions. The attempt was a failure. This was perhaps the greatest failure among black Baptists in the early twentieth century.

The failure of these conventions to reunite subsequently evidenced a period of decline in both the Lott Carey Convention and the National Baptist Convention of America. Each of these two conventions was not able to raise

Dr. Wendell C. Somerville, executive
secretary-treasurer of the Lott Carey Baptist
Foreign Mission Convention, U.S.A.

enough money to pool together for a viable foreign mission program commensurate with the needs of the conventions. Despite persistent efforts over a period of several years, any compact between the two bodies soon lost its vitality and became inoperative.

The Lott Carey Baptist Foreign Mission Convention continued a gradual decline for several years. It was not until the era of Rev. Wendell Clay Somerville, the son of the late Rev. C. C. Somerville (one of the founders of the Lott Carey Home And Foreign Mission Convention), that the convention started to show signs of growth and vitality. In the early 1940s, he accepted the challenge of leadership in the convention. At that time, the convention was in dire need of revitalization. It's foreign mission stations were in need of repair. One of the most significant ideas introduced by Rev. Somerville to revitalize the convention was the "Man of Troas" program. It was a rather ingenious idea of motivating black Baptist church leaders to contribute $1000 or more annually to the convention. He called the new program, "The Magnificent Men and Women of Troas." Several millions of dollars have been raised through this program. Rev. Somerville often referred to such monies, "Never before since the world began have this many black men and women contributed such sums of money to the cause of Christian missions."

Similarly, the leadership of the National Baptist Convention of America turned inward in an attempt to revitalize a decaying conventional movement. It organized an independent foreign mission board and several home mission projects. The National Baptist Publishing Board continued, however, to be the strongest affiliated body with the convention.

One of the strongest programs of the convention itself was evidenced in the work of the Educational Board of the National Baptist Convention of America. The Board began a program of financial assistance to the following schools: Union Baptist Seminary, Houston, Texas; Union Baptist Seminary, New Orleans, Louisiana; Conroe Normal and Industrial College, Conroe, Texas; Guadalupe College, Sequin, Texas; Florida Normal and Industrial Memorial College, Saint Augustine, Florida; Virginia Seminary and College, Lynchburg, Virginia; Morris College, Sumter, South Carolina; and Mississippi Baptist Seminary, Hattiesburg, Mississippi.

The newly organized Foreign Mission Board was able to organize mission stations in Africa, Haiti, Jamaica, and Panama. To be sure, President J. C. Sams was able to give new life to the program of the entire convention. He led the convention to a new era of growth and development.

## The Progressive National Baptist Convention

The genesis of the Progressive National Baptist Convention was the last great division within the national development of black Baptists in America. This new cooperative movement resulted from internal concerns within the National Baptist Convention, U.S.A. In other words, the question of tenure became a heated issue. Rev. J. H. Jackson, president of the National Baptist Convention, had risen to a position of great power and prestige so much so that the majority of the convention's leaders and delegates desired the continuation of his dynamic leadership beyond the tenure requirements.

However, there were some members of the convention who desired new leadership. A disturbing controversy developed in the convention over the issue of tenure. Therefore, a committee on tenure was organized to report its findings to the annual session of the convention. On Thursday afternoon, September 4, 1956, the question of tenure was debated at the seventy-sixth annual session in Denver,

Colorado. Rev. E. C. Smith was called for to make the report of the tenure committee. He in turn presented Rev. D. G. Lewis to read the report, alluding to the fact that the whole committee was not in agreement and that he was the dissenting voice. The majority report was not in favor of tenure.

The question of tenure was not debated in the convention again until September 6, 1956. At this time, it came to the convention as a part of the special committee on constitution's report. This committee attempted a compromise on constitutional changes.

President J. H. Jackson made a statement indicating his disposition concerning the compromise report of the committee. Subsequently, Rev. E. C. Smith read the president's statement that was presented to the convention in Memphis in 1955 and called on Rev. T. S. Alexander to read the committee's report. The committee recommended in substance that all officers be subject to tenure beginning in 1956; that no officer to the convention could retain his position longer than four years; and that the matter of an executive secretary be referred to a committee for further study. A tremendous controversy developed over the report resulting in a division of opinion among leading clergymen. Finally, it was moved and seconded by Rev. Burrell of Louisiana and supported by several seconds that the matter be voted on without a roll call of the states. The vote was not settled, however. After a period of prolonged confusion, Vice-president S. A. Owen asked the attorney to make a statement. Attorney A. T. Walden suggested that a committee be appointed to contact the president and suggest that he return to the building and reconvene the convention to resolve the conflict.

Again the issue of tenure failed to be resolved in the convention because President J. H. Jackson was not available for a conference to reconvene the convention in order to resolve the conflict. The issue of tenure was again delayed to a later date, supposedly Friday, September 7, 1956. Strangely enough, however, the minutes do not reflect any mention of tenure on that Friday.

The succeeding annual sessions of the convention witnessed a constant increase in the power and prestige of President J. H. Jackson. Nevertheless, the question of tenure was to agitate him for a period of time and bring renewed hostility within the convention.

The second major issue of conflict within the National Baptist Convention, U.S.A., Inc., was more political in nature. In 1954, the Supreme Court of the United States ruled that the segregation of public schools was unconstitutional. This ruling prompted several debates in the convention on the ways and means of progress in civil rights for black Americans. In 1956, a symposium was held to relate to the issue: "National Baptists Facing Integration—Shall Gradualism Be Applied?"[45] Several leading clergymen addressed themselves to the issue. Rev. C. K. Steele of Florida spoke of the bus boycott in Tallahassee and took a position against "gradualism." Rev. T. J. Jemison spoke also of his experience in the Baton Rouge Boycott in 1953. Rev. T. J. Jemison and Rev. Thomas Kilgore spoke in unqualified terms against gradualism.

After the symposium, Rev. J. H. Jackson presented Rev. Martin Luther King, Jr., president of the Montgomery Improvement Association and pastor of the Dexter Avenue Baptist Church in Montgomery, to address the convention. Rev. Martin Luther King, Jr., initially congratulated President J. H. Jackson for his support of the boycott movement. He announced as his subject, "Paul's Letter to American Christians."[46] Rev. Martin Luther King, Jr., delivered this address in a spirit strongly opposed to "gradualism" in the civil rights movement. From this point onward, a mild tension developed between Reverends King and Jackson. Rev.

J. H. Jackson tended to be more gradual or conservative in his approach to civil rights than Rev. Martin Luther King., Jr.

By 1960, significant pressure was applied within the National Baptist Convention for a new spirit of leadership. In 1961, this new spirit assumed crisis proportion. The executive meeting of the board of directors reflected tremendous sensitivity to the emerging crisis. The convention's leadership recommended that the constitution would be so amended to prohibit flagrant use of the courts against the convention by supposed members. On September 6, 1961, the crisis emerged. The stage was set when Rev. E. C. Estell was presented and read a resolution that requested President J. H. Jackson to permit his name to be renominated as president of the National Baptist Convention for 1961-1962. After the reading of the resolution, Rev. E. C. Estell moved for the adoption of the resolution. It was seconded by Rev. Levi Terril and passed by a large standing majority. However, a number of delegates voted against the motion.

Following the adoption of the resolution, disorder in the proceeding was called by a small minority who were followers of Rev. Gardner C. Taylor. The disorder became so pronounced that the director of the auditorium called for order and presented the mayor of Kansas City who made a strong appeal and asked that the delegates and visitors conduct themselves as Christians.

Subsequently, on Thursday, September 7, 1961, the crisis became so intense that President J. H. Jackson asked that the election not be held following his address as usual but be postponed until a later time in the day. There had been many rumors by the followers of Rev. Gardner C. Taylor that the election would not be held in a fair manner. In fact, some of the dissatisfied brethren had filed suit to have a court-ordered election with court supervision. Both the Jackson and the Taylor factions were being represented

Rev. Gardner C. Taylor, pastor of the
Concord Baptist Church of Christ,
Brooklyn, New York, pioneer and president
of the Progressive National Baptist
Convention. Baptist World Alliance Photo.

legally. After consultation with a local judge, it was decided that all delegates who had registered by the convention and those registered by the Taylor group would have to be certified by both groups. This was agreed upon, and most of Thursday afternoon and evening was spent in the certification of eligible delegates. After this lengthy delay, the convention finally began the voting process.

The election process was conducted by Rev. D. A. Homes as appointed by the court. The election was by states with tellers representing both sides. Alas, the Taylor faction was able to get the type of election they had desired for a long time. Nevertheless, the result was disappointing to the Taylor faction. Rev. J. H. Jackson received the majority vote and continued in the presidency of the convention.

Nevertheless, the Jackson victory did not calm the troubled waters in the convention. On September 11, 1961, a national news release was issued which electrified the black Baptists of America.

> A Volunteer Committee for the Formation of a New National Baptist Convention announced this week through its Chairman, Rev. L. V. Booth, pastor of Zion Baptist Church, Cincinnati, Ohio, that a meeting will be held November 14 and 15, 1961, at Zion Baptist Church, 630 Glenwood Avenue, Cincinnati 29, Ohio.
>
> The two-day session will be devoted to discussion on How to Build a Democratic Convention Dedicated to Christian Objectives.
>
> The keynote speaker will be Dr. William H. Borders, Pastor of Wheat Street Baptist Church, Atlanta, Georgia. Dr. Borders is one of the ten outstanding pastors expelled from the National Baptist Convention, Inc., following its notorious session at Louisville, Kentucky, in 1957, when President Joseph H. Jackson ruled Tenure unconstitutional. There has been great dissatisfaction since. . . .
>
> This movement is in no way connected with the past

effort of "The Taylor Team." It is an entirely new movement under new leadership. Persons who are concerned with redeeming the Baptist initiative and restoring a Democratic Thrust are invited.[47]

To be sure, many have questioned the accuracy of the claim that certain delegates were expelled from the National Baptist Convention, U.S.A., Inc. Nevertheless, Rev. Ralph D. Abernathy affirmed recently that he and Rev. Martin Luther King, Jr., were among a group of clergymen expelled from the convention because of their position against President J. H. Jackson's policy of "gradualism" and their support of Rev. Gardner C. Taylor's election bid for the presidency of the convention.

Unmistakably, the leading organizer of the Progressive National Baptist Convention, U.S.A., Inc., was Rev. L. Venchael Booth. Several days after the national news release, he issued a call letter to many of the greatest leaders of the black Baptist church in America to organize the New National Baptist Convention. To justify the rationale for a new convention, Rev. L. Venchael Booth noted the "all-time low in fellowship, peace and Christian dignity" in the National Baptist Convention, U.S.A., Inc.[48] Yet, some Baptist leaders still dreaded a major division within the denomination at such a critical period in the life of the race.

Nevertheless, about twenty-three black Baptist preachers moved beyond their initial fears and responded positively to the call for a new convention. On November 14-15, 1961, they convened the organizational meeting of the Progressive National Baptist Convention at the Zion Baptist Church, Cincinnati, Ohio, with twenty-three messengers registered, twenty-two churches registered, twelve states registered, and thirty-three messengers participating and fourteen states represented.

The leadership clergy of this new cooperative movement were anxious to organize a convention that would take the "crisis" of the black American experience with unconditional seriousness. They were keenly aware of the new opportunities afforded the black Baptist church to be relevant to the theological, social, and political issues of the civil rights era.

A comprehensive document relative to the rationale for the new convention was compiled by Rev. W. H. R. Powell, a former pastor of the Shiloh Baptist Church, Philadelphia. In the document, he offered a declaration of the organizational structure, principles, and aims of the new Progressive National Baptist Convention of America, Incorporated. This document was authorized at Richmond, Virginia, Thursday morning, May 10, 1962.

Several points of the document were suggestive of a crucial need to organize the new convention. First, Rev. W. H. R. Powell cited the internal disharmony within the National Baptist Convention. Second, the election of officers of the new convention should be limited by tenure. And finally, Powell affirmed that the true spirit of democracy should prevail the new convention.

The following persons were elected as officers of the new Progressive National Baptist Convention of America, Inc.: Rev. T. M. Chambers of California, president; Rev. L. V. Booth of Ohio, vice-president; Rev. J. Carl Mitchell of West Virginia, secretary; Rev. Louis Rawls of Illinois, treasurer; A. J. Hargett, director of publicity; and the Honorable William W. Parker, attorney. These men were able to lead the convention to a slow but significant progress.

As cited earlier in this chapter, the evolution of the cooperative movements among black Baptists resulted from many conflicting and yet sometimes worthy phenomena in human experiences. All conventions of this study resulted from the need for cooperative strides to face the missionary, educational, political, and sociological challenges of an oppressed people. To be sure, these cooperative church experiences served as the basis of growth and development of black Americans. Curiously enough, even the many "crises" in the cooperative movement, both locally and nationally, were not able to stop the tremendous growth of black American Baptists. By and large, the internal and external pressures of the cooperative movement, sociopolitical rather than doctrinal, caused the great divisions among black Baptists.

Fortunately, the black Baptist denominational development was spared the turbulent ordeals of doctrinal struggles that so often characterized denominational development among white Americans. White Americans inherited the bitter strife of doctrinal issues from their European background. However, the black slave experience sheltered black American Christians from exposure and participation in doctrinal battles from Europe. The great cooperative movement among black Baptists evolved out of slavery to become a vital and creative force in the advancement of the Christian faith.

# 3

# The Role of
# Black Baptists in
# Christian Missions

The story of missionary strides among black Baptists is very dramatic and sounds like a modern miracle. Its amazing reservoir of achievements in missionary endeavor under harsh and unfavorable circumstances becomes a rich heritage of courage, unfeigned faith, and self-sacrifice which should be valued by every member of the civilized world. In the first two chapters of this book, we have already seen how the evolution of plantation missions, independent or separate churches, and cooperative movements paralleled a tremendous missionary awakening among black Baptists. Actually, the black Baptist church was born a missionary movement.

Correspondingly, the missionary motivation of the black Baptist church was innate in the "being" of the church movement. Surely enough, it did draw from the great reservoir of spirit which emerged in American Baptist missions in general. The work of William Carey, the great pioneer and symbolic figure of the beginnings of modern Protestant missions, was not unknown to black Baptists at an early time. A few black Baptists were involved in the early years of the missionary idea (1789-1815) among Baptists.

Strangely enough, the foreign mission motif predates home missions in general among black Baptists. As early as the eighteenth century, black Baptists were active in foreign missions. The foreign mission involvement of black Baptists commenced in the West Indies. Rev. George Liele was America's first black missionary to Jamaica, West Indies. He was born in Virginia about the year 1750 and subsequently moved to Georgia with his master, Henry Sharpe, sometime before the revolutionary war. In 1772, George Liele was converted to Christ while residing in Burke County, Georgia, and ordained in 1775.

After his slave master died in the revolutionary war, George Liele became a freedman. Colonel Kirkland, of the British Army, advised Liele to leave the United States with him. In July 1783, George Liele departed the country and settled in the Island of Jamaica. This was ten years before William Carey went to India and twenty-nine years before Adoniram Judson went to Burma. In Jamaica, George Liele served as America's first black foreign missionary. His work began also before that of the English Baptists in the West Indies. When the English Baptists sent their first missionary for Jamaica, George Liele had a church with more than five hundred members.

The first black Baptist missionary to the Bahama Islands was Prince Williams, a freed black of South Carolina. Following the revolutionary war in 1777, he sailed in an open boat for these islands from Saint Augustine, Florida. Rev. Prince Williams preached in Nassau, baptized several natives, and organized a Baptist church about 1790. In 1801, he secured some land and built a small house of worship. Rev. Prince Williams called his new organization the Bethel Baptist Mission. An English missionary, Rev. Joseph Burton, was sent to Nassau in 1833; and by his advice Rev. Prince William, in reaction to the treachery of supposed friends, gave up his work in the Bethel Baptist Church. Subsequently, he organized the Saint John Baptist Church of Nassau where he remained until his death.

The eighteenth century was characterized by scanty missionary strides on the part of unsponsored black preachers reacting to their unique circumstances. It was not until the early nineteenth century that black Baptists developed a more structured approach to foreign missions. Rev. Lott Carey was the first to set in motion this new momentum. The seed for the establishment of a missionary enterprise was planted in Lott Carey while attending William Crane's "Colored" triweekly school, organized in 1815 in the First African Baptist Church in Richmond, Virginia. Here, Lott Carey was nurtured in the work of Rev. William Carey as taught by William Crane and received the inspiration to become a missionary. Initially, Carey organized a small church and the Richmond African Baptist Missionary Society.

## The Evolution of an African Mission

On January 23, 1821, Rev. Lott Carey acted on his desire to become a missionary. He and his little missionary church, consisting of Rev. Collin Teague, Joseph Langford, and the Carey family, left America on the *Nautilus* to begin an African mission. They departed from Norfolk, Virginia, en route to Sierra Leone, West Africa. Rev. Lott Carey and his little congregation remained, of necessity, for several months in Freetown, Sierra Leone.

It was not until 1822, that Rev. Lott Carey and his little church was able to settle at Cape Montserado to begin an African mission. Upon their arrival, the new settlers organized a colonial government. Rev. Lott Carey, the missionary, played a multiple role in the establishment of the African mission. He served as a medical officer, soldier, teacher, preacher, organizer of Providence Baptist Church of Monrovia, and builder of an educational system. The Providence Baptist Church was the First Baptist Church in Africa and one of the earliest denominational movements on the continent.

His missionary career in West Africa lasted less than a decade. Nevertheless, he was able to plant successfully a substantial Africa mission for black Baptists. Soon after Lott Carey's untimely death, several other black missionaries came to West Africa to carry on the missionary enterprise. Among these were Rev. A. W. Anderson, Rev. John Lewis, Rev. Hilary Teague, and Rev. John Day.

As previously mentioned, the evolution of an African mission was a strong motivating factor in the development of associations and conventions among black Baptists. The primary objective of most organized movements was to spread the gospel of Jesus Christ to millions of Africa's sons and daughters groping in spiritual darkness. To this end, much of the economic strength of the associations and conventions went to the support of an African mission.

The American Baptist Missionary Convention, organized in 1840, came into being as a result of many calls and requests from Africa for missionaries and means to continue the African missions commenced by Rev. Lott Carey and other pioneer black Baptists. Hence, the African mission was a strong appeal on the new convention. Due to the limited economic means, however, the convention was forced to cooperate with white missionary organizations in the support of an African mission.

Whatever the degree of involvement, however, the leadership of the American Baptist Missionary Convention took pride in their missionary work. Rev. Rufus L. Perry, corresponding secretary, mentioned this in his report to the convention:

> We have been laboring in the field of missions thirty-one years. But till our consolidation with our Southern brethren at Richmond, Va., in 1867, our labors were confined to the North and the West Coast of Africa. Now our field is the world and we are only detained mostly in the South, for the time being, by the great demand there for our work, and by our limited resources. . . . During the past year we have labored more or less in Canada, and in eighteen different states.[1]

The later work in Canada was unique in black Baptist missionary history and will be discussed extensively later in this chapter. Suffice it to say at this point that the evolution of the Canadian mission paralleled the separate church movement of the late colonial and early national periods in United States history.

Similarly, the Baptist African Missionary Convention of Western States and Territories was organized in 1873 primarily for the support of African missions. The local churches established a policy of sending their own missionaries to Africa while receiving credit for the work through the convention. Very little is known of the work of these early missionaries from the Baptist African Missionary Convention of Western States and Territories. To be sure, they paved the way for future involvement of blacks in the missionary enterprise.

By 1877, the missionary work of black Baptists in Africa had all but died out. In the report of the Consolidated American Baptist Missionary Convention, the leadership complained:

> The seal for missionary work in Africa, that characterized our Convention, some fifteen years ago, has all but died out. Our Convention ought to support a missionary in Africa. Indeed, there ought to be a foreign department to the Convention, officered or managed by a Foreign Board, to take entire charge of the Haytian Mission, and to found a Mission in Africa, or cooperate with those already established. We are too great a body, and too deeply concerned in the enlightenment of Africa, to be indifferent in regard to missionary work there. . . .
>
> Though of American birth and education, we are nevertheless sons of Africa. God has ordained it. . . . England is circumscribing the continent of Africa, with commercial posts, and acquiring the territory. God signals the intelligent men of our race, to begin to occupy the land, lest the African soon became as a wandering Jew, without Judea, and without a Jerusalem.[2]

Again, the urgency of the African mission, on the part of black Baptists, was expressed in this report to the convention. Black Baptists were not satisfied with the meager support of African missions on the part of white American

Baptists. They were aware of the relationship between black missionary involvement and the sociopolitical interests of Africans. Blacks were more in tune with the heartbeats of their African brother.

By 1879, the Consolidated American Baptist Missionary Convention was supporting the missionary work of Rev. C. H. Richardson in Africa. Apparently, the foreign board had been organized to coordinate an African mission. The Board received periodic reports from Rev. C. H. Richardson on his progress. Rev. C. H. Richardson arrived at Victoria, Cameroons, west coast of Africa, in the month of December 1878. After a brief stay, Rev. C. H. Richardson, in the company with a few other missionaries, traveled four days into the interior of Africa and established a mission station at Bakunda. The king of the region and his people received them cordially and gave them assurance of protection and aid in their work. Richardson was able to organize a school and preached regularly the gospel. By orders of the king the natives assisted in the construction of the school, and all the youth of his dominion were required to attend the school. Richardson became the superintendent of the new school. Just before the king's death, he advised his subjects: "Hear what the missionaries teach you, for I believe they bring you a message from God. I am going to God, for he has sent a multitude of people to bring me to him, and I have seen them."[3]

Also, in 1878, the black Baptists of Virginia, who had been foremost in mission work since the founding of the Richmond African Baptist Missionary Society and the Petersburg African Baptist Missionary Society, raised money and sent Rev. Solomon Crosby to Africa. He was sent to Africa to work with Rev. W. W. Colley at Abeokuta in connection with the Foreign Mission Board of the Southern Baptist Convention.

Similarly, the Black Baptists of South Carolina made an

independent attempt in African missions. At a meeting of their state convention in May 1878, the convention delegates voted to send a missionary to Africa in the person of Rev. Harrison N. Bouey. Rev. Harrison N. Bouey was able to organize an outstanding missionary work in Liberia. He organized two churches, two associations, and so aroused a missionary spirit that it subsequently led to the organization of a National Baptist Convention back in America. Bouey spent seven years working in Royesville with the Gola tribe, while still a bachelor. He built a road which runs by Royesville and is still named in his honor, "The Bouey Road."[4] When he returned to the United States, Rev. Bouey was so impressed with the possibilities of the African missions that he felt compelled to encourage black Americans to organize a national conventional effort to operate a significant African missionary enterprise.

With the development of a strong black Baptist missionary program, Rev. W. W. Colley, a missionary to Africa appointed by a white foreign missions board, returned to the United States to join in a movement for greater involvement in the African mission. Rev. W. W. Colley was born in Prince Edward County, Virginia, February 12, 1847. He was baptized September 1870, and united with the Grand Hill Church. Having entered Richmond Institute about this time, he spent his vacation of 1871 and 1872 preaching in Louisa County, Virginia. He was ordained at Alexandria, Virginia, in 1873. Subsequently, he became another pioneer missionary to Africa, appointed by the Southern Baptist Convention.[5]

In the early 1880s, the Southern Baptist Convention lost some of its momentum in West Africa. Rev. W. W. Colley terminated his work in Sierra Leone and Liberia; and subsequently the Convention ended its work in the area. With the germination of a spirit of black nationalism, the effectiveness of the work of this white Baptist body diminished. In 1898, H. J. Kletzing and W. H. Crogman argued that centuries of effort and centuries of corresponding failure fully demonstrated that the white man cannot colonize the largest part of the great continent of Africa.[6] White racism prevented them from relating to the African ethos; increasingly, Africans had become more aware of their heritage.

With the advancement of the National Baptist Convention of the United States of America and the Lott Carey Home and Foreign Mission Convention, the African missionary enterprise of black Baptists took on a new momentum. More money and personnel were utilized in the development of the African missions, more in tune with the African ethos. Most of the national leaders became electrified with a spirit to do something significant for fellow blacks in the motherland. In 1902, Rev. L. G. Jordan delivered a major address on the needs of Africa to the Negro Young People's Christian and Educational Congress in Atlanta, Georgia. He emphasized to this large delegation of black leaders the fact that black Americans were responsible for the evangelization of Africa:

> If the Negro of America will but feel his responsibility and under take the evangelization of Africa in God's name, unborn millions of Africa's sons will witness a transformed continent. . . . From that great black continent can be carved states or empires, from her cradle will come sons and daughters to rule and reign in the name of Christianity. Negroes of America, God calls you to duty; He calls you to service and He calls you now.[7]

Blacks were better equipped spiritually and emotionally to serve the unique needs of African missions. They shared the same heartbeat of oppression.

In 1883, the Baptist Foreign Mission Convention sent Rev. W. W. Colley, along with five other missionaries, to establish a missionary program in Liberia, West Africa. In December 1883, they settled in the Vey country, forty miles from Monrovia and fourteen miles from Cape Mount to organize two missions, Bendoo and Jundoo. After ten years, disease, death, and furlough decimated their numbers and finally tribal wars so endangered their lives that the remaining two, J. J. Cole and his wife, were called home in July 1893, and the mission houses were sold. For several years thereafter, the African mission of black Baptists advanced slowly.

In 1896, the Foreign Mission Board of the newly organized National Baptist Convention of the United States of America elected Rev. L. G. Jordan, pastor of the Union Baptist Church of Philadelphia, as corresponding secretary. He proved to be the right leader to establish a more aggressive and effective missionary program in Africa.

Accordingly, Rev. L. G. Jordan led the Foreign Mission Board to send to Africa the first group of five missionaries since the reorganization in 1895, beginning with Rev. R. A. Jackson and wife. During the first sixteen years following 1895, the Board sent to foreign fields twenty-six American missionaries as follows: Rev. R. A. Jackson, wife, and three children of Arkansas, 1894, to South Africa; Rev. Harrison N. Bouey and three sons of Missouri, 1902, to West Africa; Rev. A. W. Anderson, wife, and three children of Connecticut, 1902, to South America; and Rev. W. R. Richardson.[8]

Sometime near the turn of the century, Rev. J. C. Jackson, who became the father of missions in South Africa among black Baptists, was sent to work at Cape Town. Cape Town was a great city which attracted people from other areas to work on the docks of the seaport city. Many of these workers were converted by Rev. J. C. Jackson and went back to their homes in the interior carrying the gospel of Jesus Christ. This was Rev. Jackson's methodology of starting churches throughout South Africa. The nationals who came to hear him, principally from Middledrift, were instrumental in organizing new churches in South Africa.

Significantly enough, Rev. J. C. Jackson was also able to lead a Roman Catholic to join in the black Baptist missionary endeavor in Africa. Namely, Rev. J. I. Buchanan was converted by the powerful preaching of Rev. J. C. Jackson. Subsequently, Rev. J. I. Buchanan established a great church in Middledrift, South Africa. He also established an extended mission with four small churches. Buchanan also attempted to start a school in Middledrift, South Africa, but died before the realization of his dream came true in 1907. After his death, the nationals attempted to organize the school.

Another black Baptist missionary of note was Rev. James Edward East. He was born January 27, 1881, at Huntsville, Alabama, the third child and only son of James and Georgiana Bonefield East. At an early age, he was converted. Soon thereafter, he became interested in the African mission. Hence, Rev. James Edward East entered the Missionary Training Institute at Nyack, New York, in 1904, and later became a student in the Virginia Seminary of Lynchburg, Virginia. While attending the latter school, he met Miss Lucinda Thomas. She became Mrs. James E. East on October 18, 1909; he graduated the same year. James Edward East was licensed to preach July 8, 1904, and ordained September 4, 1907.

In October 1909, Rev. James Edward East and his bride of a week sailed for South Africa. Seven children were born to the union, six of whom survived him. The first four were born in Africa. For eleven years Rev. East served faithfully on the foreign field, returning to the United States in 1920. He left behind a church with 600 members at Rabula, South Africa.

In 1915, Dr. E. D. Hubbard indicated his desire to serve the African Mission. He was a native of Mississippi. Initially, he worked in Africa under the auspices of the newly formed National Baptist Convention of America, Unincorporated. He sailed for Liberia and did his first mission work near Careysburg. After clearing away trees, Dr. E. D. Hubbard erected a temporary building for a mission station which he named in his own honor. There he labored very hard to establish a mission school. However, his work with the convention was not productive due to a lack of funds for the African mission.

Subsequently, Dr. E. D. Hubbard visited the Seuhn Mission of the National Baptist Convention, U.S.A., Inc., and made application to the Foreign Mission Board to work under the auspices of the older and more established convention. Accordingly, he became one of the principal missionaries at Suehn. At Suehn, Dr. Hubbard advanced a tremendous agricultural mission to feed the national students. His outstanding missionary career was terminated by death, December, 1932.

In the meantime, Rev. James Edward East had returned to the United States from Africa and had been elected corresponding secretary of the Foreign Mission Board. To this office, he brought a wealth of experience from the foreign field. Rev. East charted a course for the National Baptist Convention, U.S.A., Inc., through the most difficult years of the black Baptist endeavor to advance an African mission. In 1925, he gave a detailed report on the challenge.

Circumstances have altogether changed in recent years. Africa has been gobbled up by some six European nations. The world has watched carefully the progress of the American Negro: the wonderful strides he has made in civilization, the rapid way he has reduced his illiteracy since the Civil War, the thousands and thousands of professional men, lawyers, doctors, teachers and business men that have developed within the last half century, the vast amount of real estate and wealth he has acquired, the number of wonderful institutions he has built; and this progress of the black man has made the white world tremble as they question themselves, "What will happen if all of Africa awakens as the black man of America awakened?"

First, a great discussion was held by the European nations as to what steps should be taken to keep the black man of Africa from coming to America, being educated in our schools and getting ideas of freedom and desires for equal opportunity for happiness and livelihood. Everything possible was done to discourage native Africans from coming to this country. Then the next step was taken to prohibit people of color from going from America, especially those who represented religious institutions and went as leaders of the people. We are now at the point where with the exception of Liberia, a Negro Republic, with about 360 miles of coastline, all of the dark continent is practically closed to Negro missionaries who go out under independent Negro churches such as the Baptist, A.M.E., and A.M.E.Z. A few years back, some of our missionaries got as far as Cape Town and were held on the boat for a while. After putting up large deposits and much pleading, we got them off on temporary permit. Now, however, the governments in question have notified their consuls representing them in this country not to issue passports, and have also notified steamship companies not to sell tickets to any colored missionaries wishing to come to parts of Africa unless they produce a permit from such countries.[9]

This report reflects the tremendous sociopolitical changes on the continent of Africa. The partitioning of Africa by European powers had reached an apex in its hindrance to the black church's attempt at a viable African mission. The Europeans were by 1925 feeling more acutely the pressure of African nationalism. Accordingly, they tried to stop black American activity on the continent hoping, at the same time, to suppress African nationalism. This became a major blemish on the missionary activity of all whites in Africa. African nationalists became more suspicious of the white man's Christianity.

Rev. James Edward East's strategy under the circumstances was to develop a model African mission in Liberia. He did not want political factors to prevent a vital witness in Africa. He observed: "One of the most effective weapons we can use to break open doors in other parts of Africa and have those European governments to open their doors and let us in, is to put on a very effective, sound missionary program for the redemption of Liberia."[10] The wise programming and perseverance of black Baptists were able to advance an African mission through such years of test. To be sure, the African mission has been the primary missionary enterprise of the denomination.

## Black Women in Christian Missions

Obviously, the tremendous potentials of black Baptist women to do meaningful missions on the foreign field were recognized by the associations and conventions of black Baptists. In general, black women have possessed tremendous strength of character as required for the development of a black Baptist missionary enterprise. As early as 1871, the Women's Baptist Foreign Missionary Society of the West was organized with its headquarters in Chicago. This organization reflected the growing awareness on the part of black women of their potentials for missions. Miss Louise C. Fleming was the first black woman missionary from America to be sent to Congo, Africa, under the auspices of this society. Miss Fleming labored extensively with the African mission.

After Miss Louise C. Fleming and other women proved their special usefulness in Christian missions, Rev. William J. Simmons, president of State University, Louisville, Kentucky, decided to inspire other black Baptist women to organize independent women's missionary societies and establish meaningful foreign mission programs. His first move was to attempt the organization of a missionary society among the black Baptist women of Kentucky and to receive the new society's endorsement. Subsequently, the women proceeded to organize themselves. The first meeting was held in the Fifth Street Baptist Church, Louisville, Kentucky, September 1883. The meeting was called to order by Rev. W. J. Simmons and a temporary organization was effected until the adoption of a permanent constitution.

Consequently, the Baptist women of Kentucky organized a convention named "The Baptist Women's Educational Convention of the State of Kentucky." These black Baptist women established three objectives for the new convention. First, to encourage the attendance of the youth of the state to attend State University under Rev. William J. Simmon's administration. Second, they decided to contribute funds for the payment of the debt on the property of the State University. Third, they planned a program of greater missionary involvement on the part of the black Baptist women of Kentucky. Soon they organized "Children's Bands" for the purpose of gathering and imparting information concerning the religious work in Kentucky, the training of children for Christ, and the collection of funds to pay the property debt at State University.

As expected, the organized program of missions commenced by the Baptist Women of Kentucky soon gained the attention of leaders outside the state. Rev. E. M. Brawley, after visiting the convention, was so impressed that he became determined to organize a similar organization in the state of Alabama. He returned to Alabama and called a meeting to organize what became known as the Baptist Women's State Convention of Alabama. The Baptist women of Alabama organized subsequently women's educational and missionary societies throughout the local churches in the state. The convention placed primary emphasis on the support of Selma University and mission work.

Similarly, the women of Arkansas organized the Women's Baptist Missionary Association in 1888 at the First Baptist Church in Little Rock, Arkansas. This general trend was followed by black Baptist women throughout the United States.

The interest of these Baptist women soon extended to the foreign fields. They became increasingly supportive of the African mission. Significant sums of money have come from the various women's conventions for the support of missionaries on the foreign fields.

One of the greatest black Baptist women who pioneered the African mission was Nora A. Gordon. She was born in Columbia, Georgia, in 1866. Her parents were formerly slaves, belonging to the well-known General Gordon from whom they received their name. Miss Nora A. Gordon attended the public schools of La Grange, Georgia, where she resided. In the fall of 1882, she entered Spellman Seminary. At Spellman, she was converted and joined a Baptist church in Atlanta.

Miss Gordon's early missionary career consisted of the organization of temperance societies, Sunday Schools, and causing family altars to be erected in the homes of her Sunday School pupils. In 1888, she completed her course of study at Spellman Seminary and became a teacher in one of the Atlanta public schools. In the meantime, Miss Gordon experienced a call or inspiration to work on the foreign fields of Africa. She obeyed the call and set sail to Africa where her labors lasted until 1893. In Africa, Miss Nora A. Gordon experienced a health problem which forced her to return to the United States. Fortunately, her health soon improved, and she married Rev. S. C. Gordon of Stanley Pool. Subsequently, the two returned to Congo, Africa.[11]

In 1898, Miss Mamie Branton went to South Africa to extend the influence of black Baptist women in the African mission. She labored faithfully in South Africa for several years. Unfortunately, Miss Branton's service was hindered by the tremendous political unrest in South Africa. Her missionary activities paralleled with the British Boer War of 1899-1900. Much of the land was in a state of turmoil. The stress severely tested the missionary zest of Miss Mamie Branton. However, she labored well under the circumstances.

The National Baptist Convention, U.S.A., Inc., was very determined in its commitment to advance a significant African mission. In the early 1900s, the convention sent several black women to the foreign fields. Among them were Miss Eliza L. Davis of Texas, Miss Susie A. Taylor of South Carolina, and Miss E. B. Delaney of Florida to West Africa. Each made significant contributions to Christian missions.

Miss E. B. Delaney's missionary work was particularly outstanding. She was sent by the Baptist women of Florida after being trained at Spellman Seminary. In 1901, Miss Delaney sailed for British East Central Africa under the auspices of the Foreign Mission Board of the National Baptist Convention and labored faithfully at Chiradzulu, Zyasaland, for five years. She was cofounder of the Providence Industrial Mission. Her labors resulted in the development of many schools in Central and West Africa and did much to inspire other black American women to rally to the cause of the redemption of Africa.

In 1905, Miss E. B. Delaney returned to the United States. To her great surprise, she was accompanied by a native African boy who was previously converted under Miss Delaney's training and teaching in Africa. The African boy slipped away from his parents and made his way through more than two-hundred miles of jungles, infested with lions and tigers, in order to follow Miss Delaney back to America. His name was Daniel Malekebu. Miss Delaney was so impressed with the youth that she encouraged Daniel Malekebu to enter the Meharry Medical School at Nashville, Tennessee.

In 1917, Daniel Malekebu graduated from the medical school and married Miss Flora Zeto of the Belgium Congo, who was a graduate of Spellman College of Atlanta, Georgia. Subsequently, Dr. Daniel Malekebu and his wife returned to Africa to advance the cause of Christian missions among their people. He became supervisor of missions of South, East, and Central Africa.

To be sure, the medical mission of Dr. Malekebu resulted from the mission work of the great black missionary, Miss E. B. Delaney. In 1912, Miss Delaney returned to Africa to work in Liberia and labored until her death in 1920. According to tradition, she went into bush areas, cleared the ground, drove down stakes, and commenced a significant work for the African mission. This sacrificial effort resulted in the founding of the Suehn Industrial Mission in Liberia, West Africa, in 1912. Miss Delaney spent a total of eight years in Liberia and three in British Central Africa. The contributions of this great woman stand out in the missionary enterprise of black Baptists.

The Women's Convention, Auxiliary to the National Baptist Convention, U.S.A., Inc., organized on September 15, 1900, in Richmond, Virginia, contributed largely to the support of Miss E. B. Delaney's missionary work in Liberia. The success of the black Baptist women on the foreign field inspired the Women's Convention to increase its financial support of the Foreign Mission Board.

As early as 1909, the Foreign Mission Board of the National Baptist Convention, U.S.A., Inc., commenced utilizing women nationals to render service to the foreign field. One of the earliest of such missionaries was Miss Mary A.

Buchanan. She was born in Capetown, South Africa. In 1900, Miss Buchanan was baptized by her father, J. I. Buchanan, at Middledrift. Subsequently, she spent five years in specialized training in the United States, commencing in June 1904. Her father had turned the young lady over to Rev. L. G. Jordan, secretary of the Foreign Mission Board, to receive a good education in the United States. In 1909, Miss Mary A. Buchanan returned to Africa to work with her people. The Wheat Street Baptist Church of Atlanta, Georgia, under the pastorate of Rev. P. James Bryant, made an arrangement with the Foreign Mission Board for the support of the young national missionary in Africa.[12]

In 1912, the Foreign Mission Board of the National Baptist Convention, U.S.A., Inc., sent Miss Susie Taylor to work in Liberia, West Africa. Miss Taylor's missionary labors were closely related to the work of Miss E. B. Delaney. She worked primarily at Grand Bassa, Liberia. Miss Susie Taylor founded the Baptist Industrial Academy, the second largest school under the auspices of the National Baptist Convention, U.S.A., Inc. In 1913, Miss Taylor returned to the United States on furlough. To be sure, this was a well-deserved furlough because she had worked manually in clearing land for the new school. Three hundred acres of land had been given to the Foreign Mission Board of the National Baptist Convention, U.S.A., Inc., for the erection of the Baptist Industrial Academy through the generosity of the Baptists of Liberia.[13] Miss Susie Taylor was assisted by Miss Eliza Davis in clearing the land.

Rightly so, Miss Susie Taylor was succeeded at the Baptist Industrial Academy (also called the Bible and Industrial Mission) by her friend and coworker, Miss Eliza Davis. Miss Eliza Davis continued the same vigorous approach to the development of this great mission in Liberia. She labored at the Academy from 1913 to 1915. Unfortunately, Miss Davis's missionary work was hampered by the severe problems and resultant split of the National Baptist Convention. After the crisis ended, she resumed the initial vigor of work at the Academy until 1938.

Another pioneer black woman in African missions was Mrs. Lucinda Thomas East, wife of Rev. James E. East. She served the missionary cause for over a half century. In October 1909, Mrs. East accompanied her husband to South Africa where they began their work under the Foreign Mission Board of the National Baptist Convention. Together, they served eleven years in South Africa at the Middledrift Mission. Mrs. East rendered a tremendous service in assisting her husband in the education of South Africans at the Buchanan Mission and Industrial School, Middledrift, South Africa. Their work was so successful that Rev. James E. East was affectionately called "one of the greatest missionaries ever sent out by the Baptist Board."[14]

In 1921, Rev. East was elected corresponding secretary of the Foreign Mission Board of the National Baptist Convention, U.S.A., Inc., and the East family settled in Philadelphia, Pennsylvania. Nevertheless, Mrs. Lucinda Thomas East persisted in her love for the African mission. She was able to inspire her daughter, Gladys East, to continue the family tradition of foreign mission service. Gladys was born while the East family was serving in South Africa and was eight years old when the family moved to the United States. She left the United States in 1944 to serve at the Suehn Industrial Mission in Liberia, South Africa.[15] Gladys East was just as aggressive as her mother in the advancement of the African mission.

Mrs. D. R. Horton, along with her husband, was sent to Liberia in 1917 by the Foreign Mission Board of the National Baptist Convention. Mrs. Horton was a graduate of Morehouse College and Spellman College of Atlanta, Georgia. The Hortons made this journey when it was very dangerous to travel on the seas due to the extensive submarine warfare. Such warfare was extensive along the Africa coast during World War I. She worked at the Baptist Industrial Academy at Grand Bassa, Liberia. Mrs. Horton was very supportive to her husband in his strides to organize several churches among the Bassa people. They were able to organize one very large church, the Saint Simon Baptist Church, at Grand Bassa. Many converts were won through the ministry of this church.

Mrs. Delia Harris was another black Woman who would not be deterred from foreign service by the world war. In 1919, she sailed for West Africa, accompanied by Miss Pricilla Bryon and Rev. L. G. Jordan, the former secretary of the Foreign Mission Board of the National Baptist Convention, U.S.A. Miss Delia Harris initially labored at the Providence Industrial Mission. Later, she moved to another area and founded the Burrough's Industrial Mission. Primarily, the Mount Carmel Baptist Church of Washington, D.C., under the leadership of Rev. W. H. Jernagin, paid the missionary salary for Miss Delia Harris.

In February 1920, the Lott Carey Baptist Foreign Mission Convention sent Mrs. F. B. Watson to labor in Brewerville, Liberia. She was a member of the First Baptist Church of Kansas City, Kansas. This church made significant contributions to her expenses in Liberia. Mrs. F. B. Watson's pioneer field of labor was at the C. S. Brown Mission at Careysburg. By 1936, Mrs. Watson was able to report some of the fruits of her labor. The mission station included: 135 converts and ten Baptist churches—seven among the Bassa and three among the Gola and Pessa tribes.

After retirement from the mission field, Mrs. Watson returned to her native church in Kansas City under the pastorate of Rev. E. A. Freeman. However, she never gave up her interest in the African mission. In fact, Mrs. Watson often made speaking tours throughout the United States, speaking to both white and black congregations on behalf of the African mission. Similarly, she entered the field of professional writing and published a book entitled *The Native Liberian Missionary Field* in 1942. To be sure, Mrs. F. B. Watson made a tremendous contribution to the black missionary enterprise.

During Mrs. Watson's missionary career in Liberia, the republic went through some tremendous sociopolitical changes. When she arrived in Liberia, the British government had the gold and rubber concession and an English bank in Monrovia. However, the world war caused the British people to abandon their economic involvement in Liberia. Subsequently, the gold and rubber fields soon grew up in bushes in the Johnsonville area. The British presence was a tremendous drain on the economy as they made no real contributions to the welfare of the Liberian government. By 1926, the Firestone Tire and Rubber Company made an appeal for and obtained a ninety-nine year concession on the rubber field. This signaled the beginning of a substantial American involvement in the economy of the republic.

The sociopolitical changes in Liberia did not deter Mrs. Francis B. Watson from the establishment of a significant mission in the republic. One of her first students in 1920 was Joel N. Talbot of the Pessie tribe. The Pessie tribe, sometimes called the Kpellie, was the great laboring tribe in Liberia. Hence, Joel N. Talbot brought to the mission school an industrious spirit. After he graduated from Mrs. Watson's school, Talbot became a major in the Liberian army.[16] Many other persons of industry and leadership were educated by Mrs. Francis B. Watson.

In 1922, Mrs. Watson worked with the Bassa tribe in Monrovia. About forty Baptist churches grew out of her work with these natives. Her work with the Bassa tribe was a tremendous success. In January 1932, she traveled into the interior to a place called Sanoquellie where she conducted a Christian service at the request of the district commissioner. Mrs. Watson refuted the claims of the Muhammadans, and her discourse led to the conversion of a native boy of the Mana tribe.[17]

Similarly, Mrs. Francis B. Watson was instrumental in helping two natives receive an education in the United States. Sarah Williams of the Bassa tribe and B. G. Dennis of the Gbandie tribe were given assistance by the Liberian government through the influence of Mrs. Watson. Sarah Williams graduated in June 1953, from the girl's high school in Brooklyn, New York. Subsequently, she entered Cornell University. B. G. Dennis studied auto mechanics and, subsequently, graduated from Lincoln University, Jefferson City, Missouri, with the B.A. and B.S. degrees. He took the Masters degree at Fisk University and was given a scholarship of $1,800 to study for the Ph.D. degree from Chicago University. B. G. Dennis later became an ordained Baptist preacher. Both Dennis and Sarah Williams returned to Liberia to work among the natives.[18]

In concomitance to regular missionary activities, Mrs. Francis B. Watson was active in bringing social change to Liberia. She was a strong supporter of woman's suffrage in the republic. Mrs. Watson argued:

> The women know how to use the ballot as well as the men and better than some of them. The women are not going to be a hindrance to the men, but a helper; not a liability, to them but an asset. There are many reforms that the women can help the men to bring about. Women of Africa have been kept down, but this administration (President's W. V. S. Tubman's administration) has brought them to the front.[19]

Mrs. Watson labored for several years on the foreign field in Liberia. When she returned to the United States, her interest did not cease for the African mission. Mrs. Watson traveled extensively in this country to speak on behalf of foreign missions.

In 1924, the Foreign Mission Board of the National Baptist Convention, U.S.A., Inc., sent Miss Sarah C. Williamson to Africa. She took over the work of the Suehn Mission Station. After spending more than a year in the position, Miss Williamson had to leave the school for the Tropical Hospital in Germany to be cured of black water fever. She soon recovered and returned directly to the work of the Suehn Mission in Liberia. In 1925, Miss Williamson reported to the Foreign Mission Board that there were almost one hundred students, including day school students from Fortsville and Hartford, attending the Bible Industrial Mission of the Suehn Mission. She organized the girls of this school into Girl Reserve clubs patterned after the YWCA in the United States. In 1932, Miss Sarah Williamson returned to the United States on furlough.

A group of missionaries were sent out by the Foreign Mission Board of the National Baptist Convention, U.S.A., Inc., sometime in 1925. Among this new group of black Baptist women were Mrs. A. P. Brown, Mrs. D. S. Malekebu, Mrs. E. H. Bouey, Mrs. J. L. Spencer, Miss Mildred Griffin, Mrs. Hattie Mae Davis, Mrs. Emma F. Butler, and Mrs. J. S. Cyrus. These women missionaries were accompanied by several black Baptist clergymen. By 1926, many of these missionaries had assumed work in different parts of Africa.

At this time, the Foreign Missions Board operated an extensive program in West Africa with twenty-six missionaries, three central schools, and eight other stations. Plans were also being developed by the Women's Convention of the National Baptist Convention to erect a hospital in Liberia, West Africa.

In 1928, Miss Ruth Occomy was commissioned by the Foreign Mission Board of the National Baptist Convention,

Miss Minnie C. Lyons, pioneer black
woman missionary to Liberia, West Africa,
for the Lott Carey Baptist Foreign Mission
Convention, and Rev. A. Russell Awkard,
pastor of the New Zion Baptist Church,
Louisville, Kentucky—one of largest
contributors to Christian missions among
black Baptists.

U.S.A., Inc., to serve as a medical missionary in Africa. She sailed for Africa to do work as a trained nurse at the hospital in Monrovia, Liberia, February 1928. Miss Occomy rendered outstanding work to the sick in Africa. She worked as a yokefellow for the missionary, Dr. Pauline Dinkens, and Dr. A. F. DeWalt, a surgeon dentist in the Carrie V. Dyer Hospital.

The Carrie V. Dyer Hospital in Monrovia, where Miss Ruth Occomy labored, was the first missionary hospital erected in Liberia, and the first in Africa ever erected by black women. It was erected by the Women's National Baptist Convention, Auxiliary to the National Baptist Convention, U.S.A., Inc. The hospital was established as a medium of hospitalization and life saving for the natives, citizens of Monrovia, and missionaries of the various stations in the Republic of Liberia. It was erected at a time of dire medical needs: natives were ignorant of hygiene and sanitation, and large numbers of witch doctors promoted cruel fetishism, exploitation, and death.[20]

Also in 1928, the Foreign Mission Board sent Miss Mildred Griffin to Africa. She set sail on December 23, 1928, to labor at the Suehn Industrial Mission of Monrovia. Miss Griffin witnessed a significant increase in the student body at the mission school. Her work was highly valued at the mission in Liberia.

Miss Naomi Crawford was another black American woman who made a tremendous contribution to the medical missions program in Africa. In 1934, she was commissioned by the Foreign Mission Board to work as a nurse at the Carrie V. Dyer Memorial Hospital, Monrovia, Liberia. Miss Crawford went to the hospital to replace nurse R. L. Turner. Prior to Miss Crawford's arrival, Mrs. J. S. Cyrus carried on the work at the hospital. That same year, Miss Mildred Griffin, returned missionary, was sent to Africa to work at the Suehn Mission.

In 1938, the Foreign Mission Board sent Miss Susan Harris, RN, of Baltimore, Maryland, to work at the Dyer Memorial Hospital of Liberia. She was supported largely by the Cosmopolitan Independent Community Church of Chicago. The church was encouraged to support Miss Harris by Miss Winifred Borroughs, a teacher at the Suehn Industrial Mission.

Black American Baptist women were not only active in the African mission but in other parts of the world as well. A good example of the work of such women was Mrs. Janie Morris. She was commissioned by the Foreign Mission Board to work in the Bahama Islands. In fact, Mrs. Morris was the pioneer woman missionary to the Bahama Islands. She saw an opportunity for an extensive work there and called this to the attention of the Foreign Mission Board.[21] In 1940, Mrs. Morris was recognized by the Women's National Baptist Convention for outstanding missionary service.

These black Baptist women were the pioneers of the great work of black Baptist women in Christian missions. They established such a noble record that the National Baptist Convention, U.S.A., Inc., the Lott Carey Baptist Foreign Mission Convention, and the National Baptist Convention of America, Unincorporated, have deemed it wise and expedient to use many other black women of such quality to labor on foreign fields. The story of their tremendous work on the foreign field should be related in more details by a subsequent researcher.

## The Role of Nationals in the Black Baptist Missionary Enterprise

Early in the evolution of the black Baptist foreign mission enterprise, the leadership of all the conventions saw the wisdom of training and utilizing nationals to participate in

Christian missions. The rise of nationalism in the twentieth century was especially significant in the decision to use nationals in the advance of the foreign mission program of black Baptists. Black Baptists realized the necessity of the development of an indigenous church movement on the various foreign missions to ensure a stable program relevant to the changes among the people of underdeveloped lands. Specifically, the Lott Carey Baptist Foreign Mission Convention has been foremost in this policy. It has an established policy of employing nationals to lead all of its foreign mission stations. The utilization of nationals was designed to facilitate the indigenuity of Christianity.

To be sure, the indigenuity of Christianity in Africa has been the crucial challenge of Christian Missions from the beginning of the enterprise. Throughout history, people have experienced the need of religion in an "at home atmosphere." Such a personal experience as one's religious faith could not be thought of indefinitely as foreign or imported. Hence, the psychological and sociopolitical needs of Africans necessitated the involvement of their own people in the reestablishment of Christianity in Africa.

Again, most of the problems experienced by white Christians in Africa centered in their lack of understanding of the African ethos, on the one hand, and, on the other, their failure to divorce Christian missions from the politics of racism. The attitude of white racists blinded many white Christians and caused them to view Africa as "the dark continent." Some even forgot the existence of primitive Christianity in Africa. In fact, Christianity existed in both North and East Africa long before it reached the island of Britain and many other parts of Continental Europe. Africa was one of the earliest locales of the Christian church and one of its most important intellectual centers. Many of the African church fathers contributed to the formative years of Christianity.

The challenge to use nationals in African missions was a radical movement designed to reestablish Christianity as a major church movement on the continent. Such a move was destined to challenge the politics of racism and gradually free modern Christianity from the bondage of the racial heresy. Just as Africa served as an early battleground between conflicting Christian doctrines, it was slowly to be pushed by Christian nationalism into another battleground for Christianity's freedom from racial heresy. White Christians could not forever look in the eyes of powerful African church leaders with any false concepts of white racial superiority.

As early as 1896, the seed was planted for the beginning of service on the part of nationals in the foreign mission enterprise of black American Baptists. Mr. Joseph Booth, a friend of Africa, brought Mr. John Chilembwe to the United States from East Central Africa. The story of this young African boy will highlight further the rationale for the indigenousness of Christianity. It has a place, characterized by a thrilling dynamism, in the annals of missionary history.

John Chilembwe was born sometime in the late nineteenth century in East Central Africa. He was a member of the Yao tribe which was a strong and aggressive people who knew what they wanted and went after it.[22] The strength of mind and persistence of resolution were manifested very early in the life of this African youth. He was expelled from the Pedo-baptist Mission in East Central Africa because he had read in the Gospel of Matthew that Jesus was baptized in the Jordan. The word for baptize in John Chilembwe's native tongue was *ambezu,* the meaning of which was equivalent to the Greek word *baptizo.* When this little African youth fastened the concept in his mind that baptizing meant dipping, a covering up, submerging in water, he refused to have water sprinkled on his head. Hence, he was expelled from the mission.[23]

Fortunately, Joseph Booth, an Englishman and friend of Africa, happened to meet John Chilembwe after he was expelled from the mission. Joseph Booth agreed to baptize Chilembwe in the Zambesi River. They became great friends afterward and on Booth's second trip to America he brought this young African with him.[24] Meanwhile, John Chilembwe had become a "cook boy" for the Booth family.[25]

Soon after their arrival in New York, Joseph Booth introduced John Chilembwe to Rev. L. G. Jordan, corresponding secretary of the Foreign Mission Board of the National Baptist Convention, U.S.A., Inc. Rev. Jordan expressed an interest in the education of the African youth. So, early in 1898, Rev. Jordan took Chilembwe to Roanoke, Virginia, where Rev. William W. Brown was the pastor of the High Street Baptist Church. The two ministers then decided to introduce John Chilembwe to Professor Gregory Willis Hayes, president of Virginia Theological Seminary and College, Lynchburg, Virginia, who adopted spiritually this African youth. In the meantime, the black Baptists of Philadelphia and Rev. William W. Brown of the High Street Baptist Church in Roanoke, Virginia, decided to sponsor Chilembwe's education at the Virginia Theological Seminary and College.

The years at college afforded a tremendous social and spiritual exposure for John Chilembwe. He was apprised of the adverse sociopolitical situation of black people in America. The growing problem of lynching was impressed upon Chilembwe's mind and spirit. Professor Gregory Willis Hayes schooled the African youth in the self-help philosophy of the struggle of blacks in America.

In 1899, John Chilembwe returned to his native land after having graduated from Virginia Theological Seminary

and College, Lynchburg, Virginia. Just prior to his departure, Chilembwe was ordained to the work of the gospel
ministry. His departure was advised by a physician because
Chilembwe had contracted asthma in America. John Chilembwe was accompanied by Rev. Charles S. Morris on the
voyage back to Africa.

Rev. Charles S. Morris was given an assignment by the
Foreign Mission Board to take over the general supervision
of the National Baptist Convention's missionary activities
in Africa, and Chilembwe, under the auspices of the Board,
was to set up his own mission in British Central Africa.[26]
Chilembwe arrived at Mbombwe, Chiradzulu, sometime in
1900, and began work on his little church and school. His
mission was initially named the Afawa Providence Industrial Mission. Later, he was assisted by Rev. L. N. Cheek and
Miss Emma Delany.

The work of the new mission grew rapidly. Chilembwe
and Cheek divided between themselves the tasks of teaching and proselytizing.[27] In the meantime, Mrs. John Chilembwe and Miss Emma Delany organized sewing classes.
The team approach to missions continued between these
missionaries for about two years. After that John Chilembwe had the sole responsibility for the work of the
mission.

Soon after 1910, the converts of John Chilembwe were
implicated in the Bambata Rebellion in British Central
Africa. In 1906, a Zulu tribal military force rebelled against
British oppression. The uprising was, however, crushed by
the British military power.[28] This signaled the beginning of
grave troubles for John Chilembwe and the Afawa Providence Industrial Mission.

The nationalistic tendencies of John Chilembwe soon
came to the forefront during the struggles of his people. In
1915, he led a conspiracy resulting in a revolt against the
authority of Great Britain. The revolt lasted only a brief

period of time and was crushed by British troops. His church was destroyed by dynamite. John Chilembwe and about forty of his leaders were killed in the revolt, and the entire mission closed.

Subsequently, the British troops made several indiscriminate attacks against several other missions for their role in the Chilembwe revolt. This was followed by a general onslaught by Nyasaland settlers groups on all missionaries in the protectorate.[29] It was not until 1926 that the Afawa Providence Industrial Mission was allowed to reopen under the auspices of the National Baptist Convention, U.S.A., Inc., which indicated the depth of bitterness the British held toward the revolt of John Chilembwe.

In the meantime, Dr. Daniel S. Malekebu, a member of the same tribe, had finished his training at Meharry Medical College, Nashville, Tennessee, and returned to East Central Africa. He was born in Nyasaland (now Malawi), East Africa, about 1890. Dr. Malekebu attended a mission school in his own country sponsored by the Foreign Mission Convention, Inc.

As one of the first students and early converts of the mission, Daniel S. Malekebu was baptized in 1902. His parents refused to give him food because he had taken on the customs of "strangers." Dr. Malekebu assisted Rev. John Chilembwe in the development of Afawa Provident Industrial Mission (the word *Afawa* was later deleted) in Nyassaland. He also founded and served as president of the African Baptist Congress, an organization patterned after the National Baptist Convention, U.S.A., Inc. The congress included churches in South Africa, Northern and Southern Rhodesia, Nyasaland, East Africa, and Portuguese, East Africa. In 1952, more than 1,000 churches were members of the African Baptist Congress with a membership of approximately 300,000.[30]

Dr. Daniel S. Malekebu's work terminated on October

8, 1978, in Saint Elizabeth Hospital, Blantyre, Malawi. His funeral service was held on Tuesday, October 10, in the village of Ntypanyama, his birthplace. Dr. Malekebu's death was a great loss to the cause of medical missions in Africa.

The first decade of the twentieth century was characterized by tremendous strides on the part of black Baptists to educate nationals to serve the cause of Christian missions. Among them were: Miss Mary Buchanan, Rev. F. Solani, Rev. Peter T. Mguquisbisa, Rev. David Tessi, Miss Jennie Sumtunzi, Rev. John Tule and wife, Rev. J. N. Menze, Rev. John Ntbahala, Rev. Evis F. P. Koti, Mr. William Jimsana, all of South Africa; Rev. Majola Agbebi, Ph.D., of West Africa; Rev. G. E. Steward of British West Indies; and Rev. Samuel Richardson of South America.

One of the early pioneers to Barbados, British West Indies, was a native of Georgetown, South America. Sometime near the end of the nineteenth century, Rev. T. E. Smith was ordained to the work of the gospel ministry by Rev. J. W. Anderson. Subsequently, he spent five years in Barbados, as a missionary, and was the first black Baptist to begin work in that island. In 1906, Rev. T. E. Smith spent some time in the United States under the sponsorship of the National Baptist Convention. In November of that year, he returned to the work of foreign missions.[31]

As mentioned earlier, Rev. F. Solani of Idutywa, South Africa, served also as an early pioneer national missionary for the Foreign Mission Board of the National Baptist Convention, U.S.A., Inc. He was a native of the "galaki" tribe.[32] Rev. Solani was an energetic and aggressive native worker in South Africa although limited in economic resources. Nevertheless, he was able to open a day school at Good Hope Mission with an enrollment of thirty-two students.[33]

The missionary work of Rev. E. B. P. Koti was also significant to the cause of Christian missions. He was born in Queenstown, South Africa. In 1897, he was baptized and ordained by Rev. R. A. Jackson. Subsequently, he made several visits to the United States and became familiar with the leadership of the National Baptist Convention, U.S.A., Inc. In 1926, Rev. Koti was able to report to Rev. James E. East, corresponding secretary of the Foreign Mission Board, that tremendous progress had been made in South Africa. He supervised the mission work in South Africa which included the Union of South Africa and Basutoland.

Adversely enough, the official government of the area had closed the doors to black Americans to operate directly in South Africa. Only nationals were able to carry on the mission work in the area.

In April 1926, Rev. E. B. P. Koti attended the Twenty-sixth Annual Assembly of the South Africa Native Association at the Qangala Baptist Church, Harding, South Africa. Several national missionaries reported to Rev. Koti on the progress of their work. Rev. F. Vockerodt reported that the Buchanan Mission, Middledrift, had 349 members, 11 lay preachers, 26 newly baptized members, 3 Sunday Schools with an enrollment of 165 students and 6 teachers. Rev. Vockerodt also reported on his work at East London, South Africa, stating that the Mission had 57 members, 7 lay preachers, and 22 members received by Christian experience and letters. At the same time, he was able to report that the Shiloh Baptist Church, Capetown, South Africa, had 46 members and a Sunday school enrollment of 46 students.[34]

At the same assembly, Rev. John Tylahla, pastor of the Xwili Baptist Church, reported to Rev. E. B. P. Koti on the status of his missionary activities. He reported 8 out-stations, 32 helpers, 29 baptisms, a Sunday School with an enrollment of 24 students, 2 day schools with an enrollment of 154 students and 5 teachers, and a church membership of 461 Christians.[35]

Similarly, the report for the Qungjwome Baptist

Church, Lebode, West Pondoland, South Africa, was given by its pastor, Rev. Josie Ntlahla. He reported 834 members, 8 outstations, 14 lay preachers, 24 baptisms, and 2 Sunday Schools.[36] Several other reports were given reflecting similar growth in the missionary strides in South Africa. The black Baptist leadership in the United States was especially edified by the report forwarded from the Twenty-sixth Annual Assembly of the South Africa Native Association by Rev. E. B. P. Koti.

The work of black Baptists was furthered in Nigeria, West Africa, through the missionary strides of another national named Rev. Samuel Martin. Rev. Samuel Martin was trained in the United States by the black Baptists of Illinois and Kansas. He was assisted in the mission in Nigeria by Mr. R. I. Anagoli.[37] Rev. Martin was the founder and director of the Pilgrim Baptist Mission in Nigeria and affectionately called by the leadership of the Foreign Mission Board the "legendary African missionary."[38] The Pilgrim Baptist Mission was named after the Pilgrim Baptist Church of Chicago, Illinois, and located in Issele-Uky, Nigeria.

Actually, the Pilgrim Baptist Mission of Nigeria became one of the greatest missionary enterprises on the continent of Africa supported by black Americans. Between 1922 and 1972, the mission experienced unprecedented growth. Its student body numbered several thousand at the time of the government takeover of all church schools in 1972. Even then, the mission continued to be one of the leading schools in the country.

Following in the spirit of pioneer black Baptist missionaries, Rev. J. J. Lepele advanced a strong mission in Swinburne, South Africa, in the early 1920s. He traveled extensively, baptizing forty natives in Orange Free State and over thirty in the Transvaal.[39] During three months of 1926, Rev. Lepele traveled from church to church preaching the gospel. He was assisted in Transvaal by Jophet Selepe of Strandertown, Philip Mahlangu of Benoni, Benson Gina of Johannesburg, and Ezekiel Selepe of Evaton. In the Orange Free State, Rev. Lepele was assisted by Stephen Khena of Harrismith and Ephrim Mokeuna of Vrede. In March 1926, Rev. J. J. Lepele opened a new church at Strandertown.

The Lott Carey Baptist Foreign Mission Convention was able to secure the services of a national for the cause of missions in South America. The Providence of God guided the destiny of Allan Carlyle Miller to be instrumental in developing a medical missionary enterprise in South America. Allan Carlyle Miller was born in Stewartville Village, West Coast, Demerara, on September 19, 1898. He attended initially a school in the village and later in Georgetown, Guyana. The religious influence of his parents was an abiding presence in Miller's life.

In the early 1900s, Allan Carlyle Miller left Guyana as a youth and attended school in the United States. In this country, he obtained the bachelor's degree in divinity at Virginia Seminary and College, Lynchburg, Virginia. A short time later, Miller graduated from Fisk University and Meharry Medical School in Nashville, Tennessee. He subsequently practiced medicine in Tennessee, Ohio, Kentucky, Pennsylvania, and New York. In the early 1940s, Dr. Miller returned to Guyana to begin a series of medical care and church activities to serve the communities from Stewartville to Beterverwagting and later Supply, Kuru-Kuru, and Long Creek. His missionary work in Guyana was supported by the Lott Carey Baptist Foreign Mission Convention and the Convent Avenue Baptist Church, Brooklyn, New York.

The great missionary career of this national in South America ended in death. Dr. Allan Carlyle Miller died on January 8, 1979, at Public Hospital, Georgetown, Guyana. His funeral service was held at the Saint George Cathedral, Company Path, Georgetown, Guyana. Subsequently, the

Lott Carey Baptist Foreign Mission Convention appointed his wife, Mrs. Erma Miller, to carry on the mission work in Guyana.

### Canadian Missions: Baptists of the Black Diaspora

The black experience in Canada reflects an interesting drama in the life of Africans transplanted from their native soil. There is a significant divergence of scholarly opinion relative to the evolution of the black presence in Canada. Were the original blacks brought to Canada as slaves? Were they merely servants who enjoyed a status radically different from their brothers in the American colonies and later in the United States? Did the majority migrate directly from the United States during slavery? What were race relations like in the early history of Canada? These are some of the questions being researched earnestly by historians interested in the black experience in Canada.

To be sure, these questions require extensive examination and evaluation of the antiquarian documents of Canadian history to render acceptable answers. However, only a brief perusal of early Canadian history is in the scope of this study. Such a perusal is designed to reflect the sociopolitical milieu of the evolution of the black Baptist witness in Canada.

The early history of Canada was dominated by France. Until about 1760, Canada was known as "New France." Some historians believe that blacks came to New France almost as early as did the Frenchmen. However, Oliver Le Jeune was the first black (of whom adequate historical data reflect) that came to New France. He was a slave who reflected on his condition in response to claims of Christian freedom made by a Jesuit missionary named Paul Le Jeune in 1632.[40]

Between the years of 1628 and 1760, slavery evolved

slowly in New France. Several reasons have been offered for the slow evolution of slavery in New France. Initially, panis (or Indian) slaves were utilized by the Frenchmen. Blacks were only introduced when it was not physically and politically feasible to utilize the panis. The panis were not able to survive the disease of the Frenchmen. Hence, a few Frenchmen pointed to the quality of labor rendered by blacks in the West Indies. But only a limited number of Frenchmen desired slaves in New France. They were concerned that the cold climate was not condusive to black slaves. The few who desired slaves used them primarily as domestic servants.

The second reason for the slow growth of slavery in New France was the legal difficulties encountered in establishing it as an institution. It was very difficult to obtain a clearly defined policy toward slavery from France. The French monarchs of the period showed very little interest in such an institution in New France. Their primary concern was with slavery in the West Indies.

More important, the commerce and industry of New France were not condusive to the widespread usage of black slaves. The soil was not rich like that of the West Indies and the United States' later cotton belt. Neither cotton nor sugar production was feasible in New France. Therefore, black slaves were not required to contribute significantly to the economic development of New France.

It was not until the British came to power in Canada that slavery gained a significant momentum. In the early 1760s, black slavery in Canada was "virtually at its midpoint, for the British gave it new life."[41] Principally, the new momentum resulted from the influx of loyalists from the rebellious British North American colonies. A significant number of these loyalists brought with them the spirit of slavery as an institution. Some brought their slaves with them to Canada.

The American Revolution also contributed to the presence of free blacks in Canada. The British offered freedom to black slaves who would aid them in the war effort. These blacks served as boatmen, woodsmen, general laborers, buglers, and musicians.[42] Still the black slave and free population remained rather small in Canada until the early and middle nineteenth century.

The rise of the abolitionist movement in the United States and to a certain extent in Canada ushered in a new era in the influx of blacks to Canada. The Underground Railroad became a significant means for the practical promotion of emancipation of slaves from the United States to Canada. The harsh nature of such slavery made many fugitives seek freedom in a land they viewed as a "haven."

Moreover, the passage of the drastic Fugitive Slave Law of 1850 radically increased the influx of blacks to Canada. This law made their experience even in the North a precarious freedom. The freedom line was thus moved to the very borders of the United States. To be sure, the lure of Canada increased its intensity and the work of the Underground Railroad increased accordingly. Christian churches were vital parts of the movement. Miles Mark Fisher alluded to a church in Boston as the "church of the fugitive slaves through which many Blacks escaped into Canada for freedom."[43]

Within such a historical milieu, the black Baptist witness in Canada evolved. The unique nature of the Canadian experience tended to be reflected in the nature of such an evolution. Initially, black Baptists, like those of Colonial America, worshiped with their white masters. The basic difference was the fact that there were no plantations like those of Colonial America. Hence, the development of plantation missions did not take place in Canada. Both slave and free blacks worshiped with white Baptists.

It was not until the rise of separate black Baptists

churches in the late eighteenth and nineteenth centuries and the influx of black Baptists from the United States that Canada became the scene of separate churches based on race. Hence, there were definite links between the separate church movements in the United States and Canada. The links may be described in terms of the black Baptist diaspora in Canada.

The impact of the missionary strides of black Baptists from the United States did not reach Canada until rather late. Most black Baptists from the United States were primarily interested in the African mission. Very little attention was given to the development of Christian missions in Canada. Some few from Detroit and New England seem to have shown some interest and direct involvement in Canadian missions. However, the real impact was more or less indirect. Black Baptists migrated from the United States carrying with them witness and a desire to live indefinitely in Canada. Consequently, their witness evolved in ways similar to that of the ancient Israelites and early Christians of the Diaspora. Black Baptists who decided to make their home in Canada participated in development of Christian missions in the land.

One of the earliest black Baptist preachers to arrive in Canada was Rev. William Wilks. He was born in the Congo and first came to Canada from the United States in 1818. Initially, Rev. Wilks landed at Amherstburg in 1818 and traveled to Colchester a year later. He bought forty acres of land and constructed a small church for the black Baptists of the area. The new church was located about five miles north of the shore of Lake Erie. On the first Friday in October 1821, he was ordained by two white Canadian Baptist ministers, and the First African Baptist Church of Colchester was officially organized.[44] This church, like others to follow, remained rather small. Its membership increased very slowly. In 1830, there were approximately 36 members,

62 in 1835, 69 in 1836, and rose to its zenith of 90 in 1845 after which internal difficulties occurred, and the church rapidly declined.[45] Internal difficulties sealed the fate of the church at Colchester. It struggled for survival until in 1906 the church became extinct.

Another pioneer black Baptist preacher was Rev. Washington Christian, a native of Virginia, who migrated to Toronto. Prior to his arrival in Toronto, Rev. Christian had been ordained by the Abyssinia Baptist Church of New York City in 1822 and subsequently set himself to the task of aiding his brethren in Toronto and elsewhere. He organized the First Baptist Church ever to be instituted in Toronto and the first black institution of the city. Hence, First Baptist Church was the primary black institution in Toronto. Initially, the church did not have a meetinghouse and worshiped outdoors and in various homes. In 1827, it leased Saint George's Masonic Lodge for a house of worship. The following year, a small chapel was built on Lombard Street, Toronto.

In 1841, the First Baptist Church of Toronto erected a new church on the corner of Victoria and Queen Street. The property was donated to the church by the family of Squires McCutcheon. On March 28, 1841, the First Baptist Church of Toronto occupied its new site. Rev. Washington Christian thus led the church to realize a tremendous growth materially. He remained pastor until his death on July 3, 1850.[46]

Internal difficulties within the First Baptist Church of Toronto erupted in the congregation soon after it moved to its new church site. The new property was left in the hands of a board of trustees elected for life who usurped unreasonable authority over the deacons and pastor. The result of this controversy was the organization of a new church in 1855. This new church became known as the Coloured

Regular Baptist Church and was located on the corner of Terauley and Edward Streets.

Both churches sought to retain the status of the First Baptist Church of Toronto. They appealed to the Haldimand Association for such recognition. The association recognized the members of the Terauley and Edward Streets location as the First Baptist Church.[47]

After the division within the First Baptist Church of Toronto, Rev. William Mitchell, a native of North Carolina, served the pastorate of the First Baptist Church that was recognized as such by the Haldimand Association. He came to Toronto in the late 1850s, pastored at First Baptist Church for a brief period, then left for England on a fundraising tour. While in England, Rev. Mitchell wrote and published a book entitled *The Underground Railroad from Slavery to Freedom.*

Still another pioneer black Baptist preacher moved to Canada to extend the black Baptist witness. His name was Edward Mitchell (1794-1872). Mitchell was a native of Martinique, West Indies. The president of Dartmouth College observed the outstanding possibilities in this black man and brought him initially to Hanover, New Hampshire, to be educated at the college. After graduation in 1828, Edward Mitchell was ordained in 1831 and preached for five years to white congregations in New Hampshire and Vermont. Subsequently, he migrated to Canada where he spent the rest of his life preaching to blacks in Eaton and Magog, Canada.

The year 1841 ushered in a new era in the development of black Baptist missions in Canada. Several significant events began to transpire which affected the spread of black Baptists in Canada. First, larger numbers of black Baptists began to migrate from the United States to Canada. Second, the black Baptists of Amherstburg organized the first cooperative venture, the Amherstburg Baptist Association. This association assimilated most of the black Baptist churches formed prior to 1841 and contributed significantly to the subsequent organization of separate black Baptist churches. The boundaries of the new association were racial rather than geographical; hence, the body became international with member churches on both sides of the Canadian-American border. It also overlapped areas in Canada previously influenced by Baptist associations organized by white Canadian Baptists. This was the first sign of racial tension between black and white Baptists in Canada.

With the development of their first cooperative venture, the black Baptists of Canada later saw the need to get more involved in the political affairs of the race. Hence, they soon organized the Canadian Anti-Slavery Baptist Association. This new association became involved in the abolitionist movement. Previously, in 1833, slavery was abolished throughout the British colonies by an act of Imperial Parliament, passed on August 28 to take effect on August 1, 1834. The legal authorities of Canada had already virtually ended slavery in Canada. This was why blacks from the United States found freedom in Canada. This spirit was taken up by the new antislavery association, and Canadian black Baptists sought the abolition of all slaves within the reach of their influence.

In Nova Scotia, the black Baptists were particularly inclined toward activism. Rev. Richard Preston, a strong black Baptist leader, organized in 1842 an Anglo-African Mutual Improvement and Aid Association. One of his earliest strategies was to appoint a committee responsible for political action. Under his leadership, the black Baptists of Nova Scotia and New Brunswick were able to exert significant political influence. One reason for this was that there was a rather large concentration of blacks in the area. At one time, blacks outnumbered the white population of Nova Scotia.

In 1846, Rev. Richard Preston organized yet another politically oriented organization, an Abolitionist Society. For a brief period, this organization cooperated with other integrated abolitionist groups. The group parted ways later due to some doctrinal differences with "the mainstream of general Baptist development in the province."[48]

Subsequently, in 1854, Rev. Richard Preston established the African United Baptist Association. This association was to serve the same general purpose as the older Amherstburg Association. Nova Scotia shared with Ontario the distinction of a sizable black Baptist presence. As early as 1840, there had been seven black Baptist churches in Nova Scotia with 273 members; in 1897, there were twenty-two churches and 2,440 members.[49] Currently, there are more than ten thousand black Baptists in Nova Scotia. These black Baptists have united across the years to advance the race politically.

Similarly, the black Baptists of Canada were interested in other matters affecting black Christians. Almost from the beginning of the separate church movement, black Canadian Baptists involved themselves in the educational and social uplift of the race. They participated in the organization of local schools for blacks and temperance societies. Black Canadian Baptists were well aware of the face that intellectual development and strong morals were essential to the progress of the race.

Interestingly enough, the first black Baptist churches never discriminated against anyone on the basis of race and were interracial as at Colchester after 1830, at Niagara in 1831, and in Toronto until 1829; but few remained so past the early 1840s.[50] After 1841, racial lines began to be drawn. Both white and black Baptists were responsible for the new development in Christian race relations. As the number of white Baptists increased, these white Baptists became more concerned with the development of strong churches of their own race. On the other hand, Canadian black Baptists, especially fugitive slaves, became more racially conscious and desired "to restrict membership to blacks lest the pharoahs from whom they had fled infiltrate them."[51]

The black Baptist separate movement spread in Canada wherever there were significant numbers of Canadian blacks. Churches were organized in Amherstburg (ca. 1841), Sandwich (ca. 1840) and (1851), Chatham (1843), (1846), and (1856), North Cayuga (1848), London (ca. 1842), Second Baptist of London (ca. 1850), New Canaan Baptist of London (ca. 1854), First Baptist of Windsor (ca. 1855), First Baptist of Shrewsbury (1960), First Baptist of Daun (ca. 1855), First Baptist of Dresden (date not known), First Baptist of Braxton (ca. 1851), Second Baptist, and the Third Baptist of Braxton (dates not known). These were some of the earliest black Baptist churches in Canada.

The black Baptist witness continued to grow slowly until the end of the Civil War in the United States. At the close of the War, the influx of fugitives into Canada ended. In fact, a significant number of black Baptists returned to the United States. This was a serious blow to the growth of separate churches. Some churches closed because of a decrease in membership. By the turn of the century, Canadian black Baptists sought closer ties with the black Baptists of the United States. With such ties, they have experienced a new dynamism in church growth. Presently, Canadian black Baptists can not be overlooked in any significant chronicle of Baptists. They are a significant movement in the life of the Church.

## Recent Strides in Foreign Missions

The rise of the so-called Third World nations has caused a tremendous change in the missionary enterprise of the Christian church. Intellectuals and political leaders from these nations have slowly rejected any missionary motif or methodology which reflects any connection with Western imperialism and racism. Dr. Jeremiah Walker, superintendent of Lott Carey Missions in Liberia, remarked recently in an address at the First Baptist Church of Baltimore:

> Africa is from the first world. We are not the third world. I don't know who gave us the concept of the "Third World" nations. This idea or concept is a form of discrimination, meaning that you are a third-class people. Surely, a black man did not come up with the idea of the "Third World" nations.

This trend has deep significance for the development of a new approach to Christian missions in the developing nations of the world.

To meet the new challenge of missions in the developing nations, the black Baptists national organizations have sent out missionaries specially equipped to encounter and enhance the spirit of nationalism and enlightenment. To be sure, black Baptists have welcomed and motivated the changes in the developing nations. They have come to realize that the progress of the black church in America is linked to the changes in these developing nations.

Specifically, the Lott Carey Baptist Foreign Mission has attempted to enhance its policy of utilizing nationals and black Americans who are in sympathy with the new movements in the developing nations of the world. It has revitalized the work of such missionaries. Under the leadership of Dr. Jeremiah Walker, the convention operates the R. L. Hollomon School in Bopola, Liberia, the Brewerville Station, and several other schools and churches in Liberia. In India, the convention operates several medical clinics, churches, and a special leprosy clinic, namely, the Karnal Leprosarium. In Nigeria, the convention's work is managed by Rev. Charles E. Ebong, consisting of churches, schools, and medi-

Dr. Samuel T. Ola Akande, general
secretary-treasurer of All Africa Baptist
Fellowship and general secretary of the
Nigerian Baptist Convention. Baptist World
Alliance Photo.

cal clinics. Similarly, the Guyana Mission consists of the Campbellville Mission Station, the M. L. Wilson Chapel, the Guyana Hospital, and the Beterverwagting Mission Station.

Presently, the National Baptist Convention of America, Unincorporated, operates a medical mission in the Republic of Cameroon, the Butaw Station in Liberia, a church in Rio Abajo of the Republic of Panama, and several churches in Jamaica, including Greater Mount Zion Baptist Church, Kingstown; Zion Baptist Church in Clark's Town; and the Mount Sinai Circuit which comprises six churches. The foreign mission program of this convention is experiencing a new vitality under the leadership of Rev. Robert H. Wilson, executive secretary of the Foreign Mission Board.

The Foreign Mission Board of the National Baptist Convention, U.S.A., Inc., sponsors approximately 850 churches in ten mission fields, along with elementary and secondary schools, hospitals, and a theological seminary. The Board has missionary programs in seven African nations including Liberia, Malawi, Lesotho, Ghana, Swaziland, Sierra Leone, and the Republic of South Africa; and three countries in tropical America, including Jamaica, the Bahamas Out Islands, and Nicaragua.

The youngest black Baptist convention to establish a foreign mission enterprise is the Baptist Foreign Mission Bureau of the Progressive National Baptist Convention, Inc. This Foreign Mission Bureau has operated initially an "in-kind support" for foreign missions. Such support programs have become something of a new style for missionary endeavor.

The convention's program of "in-kind support" dates back to 1970 when several of its churches initiated a program of sharing with fellow church leaders in Africa and Haiti in the construction of new church buildings. For example, Rev. S. Amos Brackeen, pastor of the Philippian

Dr. William R. Tolbert, Jr., former president
of the Republic of Liberia, West Africa, and
former president of the Baptist World
Alliance. Baptist World Alliance Photo.

Baptist Church of Philadelphia, Pennsylvania, was inspired to encourage his congregation to share in the cooperative ministry after a trip to Africa in 1972.

Subsequently, the church contributed $9,000 to construct the Philippian Baptist Church, Idumje Unor, one of the many churches connected with the Pilgrim Baptist Mission of Issele-Uku, Nigeria.

Similarly, Rev. A. Patterson Jackson, pastor of the Liberty Baptist Church of Chicago, heard an appeal for funds to rebuild the First Baptist Church of Dubray, Haiti, and made a pledge of $5,000 toward the project. In August 1977, the actual construction work began on the church to meet some of the spiritual needs of the Haitian Baptist Mission's constituency.

Yet another example, Rev. James A. Winston, Pastor of the Northern Baptist Church of Saint Louis, Missouri, led his congregation to raise $5,000 for the completion of the Saint James Baptist Church of Issele-Mkpitime, a part of the Pilgrim Baptist Mission of Issele-Uku, Nigeria. This contribution enabled that African congregation to complete its new edifice.

The Progressive National Baptist Convention, Inc., has also adopted a program of economic aid to the Haitian Hospital Morne Pele, Cap-Haitian, Haiti. In 1978, the convention contributed $32,067.21 to the hospital. Hence, the convention has sought to develop a program of economic aid to signal its interest in medical missions.

In conclusion, the story of modern missionary strides on the part of black Baptists is suggestive of the tremendous impact of such endeavors on the advancement of Christian civilization. There are many dedicated black Baptist missionaries meeting the challenge of modern missions in the world.

# 4

# The Role of
# Black Baptists
# in Education

One of the most crucial debates of the twentieth century is the issue of education for blacks in America. Primarily, the 1954 Supreme Court's decision which ended legal segregation in public education ushered in a lively debate of tremendous intensity. It is as intense as the historic abolitionists versus proslavery debates in American history. Many whites hold tenaciously to a negative anthropology of black inferiority, manifesting itself in the rise of private "Christian" schools and the utilization of test scores to support their claims. Other whites hold that the quality of black education is dependent on exposure to white education. Much of the rationale for integration in public education comes from ideas of white superiority. Hence, even some white integrationists approach black education with vestigial presuppositions of a negative anthropology relative to black Americans. To be sure, they still use "white" anthropology as the evaluative norm for "quality" education in America.

Black educators, on the other hand, are rapidly becoming cognizant of these vestigial presuppositions in evaluative programs of American education. They are arguing that the standardized tests reflect the culture of middle class white America. The lack of exposure to this culture on the part of blacks constitutes their lack of good performance rather than any supposed mental deficiencies. If a synthesis of all American cultures were reflected in the standardized tests, blacks and other minorities would accordingly score higher. All in all, the real issue of test scores is designed to reawaken historic anthropological debates among academicians. The outcome of the debates, however, has tremendous implications for black survival.

The important thing to remember is that the underlying issues of the debate cannot be properly focused without a synthesis of black history and general American history. Today it is critically important for us to relate the historic experience of blacks in American education. Several black intellectuals have already made significant contributions to the literature on the subject of historic black education. One good example is the monumental work of Allen B. Ballard entitled *The Afro-American's Struggle for Knowledge in White America.* He carefully traces "evidences of racism" throughout the entire black experience in American public education. However, Ballard failed to relate the dynamic role of the black church as a counterracist movement in American education. Therefore, the purpose of this chapter is to relate and evaluate the role of the black church, the black Baptist church in particular, in the progress of American education among blacks.

Initially, it should be pointed out that blacks did not come to America devoid of all culture and education. The truth is that beginning in 1619 blacks brought with them the influences of African education and culture. To be sure, these and other transplanted Africans were not devoid psychologically of their "inner child of the past" when they landed in the New World. To the contrary, the internalized African culture was very much a part of these Africans' reaction to American slavery. Unfortunately, white Americans were generally not appreciative of the African education or culture.

The vestigial evidence of African education operative on American soil has been documented by Abraham Chapman, editor of *Steal Away: Stories of the Runaway Slaves.* The slave narratives relate memories of African childhood, firsthand reports on slave ships, and introduction to America's "peculiar institution." A good example of vestigial evidence of African education is found in the narrative by Gustavas Vassa, born 1745 in Guinea, West Africa. Vassa recalls freely the *Embrenche* (a term importing the highest distinction or "a mark of grandeur") cultural tradition among his people, the judicial system of the tribe, and the ethics of marriage and family.[1] Vassa talks about how his tribe excelled in the arts: "We are almost a nation of dancers, musicians and poets."[2] Even the religious traditions of the African tribe live on in Gustavas Vassa as he relates, "As to religion, the natives believe that there is one Creator of all things, and that he lives in the sun, and is girted round with a belt; that he may never eat or drink, but, according to some, he smokes a pipe, which is our own favorite luxury."[3]

There are many similar slave narratives reflecting vestigial evidence of African education operative in America. Such stories tend to justify our claim that many of the Africans brought to America were intelligent people. To be sure, they had received varied educational experiences prior to exposure to American slavery. This fact counters the prevailing idea of the ignorance and lack of intelligence of people from the so-called "Dark Continent."

However, it is evident that the early educational experiences of blacks in America consisted primarily of oral instruction. To this extent, their experiences were similar to that of the early Christians. Like the early Christians, black Baptist preachers, as well as other black preachers, developed an "oral period" in the education of the race. These preachers themselves had primarily received their education from listening to and imitating whites on the plantations and their surrounding chapels or churches. It was quite rare for any black person to receive anything other than an education based on "oral traditions" or learned conversations between white "gentlemen" overheard by these black preachers. Hence, the early black preachers simply communicated in their venacular what they had learned about the Bible and other subjects to their fellowmen in bondage.

The black Baptists were very active, along with other denominations, in the great work of uplifting mankind, especially that part of mankind with which the church was ostensibly identified. No other pulpit movement ever had a more difficult task or labored under greater disadvantages than the black Baptists. In the very beginning, the pulpit had the leadership and the enlightenment of the race in spiritual and intellectual knowledge thrust upon it, when it was neither qualified nor regularly organized to perform such tasks. Nevertheless, the educational movement was advanced even during the slave period of American history. With the rise of independent churches, the intellectual development of the race progressed slowly. Most churches served as weekday schools and houses of worship on Sundays. Hence, early blacks experienced the oneness of their churches and schools.

Moreover, the progress of independent black Baptist churches gave new momentum to other emerging institutions of intellectual and cultural development. As noted, the denominational schools, primary through college, grew up in direct relations to local churches. This was especially true of the primary and secondary schools. Black colleges were only indirectly related, for the most part, to local churches. The black press was the other great institutional movement that developed concomitantly with the independent churches. The purpose of this chapter, then, is to relate the role of black Baptists in the black press and black college movement as institutions of intellectual and cultural development for the race.

## The Black Press

The emergence of separate black Baptist churches signaled a tendency to unite the religious and social experiences of the race. These churches soon took on the characteristic of multipurpose community centers from which emerged some great minds that paved the way for the acceleration of literary or intellectual development among the race. Black leaders soon realized the importance of education to moral, social, and political progress of free blacks and the peaceful emancipation of the enslaved "brothers in Black."

To be sure, the primary locale of this new intellectual awakening was in the North. The black press movement was a northern phenomenon among free blacks. During the later part of the eighteenth century, the revolutionary war resulted in a large number of manumissions. An increasing number of these free blacks were becoming economically successful and some managed to get an education. From this class emerged the spirit of the black press movement. These were the men who began the political discussions and organizational efforts to effect the intellectual development and liberation of the race.

By the end of the 1800s, the American Christian experience witnessed the emergence of "The Afro-American Press" (commonly called today "The Black Press"). The first newspapers were published March 16, 1827, by free blacks in New York City entitled *Freedom's Journal* and *Rights of All*. These two papers were edited by Mr. John B. Russwurm.[4] The social climate was not very encouraging to this early press movement. I. Garland Penn remarked:

> Of course, any paper established by Afro-Americans at that time and for the succeeding forty years would have fought absolutely in the interest of abolition of slavery. As a matter of fact, this publication by Mr. Russwurm met with more and greater obstacles than did any other paper ever published upon the Continent. Besides having to fight for a cause which then had few advocates, it could see in the popular mind no indication of support.[5]

Similarly, Frederick G. Detweiler reached the conclusion that it was "only the anti-slavery agitation that made the press possible to the Negro in this period."[6]

Despite the social climate, free blacks soon advanced the spirit of the black press movement. Initially, most of the papers were published in New York City and state, but others came early from Pittsburgh, Cleveland, Cincinnati, and San Francisco. These papers did much to change opinions among the oppressed and the oppressors. They provided the necessary learning experiences which encouraged individuals to accept new opinions relative to the liberation of black Americans. Free black editors continued this momentum even under most adverse circumstances until the Civil War experience. Their editorials constantly offered new intellectual options to the development of public opinion.

In the early 1860s, black Baptists and other denominations became more directly involved in the black press movement. Black church leaders soon realized the urgency for creating and organizing public opinion on progressive issues and for looking after the "special" interests of black Americans. The abolition of slavery and the close of the Civil War ushered in tremendous problems of political orientation for blacks complicated by poverty, illiteracy, and general social disorganization.[7] But more than mere political interests necessitated the direct black church involvement in the black press movement. The decade of the 1860s was a time of church building and denominational expansion. Hence, the new motif of denominational growth and development entered the "voice" of the black press. Independent publications along denominational lines soon emerged to challenge and shape public opinion.

The first black Baptist to advance directly the press movement along denominational lines was Rev. Rufus L. Perry. He edited an initial paper entitled *The Sunbeam* with its headquarters in Brooklyn, New York. By 1870, Rev. Perry had advanced two other papers, *The People's Journal,* a juvenile paper which had 10,000 subscribers, and *The Na-*

*tional Monitor*.[8] He utilized these papers to advocate the moral, spiritual, and educational advancement of the race.

Rev. Rufus L. Perry was a native of Smith County, Tennessee. His educational experiences excelled the usual degree of others in the Baptist leadership. Along with his academic degrees, Rev. Perry held two honorary degrees. Hence, he was a writer of vast learning and experience.

The pioneer work of Rev. Rufus L. Perry was soon followed by other black Baptists. The organization of various conventions among the race gave new impetus to journalism among Baptists. Consequently, black Baptists across the nation took up the pen. Accordingly, Rev. William J. Simmons edited and published a magazine at Louisville, Kentucky, known as *Our Women and Children*.[9] He established this new publication in 1888. The purpose of the magazine was the uplifting of the black American, particularly black American women and children.

Being devoted to this kind of work, the magazine was able to do more than all the black American papers together in bringing to the front the latent talent of black women writers. Its columns were open to black women beyond denominational lines to contribute articles on the particular questions which affected the homelife of black Americans, especially the mothers and children. By the efforts of its editor it was thus given to the world as a unique journalistic production with a bright array of female writers relating to different questions previously unknown to the literary world.

With the organization of educational boards, the black Baptist denomination became directly involved in journalism. Accordingly, the Missionary State Convention of Mississippi led the way with the publication of *The Baptist Signal*. This denominational paper was edited by Rev. G. W. Gayles. Possibly no man connected with black American journalism had a brighter and more honored career than this versatile writer.

Rev. G. W. Gayles was born in Wilkinson, Mississippi, January 29, 1844, of slave parents, Perry and Rebecca Gayles.[10] Initially, he was a house servant and, as such, was given special privileges. As house servant, young Gayles was taught the alphabet by a lady who was employed as private tutor in Mrs. Nancy Barron's family. This was done on account of his diligence. He soon gained the ability to read the Bible and his hymnbook, which attracted the young boy's greatest attention.[11] This was the beginning of his brilliant intellectual development.

In 1867, Gayles was called into the gospel ministry and by vigorous work became a tremendous preacher of the Word. He soon was appointed to some of the most prominent places in Mississippi. In 1869, Gayles was appointed, by George A. Ames of the United States Army, a member of the board of police for the third district of Bolivar County, Mississippi. In 1870, Governor J. L. Alcon was instrumental in helping him to become justice of peace for the fifth district of Bolivar County. Subsequently, Gayles was elected to the state legislature for four consecutive years and was returned in 1877 as state senator for the twenty-eighth senatorial district of Mississippi.[12]

Rev. G. W. Gayles did not allow these political accomplishments to deter him from advancing a significant ministry for the black church. He served as corresponding secretary for the Missionary State Convention and later served as the convention's president. Hence, Gayles had a wide experience in religious, political, and general affairs which served to make him a grand force in journalism. He utilized such experiences to interpret the current events of the day in the light of God's action in history.

In the early 1880s, Rev. J. E. Jones, a native of Virginia, entered the field of journalism. He was born in Rome, Virginia, October 15, 1850, of slave parents and was himself a slave until the end of the Civil War.[13]

Rev. J. E. Jones began his career in journalism as a staff editor for the Baptist State Convention of Virginia. The name of this official organ of the black Baptists of Virginia was *The Baptist Companion.* He was elected corresponding secretary of the Baptist Foreign Mission Convention of the United States and started an official journal for this convention known as *African Missions.* This paper was very successful in promoting the African mission on behalf of the convention.

In May 1888, another black Baptist named Charles B. W. Gordon entered the field of journalism. Born of humble parentage in the State of North Carolina, Gordon was able to develop his intellectual abilities in a school under the guidance of Thomas Mixon on Roanoke Island, North Carolina. After his conversion to the Christian religion, Gordon entered the Richmond Seminary at Richmond, Virginia, in 1881. In 1883, Rev. Charles B. W. Gordon graduated from this school and became pastor of a large church in Petersburg, Virginia. In 1884, he published a book of sermons.

Rev. Gordon's career in the black press began with the launching of a monthly religious sheet, May 16, 1888, named *The Pilot.* It became the paper of the Virginia Baptist State Convention after the suspension of *The Baptist Companion* at Portsmouth, Virginia. The founding of *The Pilot* afforded the convention a new means of communication. The popularity of the new publication became evident, and *The Pilot* soon became a weekly paper.[14] In March 1889, a writer for *The Indianapolis Freeman* paid tribute to the work of Rev. Charles B. W. Gordon.

To write a full and elaborate estimate of the brilliant and growing subject of this sketch, would be impossible in an ordinary newspaper article; therefore, suffice it to say, that as an author, orator, poet, essayist and divine, the negro race in this country has hardly produced his equal, at his age, 28.[15]

Rev. W. J. White was the next major black Baptist leader to enter journalism. He was born in Elbert County, Georgia, December 25, 1831. Fortunately, he was able to receive some educational experiences at an early age. White served as an apprentice under W. H. Goodrich, an extensive house builder, and later worked at the carpenter's trade for about seven years.

In the early part of 1866 the Republicans of Augusta, Georgia, started a newspaper called *The Colored American* which was the first black paper ever published in Georgia. The paper's name was later changed to *The Loyal Georgian,* and Rev. W. J. White was elected secretary of the new publication. A few years later, the Missionary Baptist Convention of Georgia established a new paper known as *The Georgia Baptist* and designated him the manager.

Unfortunately, the Missionary Baptist Convention of Georgia did not appropriate sufficient funds to operate the new venture in journalism. Hence, Rev. W. J. White was left to develop his own financial program. He organized a stock company and provided the physical facility for the publication. Soon he became proprietor and editor of *The Georgia Baptist.* Subsequently, the black Baptist conventions and associations adapted the publication as their official organ. Rev. W. J. White was favorable to this new development and used the paper to defend the creed and doctrine of black Baptists of Georgia.

The first issue, October 28, 1880, consisted of 1,000 copies. The number gradually increased until the average for the succeeding three months was 3,240.[16] *The Georgia Baptist* experienced a very wide circulation reaching as far as

England and Africa. People at home and abroad were impressed with the versatility of this black Baptist publication. Many articles circulated in this paper ranging from Baptist doctrine to prohibitionist thought. *The Georgia Baptist* became one of the most successful publications in the black press movement.

In the early 1880s, another black Baptist preacher of tremendous intelligence and social refinement entered the black Baptist strides in journalism, Rev. William B. Johnson. He was born in Toronto, Canada, December 11, 1856. Having migrated to the United States, he spent the major portion of his youthful days in the schools of Buffalo, New York. Subsequently, Johnson attended the Wayland Seminary of Washington, D.C., where he graduated with honors in the class of 1879.

After a call to the gospel ministry and graduation from Wayland Seminary, Rev. William B. Johnson was called to the pastorate of the First Baptist Church of Frederick, Maryland, and served this church several years. Subsequently, Johnson resigned the charge to accept an appointment by the American Baptist Home Mission Society to be a general missionary for the states of Maryland, Virginia, West Virginia, and the District of Columbia.

In 1887, Rev. William B. Johnson made his first attempt in the field of journalism. He read a paper entitled "Religious Status of the Negro" during the annual session of the Baptist State Convention of Virginia which convened at Lynchburg, Virginia. The leadership of the convention was so impressed with the paper that it decided to publish Johnson's "Religious Status of the Negro." His literary ability soon became nationally known.

In 1893, Rev. Johnson was elected managing editor of the *National Baptist Magazine,* the literary organ of the National Baptist Convention, U.S.A. This magazine was one motivating force which later gave birth to the National Baptist Publishing House. It was, perhaps, the most impressive periodical published by black Baptists in the nineteenth century. The strongest minds of the denomination published articles in the *National Baptist Magazine.*

About the same time Rev. Johnson entered journalism, Rev. Joseph A. Booker of Portland, Arkansas, directed his attention to the black press movement. He became editor of *The Baptist Vanguard* which became the denominational organ for the black Baptists of the state. Joseph A. Booker was born in Portland, Ashley County, Arkansas, December 26, 1859. His mother died when he was only one year old. Two years later, Booker's father, a man of some literacy ability, was whipped to death for teaching other black Americans and thus, in the minds of some members of the community, "spoiling the good niggers."[17] Subsequently, young Booker was placed in the hands of his maternal grandmother, who carefully nurtured the youth and looked after his educational interests. When the free school system was inaugurated in the state, Booker's grandmother saw that he was one of the first pupils to be enrolled. After seventeen years of instruction, young Booker became a teacher and furthered his education at Norman School of the University of Pine Bluff, Arkansas, under Professor J. C. Corbin, the noted linguist of that time in the state's history. After being called to the gospel ministry, Rev. Joseph A. Booker became managing editor of *The Baptist Vanguard,* published on the campus of Arkansas Baptist College where Booker served also as college president. The new publication won many friends in the state for the college and the Baptist denomination in general.

The year 1887 witnessed the journalistic strides of another black Baptist, Rev. Calvin S. Brown of North Carolina. He became editor of a journal called *The Samaritan Journal,* the official organ of the Samaritan Society of the state. This was just the beginning of the literary works of this black Baptist preacher.

Calvin S. Brown was born in Salisbury, North Carolina, March 23, 1859, the son of Henry and Flora Brown. He was able to receive a good education. After receiving a call into the gospel ministry, Brown studied at Shaw University, Raleigh, North Carolina.

After graduating valedictorian of his class, Rev. Calvin S. Brown became the pastor of a large rural church in Winton, North Carolina. While pastoring this church along with four other churches, he decided to organize an institution of learning for the blacks of eastern North Carolina. To enlist the sympathy and help of the community in Winton, Rev. Brown began to issue monthly a paper known as *The Chowan Pilot.* The circulation of this paper spread and aroused the community to the support of the school project. Within eighteen months, he was able to lead the community to erect a two-story school building. Soon Rev. Calvin S. Brown became a reputable journalist and educator throughout the state of North Carolina.

To be sure, the influence of these pioneer black Baptists in the black press movement was a potent factor in the tremendous educational and social advancement of black Americans. It has been argued that the black press surpassed the pulpit in influence. Robert T. Kerlin remarked in *The Voice of the Negro:*

> The Negro seems to have newly discovered his fourth estate, to have realized the extraordinary power of his press. Mighty as the pulpit has been with him, the press now seems to be foremost. It is freer than the pulpit, and there is a peculiar authority in the printer's ink. His newspaper is the voice of the Negro.[18]

The black press sought to fulfill the true role of journalism in the interpretation of the "black experience." It sought to communicate accurately to all Americans what black people did, felt, and thought about the many adverse transitions in their experiences. Real attempts were made to avoid error, bias, prejudice, and false color in the articles and editorials of the black press. The most reliable accounts of the historic events were sought by the men and women of this great movement. They were ever aware of their role as purveyors of information, interpreters, and molders of public opinion. The latter was of paramount importance. For public opinion relative to the social, religious, political, and economic progress of the race was crucial to racial pride and acceptance in the broader American experience.

The black press, particularly the religious press, served as a medium of cultural exchange between the various black regions of the nation. It was through newspapers, denominational journals, books, and magazines that black church leaders were able to impact the cultural development of black Christians in other parts of the nation. A sermon or address published in such media was able to reach far beyond the regular pastoral or evangelistic pulpit ministries. Rural and urban Christians were able to share equally in the religious thoughts of black leaders on the crucial events of their experiences. Surely then, the black press has served as an extended ministry of great potency to the black church in its attempt to enlighten the minds of men in general and to enhance the theological sophistication of black Christians. This was partially accomplished by converting the masses of black Baptists into readers. Large numbers who formerly read nothing began reading the various articles of the press movement. For the first time, then, large numbers of black Christians were exposed to the best theological minds of the church.

## Black Baptist Schools

The great journalistic strides of black Baptists precipitated the organization of educational boards within the denomination and, subsequently, the emergence of educational institutions for the progress of the race. The intellectual leadership of the denomination saw the need of education for black Americans and initiated, with the help of white Christians and philanthropists, a strategy for the achievement of literacy on the part of the black population. The education of the race was a tremendous undertaking.

At the close of the Civil War the percentage of illiteracy among the black population tended to overwhelm the race. The experience of slavery had been devastating to black education. In 1850, there was a total free black population twenty years of age or over of 219,520, of these, 90,522, or 41.2 percent, were reported as unable to read and write, leaving nearly 60 percent in the literate class. There were 113,629 free Negroes in the South; of these, 49 percent or approximately one half were literate.[19] Complicating the problem, the former slaves emerged from the Civil War almost completely illiterate. Hence, the need for an aggressive program of education was both critical and urgent for the survival of the race in America.

Fortunately, the end of the Civil War ushered in a new era of opportunities for black Americans to receive an education. Initially, the federal government involved itself through the Freedmen's Bureau. General Oliver O. Howard, appointed commissioner of the bureau by President Abraham Lincoln, was first to recognize the need for government involvement in the establishment and support of schools for the freedmen. He requested the US Congress to pass legislation designed to broaden the role of the bureau to include black education. Congress acquiesced and passed such a bill over the veto of President Andrew Jackson, and the bill became a law on July 16, 1866. Subsequently, the Freedmen's Bureau spent significant sums of money toward the organization and development of schools. Not only did the bureau organize schools itself but participated financially with benevolent agencies already engaged in such work, especially the American Missionary Association.[20]

The tendency toward cooperation on the part of the Freedmen's Bureau gave new momentum to benevolent agencies and denominational missionary organizations to expand their involvement in black education. One of the problems faced initially by such groups was the menace of violence from radical rebels in the South. Black and white teachers alike were often victims of mob violence. After the federal government offered them protection, their work was enhanced in the South. To be sure, the Freedmen's Bureau viewed the protection of educational movements for blacks as a vital part of its function.[21]

The sensitivity of the Freedmen's Bureau to the protection of black schools heightened by the end of the decade. In 1868, southern white opposition to black education took on the style of an organized movement. Educators in Charleston, West Virginia, received an initial warning from the Ku Klux Klan to stop their labors among blacks. Local white families feared any signs of support to those educators. In fact, several teachers in nearby Maryland were ordered to leave certain areas or suffer violence. Throughout the South, many teachers of blacks were victims of violence and some school buildings were burned.[22]

In such a social milieu, churches advanced their educational strides for blacks.

Significantly, black Baptists were among the pioneers of black education. They realized that the reduction of the illiteracy rate among blacks was absolutely necessary for the progress of the race. Hence, black Baptists committed themselves, in cooperation with other groups, to the development of an aggressive educational enterprise. This became one of the greatest contributions of the black church to the advancement of civilization.

The evolution of educational institutions among black Baptists may be classified into two groups: cooperative schools with whites and the independent black Baptist schools. As early as 1865, black Baptists enjoyed the privilege of attending a Baptist institution organized specifically for the race, the Wayland Seminary in Washington, D.C. The American Baptist Home Mission Society was very aggressive in its cooperative ministries with black Baptists for the cause of Christian and general education for black Americans. These white Baptists participated either directly or indirectly in the rapid succession of organized black Baptists schools: Richmond Theological Seminary, Richmond, Virginia, founded 1867, incorporated 1876; Shaw University, Raleigh, North Carolina, founded 1865, incorporated 1875; Atlanta Seminary, Atlanta, Georgia, founded originally at Augusta in 1867, transferred to Atlanta in 1879; Roger Williams University, Nashville, Tennessee, 1864; Leland University, New Orleans, Louisiana, 1870; Benedict College, Columbia, South Carolina, 1887; Bishop College, Marshall, Texas, 1881; Selma University, Selma, Alabama, 1878; State University, Louisville, Kentucky, 1873; Hartshorn Memorial College, Richmond, Virginia, 1884; Florida Institute, Live Oak, Florida, 1873; Spellman Seminary, Atlanta, Georgia, 1881; Arkansas Baptist College, Little Rock, Arkansas, 1887; Home Institute, New Iberia, Louisiana, 1888; Mather School, Beaufort, South Carolina; and the Bible and Normal Institute, Memphis, Tennessee.

To be sure, the American Baptist Home Mission Society played a major role in the intellectual and cultural development of blacks. Its work among black Baptists consisted mainly of: first, sending missionaries to work among blacks; second, establishing and supporting schools; and third, support for teachers among freedmen. The major involvement of white Baptists was in the area of black higher education. Most of the earliest black Baptist colleges were financed, administered, and staffed by white American Baptists. Only gradually did black Baptists assume responsibilities in these important areas. Black Baptist churches, associations, and conventions did, however, provide some funds and moral support to the colleges established by the American Baptist Home Mission Society. Some black Baptist intellectuals were also to be found at these schools.

In 1884, another group of black Baptist schools grew up in concomitance with those organized by the American Baptist Home Mission Society. The first independent black Baptist school was Guadalupe College. Subsequently, others appeared in rapid succession: Houston College at Houston, Texas, in 1885; Virginia Theological Seminary and College at Lynchburg, Virginia, and Walker Baptist Institute at Augusta, Georgia, in 1888; Western College at Independence, Missouri, in 1890; Friendship Baptist College at Rock Hill, South Carolina, in 1891; Meridian Baptist Seminary at Meridian, Mississippi, in 1897; Central City College at Macon, Georgia, in 1899; Central Texas College at Waco, Texas, in 1903; East Texas Normal and Industrial Academy at Tyler, Texas; and Morris College at Sumter, South Carolina, in 1905.

Most of the independent black Baptist colleges were founded in the South where the largest population of the race resided. However, a limited number was attempted in the North and West. In 1901, the Colored Baptist Convention of Maryland organized the Clayton-Williams Academy and Biblical Institute at Baltimore, Maryland; the Maryland Baptist Missionary Convention organized in 1914 the Lee and Hayes University at Baltimore, Maryland; the Independent Colored Baptist Convention organized in 1928 the Williams and Jones University at Baltimore; and the United

Baptist Missionary Convention organized in 1942 the Maryland Baptist Center and School of Religion, also at Baltimore. These Baltimore schools were largely the result of convention rivalry and lived only a few years. However, the latter school still exists as an extention school of the Virginia Seminary and College, Lynchburg, Virginia. Similarly, two northern black Baptist associations established in 1921 two additional institutions for the advancement of an educated ministry; Central Baptist Theological Seminary at Topeka, Kansas, and Northern Baptist University at Rahway, New Jersey.

Likewise, the decade of the 1880s witnessed the evolution of many independent black Baptist schools for secondary education. As previously mentioned, blacks depended largely at the close of the Civil War upon the public schools and those organized by the Freedmen's Bureau for the early education of their youth. It was not until after the reconstruction period that blacks began independent strides in secondary schools. Most of the schools were organized in churches, log cabins, and abandoned buildings.

The state of North Carolina was foremost in the attempts of its Black Baptists to organize private secondary schools. The establishment of Shaw University paved the way for the widespread development of high schools. Some of the teachers and preachers who graduated from Shaw University organized the first such schools in the state. First among these were Alexander Hicks, of Plymouth, North Carolina, and E. H. Lipscombe, of Dallas, North Carolina. This school at Plymouth developed into a State Normal School while the one at Dallas existed for several years and became extinct. These two pioneer movements inspired local black Baptist associations to get involved. Other high schools were organized by Baptist associations throughout the state. Unfortunately, the vast majority of these private schools closed with the rise of substantial state support for secondary schools.

By 1943, most of the black Baptist high schools had been discontinued. All of the high schools in North Carolina have been discontinued. Among those still in operation were: Marion B. Academy, Marion, Alabama; Bethlehem Academy, Monroeville, Alabama; Northern Neck Academy, Chatham, Virginia; Bluestone Harmony Academy, Keysville, Virginia; Tidewater Institute, Cape Charles, Virginia; Thomaston N. & I. School, Thomaston, Alabama; and Union Baptist Institute, Athens, Georgia. These schools soon showed signs of decay as public education became the order of the day.

Moreover, independent black colleges were affected by the increase of state support to black education. The rise of state colleges soon began to limit the growth of church-related schools. Hence, several of the black Baptist colleges and seminaries closed gradually. Fortunately, a few were able to survive through merger and vigorous leadership in those that remained separate.

The organization and development of the schools that survived either through mergers or as separate institutions were unique in higher education. They represented the sort of drama that became a unique American experience for blacks and whites who sympathized with the cause of black higher education. The drama has been full of struggles against oppressions, failures, and triumphs. A brief survey of these independent stories will reflect such an intense drama.

## Wayland Seminary

The Wayland Seminary was a pioneer educational institution for the intellectual and moral development of black Americans. It was opened in the Nineteenth Street

Baptist Church of Washington, D.C., under the auspice of the American Baptist Home Mission Society of New York City. The school was named in honor of Dr. Francis Wayland who was quite instrumental in the organization and maintenance of the seminary.

The seminary came as the result of a series of social developments at the end of the Civil War. The leadership of the American Baptist Home Mission Society observed, in its meeting at Saint Louis, May 18, 1865, that nearly four million freedmen were "thrown like waifs on the sea of political strife."[23] So viewed, the society sought to detail the situation of freedmen in its report entitled "Work Among the Freedmen—The New Era."

> They are houseless, penniless, without business experience, without capital or credit, their social, civil, and religious condition chaotic. How to evolve order; how out of the mire of servile degradation to produce the lilies of the Christian virtues; how to fit them for citizenship; for the duties of Church organization; how to displace superstition with truth; how to educate them to read and think for themselves; how to provide them with meeting-houses, of which they have but few; how to train the ministers, most of whom cannot read a sentence in the Scriptures;—these are some of the problems confronting American Baptists at the meeting of the Society in 1865. It is estimated that at the close of the war, nearly 400,000 of these people are Baptists. The South is impoverished. The black man is ground between the upper and nether millstones of poverty and politics.
>
> To the close of the war, the common school system is unknown in the South. The door of no schoolhouse opens to the children of these emancipated millions. They need the schoolhouse and the schoolmaster, the meeting-house and the missionary, in a thousand places. How and by whom shall these be provided? Such are the questions to be considered at the St. Louis meeting.[24]

In light of the foregoing, the society was challenged to "determine its line of operation in the South".[25]

There was already existing within the denomination a certain movement which began an independent effort to work among the freedmen. The National Theological Institute, organized at Washington, D.C., in 1864 and commenced operations early in 1865, took specific actions in issuing "its circulars and appeals for educational and religious efforts among the freedmen, announcing before the Society's annual meeting that schools had been planted in several places."[26] The society was somewhat embarrassed over such premature labors.

However, the two separate educational enterprises existed in concomitance for a brief period of time, that is, the Wayland Seminary and the National Theological Institute. In 1869, the two schools merged under the name of "Wayland Seminary." After the merger, Dr. G. M. P. King became president of Wayland Seminary. In 1876, a new building on Meridian Hill, near Sixteenth Street, was completed and occupied. Subsequently, the growth of this new educational institution was constant and sustained. Many of the great leaders of the black race were educated at Wayland Seminary. In 1874, it was stated that "more than five hundred freedmen have been pupils in Wayland Seminary."[27] Again these men were spoken of as "eminently useful on their field of labor."[28]

The course of instruction at Wayland was adapted to the needs of the freedmen. The curriculum combined academic, normal, and theological courses to prepare the freedmen for American citizenship. Wayland Seminary continued as a growing institution until 1889 when it was decided to merge the school with the Richmond Theological Seminary under the new name of Virginia Union University at Richmond, Virginia.

## Virginia Union University

The Virginia Union University was founded in 1865 by the American Baptist Home Mission Society. This bold venture reflected the evolving policy of the Society toward black Americans and their educational plight. It was the society's first attempt at such an organized work in the South—Richmond, once the capital of the Confederate States of America.

Virginia Union University's early evolution was inextricably related to several other educational movements. Near the end of 1865, Rev. J. B. Binney, former president of Columbia College in Washington, came to Richmond and started a night school, Richmond Theological Institute for Freedmen. Initially, he encountered so much difficulty in attempting to find a permanent location for the night school that he abandoned his effort "after eight months and became a missionary in Burma."[29]

Fortunately, the work was continued by Rev. Nathaniel Colver, an abolitionist and biblical professor at the University of Chicago.[30] In 1867, he was asked to continue the work and secure a permanent site. Rev. Colver succeeded in this endeavor by leasing the Lumpkin's Slave Jail property from its owner. The new site was named the Colver Institute. Subsequently, the trustees and other officials of the American Baptist Home Mission Society decided to make it a school for ministers only; hence the name was changed to the Richmond Theological Seminary.[31] The society elected Rev. Charles Corey to serve as the president, and he remained in this capacity until 1899.[32]

The school was strategically located in an area densely populated by blacks. This factor contributed to the rapid growth of the new educational movement. Several years after its successful operation, Rev. Charles Corey reminisced:

The historic Pickford Hall, administration building at Virginia Union University, Richmond, Virginia.

Of students there have been in attendance nearly 1,100; total preparing for the ministry, 540; graduates with diplomas from Richmond Institute, 73; total graduates with degree of B.S. from Richmond Theological Seminary, 27. Some of these graduates are now in charge of institutions of learning, others are professors in seminaries and Universities. Six entered the foreign mission field. The former students of the Richmond Theological Seminary are to be found from Canada to Texas, and in the lands far beyond the sea.[33]

The initial decade of the school's mission was very fruitful in the progress of the race.

In 1870, the school moved to a new location at the old Union Hotel in Richmond. It remained in this location until 1898 when the Home Mission Society decided to move Wayland Seminary to Richmond and merge it with Richmond Theological Seminary.[34] The merger was then named the Virginia Union University. With the sale of the Wayland Seminary property in Washington, the society was able to use the funds to purchase a new location for the University at Sheep Hill—the old site of Nathaniel Bacon's plantation.[35]

The Virginia Union University soon assumed its university structure. Wayland Seminary became the men's college while Richmond Theological Seminary became the graduate school in religion.

In 1932, Hartshorn Memorial College, a women's Christian school, merged with the growing and viable institution of higher learning. The last school to join the "union" was Storer College in 1964. It was the oldest institution dedicated to the education of blacks in West Virginia. Initially, this American Baptist school was closed in 1955 and officially merged into Virginia Union University in 1964.

Each of the several institutions of the "union" was initially led by white Baptists. The American Baptist Home

Dr. John M. Ellison, first black president of
Virginia Union University, Richmond,
Virginia.

Mission Society delegated the management of Virginia Union University to its various trustees and administrators. Even the faculty consisted largely of white teachers. However, the black Baptists of the Baptist General Convention of Virginia gradually assumed greater responsibility for the operation of the university. In 1936, Dr. John Malcus Ellison, born in Virginia in 1889, became the first black Baptist president of Virginia Union University.

Very significantly, Virginia Union University has developed into one of the few church-related schools for blacks to be accredited by the Southern Association of Colleges and Secondary Schools. It shares only with Howard University School of Religion and Interdenominational Theological Center of Atlanta University the distinction of accreditation by the American Association of Theological Schools.

Moreover, Virginia Union University represents a symbol of cooperation between American Baptists (formerly Northern Baptists), Southern Baptists, and black Baptists to facilitate quality education for the race. Southern Baptists, though somewhat late, joined with these groups in the development of the university. Specifically, the Woman's Missionary Union, Auxiliary to the Southern Baptist Convention, has erected on the campus a small dormitory for young women interested in full-time Christian service at an approximate cost of $100,000. By 1960, the facility was housing the Department of Religious Education. The Woman's Missionary Union has provided the salary for the director and assistant director of the Department of Religious Education, special scholarships for girls, and contributed large sums of money toward the general operation of the school.[36] To be sure, black colleges attest the authenticity of a rationale of cooperation among all Baptists.

## Shaw University

In 1865, Shaw University was established by Rev. H. M. Tupper of Massachusetts under the auspices of the American Baptist Home Mission Society. Initially, Rev. Tupper began a theological class of freedmen in the old Guion Hotel, in Raleigh, North Carolina, December 1, 1865. Out of this theological class, Rev. Tupper conceived the idea of establishing a university. The actual university was started "in a very humble way in a negro cabin on the outskirts of the City."[37]

The work of developing the university progressed slowly. However, Rev. H. M. Tupper made appeals to other white men who sympathized with the plight of black Americans. The construction of a building to house the university was made possible by liberal contributions from Elijah Shaw of Wales, Massachusetts, J. Estey and Company, Gen. Andrew Porter, George M. Moore, and other men from New England. Several black men of the city of Raleigh also contributed to the construction of the first building which was erected at the corner of Blount and Cabarrus Streets in Raleigh.[38] The school remained in this location for several years under the name of Raleigh Institute. From its inception until 1870 approximately 2,000 men, women, and youth received instruction at Raleigh Institute in the day, night, and Sunday Schools.[39]

Rev. H. M. Tupper encountered some severe problems in the early years of the development of Raleigh Institute. The white citizens of Raleigh were generally antagonistic toward the education of black Americans. This tendency, constant and unchanging, was related by Rev. J. A. Whitted, a pioneer black Baptist historian, when he observed:

> President Tupper and wife spent a night in a corn field in the rear of their humble cabin, having been threatened by the Ku Klux. Every moment of these hours of anxious sus-

pence they expected to see the flames consume their home and all their earthly effects, but a kind, all-wise Providence guarded them through the long night watches, and when the welcome dawn tardily appeared the humble cabin was still standing and in devout thanksgiving they returned to its kindly shelter.[40]

In 1870, a new day dawned for Raleigh Institute. The Barringer property, comprising about ten acres with a mansion, was bought for $15,000 to house the expanding school.[41] In 1872, nearly one half of the Shaw building was completed at a cost of $15,000. Two years later, the Estey building, a school for girls, was finished at a cost of $25,000. In 1875, the school was incorporated as Shaw University. It became the first college for blacks in North Carolina to receive the *A* rating by the state Department of Education and the first such institution south of Washington to limit itself strictly to college and theological work.

After its incorporation in 1875, Shaw University was expanded to reflect university status. President Tupper first envisioned the establishment of a medical department. By 1908, the university had developed the Leonard Medical School in addition to normal, college, and industrial departments, and the schools of law, theology, and pharmacy. The medical school was led by prominent white physicians in the city of Raleigh.

To be sure, the initial years of Shaw University were full of crises. By 1914, a rather severe crisis developed in the area of finances. President Charles Francis Meserve decided that the financial situation of the university necessitated the termination of two important professional schools—the Leonard Medical School along with its new Leonard Hospital and the Law School. All that remained of the medical school was the continuation for a brief period of time of a two-year course in pharmacy. During its brief lifetime, the

Leonard Medical School graduated 396 black medical students.[42]

Another crisis in the life of Shaw University centered around racial issues. Early in the twentieth century, black students at Shaw became increasingly aware of the prominence of white leaders on the campus. Several of the student leaders began organized efforts to obtain greater black control of the university. In 1914, a student protest movement erupted. It was designed to remove President Meserve and obtain the services of a black president of the university. Some students even left Shaw to enroll in other schools because of the tension at the school.

On January 21, 1914, T. L. McCoy of the Norfolk *Journal and Guide* surveyed the aftermath of the student protest movement at Shaw University. This editor sided with the school's administration and suggested that the "student uprising" was more hurtful to the cause of black education then to the university. Such support was very encouraging to the administration until 1919. Only gradually did black Baptists gain greater control over the university.

Meanwhile, the university shifted its emphasis from the professional schools to liberal arts education and the Shaw Divinity School. It specialized, more or less, in the field of education. For many years, it provided most of the black teachers for the state. Many of Shaw's alumni, among them such distinguished persons as Ms. Angie Brooks, a world leader of the United Nations from Liberia; Dr. James E. Shepard, founder of North Carolina Central University at Durham; and James Y. Eaton, member of the North Carolina Legislature in 1899, have served the religious and sociopolitical movements of the world.

In the mid 1960s, Shaw University experienced perhaps its most important period of growth and development. President James E. Cheek, a young black scholar, led the university to redevelop its total curriculum and to expand the physical facilities. He was able to attract large sums of federal monies to Shaw which were utilized to construct several new buildings and to upgrade the academic programs.

The key word in the Cheek administration was *renaissance.* Its impact was felt everywhere in the life of the university. Within three years of Dr. James E. Cheek's administration, the faculty increased from 36 to 71 and the student enrollment from 667 to 1,052.[43] Similarly, he made plans to raise faculty salaries by approximately 30 percent and to increase the capital outlay for new construction to approximately five million dollars.[44]

It was also during Cheek's administration that the university adopted a growth posture still operative. He defined such a posture succinctly:

> For us at Shaw, academic freedom refers not only to the freedom to teach and learn within the canons of scholarly inquiry, but also to change, to determine our own internal policies and philosophy; to create that curriculum and those programs which we deem most necessary for the welfare of our students; and to decide for ourselves the role Shaw must play as a center of learning.[45]

In this statement, Dr. Cheek addressed himself to the underlying issue of too much denominational control over the university. He tried to accomplish two things in the address: on the one hand, to encourage the financial support of the General Baptist State Convention of North Carolina, yet, at the same time, to limit the direct involvement of church leaders in the internal affairs of the university.

The tremendous success of the Cheek administration still is viewed with great pride at the university. Dr. James E. Cheek was succeeded by his brother Dr. King Cheek. Both men gave the school quality leadership. Later, Dr. King Cheek left Shaw for a new job in Maryland.

Currently, the leadership at Shaw University is still characterized by the sort of quality initiated by Dr. James E. Cheek. The entire campus is going through a renewal. The university stands as one of the great institutions of learning for black Americans. The black Baptists of North Carolina take particular pride in the quality of Shaw University.

## Roger Williams University

The beginning of the work of the American Baptist Home Mission Society in Nashville was in 1864 when Rev. H. L. Wayland was appointed as a missionary-teacher for the city of Nashville. After eight months he resigned; and Rev. D. W. Phillips, who in August 1864 had been appointed to Knoxville, took his place.

Initially, Rev. D. W. Phillips organized a class for black youth in his house, the later one in the basement of the First Colored Baptist Church of Nashville, Tennessee. In 1866, Roger Williams University was organized and housed in an abandoned government building. The school opened with accommodations for about forty-five young men and twelve girls. For ten years Roger Williams University remained in this building.[46]

In 1882, the Board of the Home Mission Society decided to incorporate the institution, but the incorporation was not effected until January 1883. Initially, the school was named Nashville Institute and later changed to the Roger Williams University after its incorporation.

The American Baptist Home Mission Society contributed the largest portion of the funds for the development of the new university. However, in 1905 the principal buildings were destroyed by fire. This destructive event led to the direct involvement of black Baptist leaders in the financial support and subsequent administration of the institution. In 1908, Roger Williams University was reopened, and the responsibility for its direction was transferred from the American Baptist Home Mission Society to the Negro Baptist Missionary and Educational Convention of the state of Tennessee.

Fortunately, the Roger Williams University, from the very beginning, maintained a high reputation for thorough academic training. In addition to the training of black Americans, Roger Williams University was one of the pioneer institutions in the state for the education of Indian Americans.

Unfortunately, the Roger Williams University soon experienced financial difficulties. By 1929, it began showing significant signs of general decay. Low enrollments, budget deficits, and administrative problems led to a survey committee on Negro colleges and universities by the US Department of the Interior. Subsequently, the government recommended that the Negro Baptist Missionary and Education Convention of the state of Tennessee should seriously consider the advisability of discontinuing the institution. Very soon thereafter, the fate of the university was sealed.

## Leland University

In 1870, Leland University was founded in New Orleans, Louisiana, for the education of black men and women to prepare them for Christian citizenship, either as ministers, teachers, or tradesmen. The school was open to all qualified persons without distinction of race, color, or religious opinions.

Initially, the school was developed out of the labors of two American Baptist missionaries, Rev. J. W. Horton and Rev. Jeremiah Chaplin. These men were appointed by the American Baptist Home Mission Society to "engage in the work of instructing colored ministers, and students for the ministry."[47] In 1869, Holbrook Chamberlain and his wife, of the Baptist Free Mission Society, arrived on the scene and assisted the missionaries in the establishment of the school. The new school was named Leland University after the maiden name of Mrs. Chamberlain, who was a direct descendent of Rev. John Leland.

The curriculum of Leland University consisted of courses necessary for quality in normal and industrial education. However, the school also maintained a strong program of religious studies since the great aim of its founding was for the education of black preachers. Equally important, the school served as a center for Protestant polemics against the strong Roman Catholic influence in the city of New Orleans.

## Benedict College

During the early days of reconstruction in South Carolina, the Baptist denomination did very little in an effort to begin one strong institution for higher learning for the freedmen of the state. It was not until 1870 that a substantial effort evolved. That year a desirable site for an institution of higher learning was found available at Columbia, South Carolina. The site seemed ideal since Columbia was the state capitol. Funds were made available for the purchase of this site through the generosity of Mrs. B. A. Benedict of Providence, Rhode Island. It consisted of approximately eighty acres of land.

The American Baptist Home Mission Board led the way in the establishment of this school. Due to the large contribution from Mrs. Benedict, the Board decided to name the new school Benedict Institute in honor of the deceased husband of the donor, Deacon Stephen Benedict. In 1871, the school was opened under the presidency of Rev.

Timothy D. Dodge. The school was later incorporated under the name Benedict College.

The founding of Benedict College signaled a new era in educational opportunities for the black people of South Carolina. According to the census of 1880, there were 604,332 black people living in the state. Many of these people were illiterate. Benedict College played a major role in decreasing the problem of illiteracy in South Carolina. The student body of Benedict College more than doubled in the early 1880s. Blacks, young and old, took advantage of the quality of education offered at the school.

Initially, the focal point of concern at Benedict College was the education of teachers and preachers for the large black population of South Carolina. A strong program in Christian morals permeated the entire curriculum of the institution.

By the turn of the century, the curriculum of the institution was greatly expanded in the liberal arts. Gradually, the general program of the school developed into a very strong institution of higher learning. The growth of the institution was reflected in a legal move. On November 2, 1924, the school was legally incorporated and became a chartered institution, possessed of full college powers, under the laws of the state of South Carolina.

Presently, Benedict College is organized into two schools—the College of Liberal Arts and the School of Theology. Each school is designed to meet the unique needs of blacks, especially black Baptists.

## Bishop College

The need for an institution of higher learning for black people of the Southwest, beyond the Mississippi River, was recognized during an early period of the reconstruction era. Dr. Nathan Bishop, a former secretary of the Home Mission

Society of the American (Northern) Baptist Convention, was first to articulate this concern concretely: "I have 10,000 to put into a school in Texas, when the time has come."[48] This was the inspiration of the movement to establish such an institution in the state.

In 1881, the college was founded through a cooperative effort of white Baptists, North and South, and the black Baptists of the state. It was located in the city of Marshall, Texas. This was a pioneer movement with cooperation among the separate Baptist groups in the United States. Hence, the founding of Bishop College represented the beginning of a slow but determined effort of the Southern Baptists, Northern Baptists, and the black Baptists of America to cooperate on important issues affecting the good of race relations. It signaled a greater involvement of Southern Baptists in the general uplift of the blacks of the South.

The college was established as a liberal arts school, but it provided educational opportunity for children and adults from the kindergarten through the undergraduate years. During the administration of its first president, S. W. Culver, the institution was chartered in 1886 under the laws of the state of Texas. Incorporators were members of the American Baptist Home Mission Board, representatives of the Southern Baptist Convention, and several black Baptist associations in Texas.

The academic program of the school was geared to prepare preachers and teachers and to provide professional training for lawyers, physicians, and dentists. In 1892, during the administration of N. Wolverton, the college's second president, an affiliation was effected with the Richmond Theological Seminary, Richmond, Virginia, making it possible for advanced students to enter the seminary, and with Shaw University, Raleigh, North Carolina, to accept the preprofessional students at Bishop College for admission to the schools of law and medicine at Shaw. Hence, black

Baptists beyond the Mississippi River were linked with those of the East in cooperative educational programs.

Bishop, like many other private black colleges, was initially administered by white presidents. It was not until 1929 that Bishop College elected its first black president, Dr. Joseph J. Rhoads, a native of the local community and a graduate of the college. Under Dr. Rhoads's leadership, the high school department was terminated, and Bishop College was given unconditional rank as a senior college by the Texas State Board of Education. Subsequently, Bishop College became one of the two black colleges west of the Mississippi River to be rated at that time by the Southern Association of Colleges and Schools. Significantly enough, this academic distinction was accomplished under the leadership of a black administration.

Several other achievements of the Rhoads administration include: a junior college extension opened in Dallas in 1947; a graduate program leading to the Master of Education degree initiated in 1947; and the organization of the Lucy Kirk Williams Ministers' Institute. The latter has come to share with the Hampton Institute Ministers' Conference as the two greatest short-term training centers for in-service ministers and lay black church leaders in America. Also, Bishop College joined the United Negro College Fund in 1944.

In May 1951, Dr. Earl L. Harrison, pastor of Shiloh Baptist Church, Washington, D.C., and a member of the board of trustees, was named interim president during the illness of Dr. Joseph J. Rhoads. Following the retirement of President Rhoads in August 1951, Dr. Harrison assumed full duties of the presidency but declined permanent appointment. He served until February 29, 1952. During this brief administration, Dr. Harrison succeeded in realigning the Baptist Missionary and Educational Convention of Texas with Bishop College. Earlier concerns had resulted in the withdrawal of some support on the part of this convention. However, the realignment brought back the support of many strong black Baptist leaders.

In December 1951, the board of trustees elected Dr. M. K. Curry, Jr., to the presidency of Bishop College. His long tenure was crowned with many accomplishments. The administration eliminated the graduate program in teacher education, raised the minimum endowment of $300,000 in 1952-1955, upgraded the faculty, and renovated the campus with funds from the United Negro College Fund Capital Campaign of 1952-1955. More significantly, the greatest accomplishment of this administration was the relocation of the college in Dallas in 1961.

The college has made many outstanding contributions to the intellectual, religious, and social life of Dallas and the nation. Early in January 1964, Bishop College participated in the organization of the Dallas-Fort Worth Metropolitan InterUniversity Council composed of administrators from nine of the colleges and universities in the area and the Southwest Center for Advanced Studies to promote interinstitutional cooperation. The college also participated in the organization of the Texas Association of Developing Colleges, a consortium of six traditionally black colleges committed to improving the quality of undergraduate instruction, reducing unnecessary duplication of course offerings, and promoting cooperation among the participating institutions.

Currently, Bishop College, with property valued at $15 million, remains a church-related institution of higher learning dedicated to the liberal arts. It is related to black Baptists but nonsectarian and interracial in its selection of students, faculty, and staff. All in all, Bishop College is simply continuing its long-time record as an equal opportunity employer and a quality institution of higher learning.

## State University of Louisville

State University of Louisville, Kentucky, founded in 1879 as the Kentucky Normal and Theological Institute (later named Simmons University), was one of the pioneer independent black Baptist institutions of higher education in the United States. It grew out of a general discussion among black Baptists at the close of the Civil War relative to the best means of elevating the race and teaching true citizenship. These black Baptists of Kentucky organized themselves into a "General Assembly" for the purpose of "establishing a college for the education of ministers and teachers."[49] In 1866, they purchased a site at Frankfort but were too poor to start the school. In 1869, these black Baptists changed their name to the General Association of the Colored Baptists of Kentucky and, by a bare majority, decided to change the location for the new school project from Frankfort to Louisville. The actual founding of the Kentucky Normal and Theological Institute was the culmination of almost a decade of planning. In the annual session of the General Association of the Colored Baptists of Kentucky held at Lexington, Kentucky, the leadership of the convention drew up an application and petitioned the state legislature for a charter. This was granted, and the leadership of the convention soon raised sufficient funds to purchase grounds and buildings for the school. It was finally opened in February 1879.

Rev. E. P. Marrs and his brother H. C. Marrs were especially instrumental in the development of the new school. They were the first administrators of the institution. Specifically, Rev. E. P. Marrs served as manager and his brother the assistant manager. The first teacher was Rev. W. R. Davis. William H. Steward, who was employed in the Louisville post office as carrier, was elected chairman of the board of trustees. His large financial contributions were responsible for the economic growth and stability of the school.

Other pioneers in the growth and development of the school, later called State University, included Rev. William J. Simmons, the first president; Rev. Charles L. Purce, who succeeded Rev. Simmons as the second president; Professor R. S. Wilkinson, professor of Languages and Political Science; Professor W. H. Huffman, Mathematics and Natural Science; Professor A. G. Gilbert, MD, English and Hygienic Science; Professor L. M. Seeley, English and Cognate Branches; and Mrs. M. E. Steward, instructor of music.[50] These black Baptist leaders led in the establishment of State University as one of the leading independent colleges among the nineteenth-century black colleges.

In 1884, the school's name was changed to the Baptist State University. It operated under the new name until 1918 when Simmons University was the name given to the school.

By 1929, Simmons University consisted of a liberal arts college, a theological department, and a preparatory school. It was also recognized as a standard college by the Kentucky State Department of Education.

Simmons University enjoyed significant growth for several decades. Under the leadership of President C. H. Parrish, the university enjoyed unprecedented growth. In 1922, it had an enrollment of 467 students, 33 theological students, and property valued at $750,000. The *National Baptist Year Book,* compiled by Dr. C.H. Parrish, reported also that year the university's endowment of $54,000.

Unfortunately, the following decade witnessed a gradual decline in the vitality of Simmons University. In 1943, the *National Baptist Bulletin,* edited by Roland Smith, reported the school as merely a theological institution with only 73 students. Fortunately, the decline did not continue, and stability came to this pioneer black Baptist educational institution. This school still operates in Louisville and is now called Simmons Bible College.

## Selma University

In 1873, the Colored Baptist Convention at Alabama decided, while in session at Tuscaloosa, to establish a school for preachers and other church leaders. The leadership of the convention was anxious to develop an educated black Baptist ministry in the state. In this endeavor, they asked the assistance of the white Baptists; but the white brethren said that "the scheme was impracticable." Nevertheless, the black Baptists went to work among themselves and succeeded in opening a school at Selma, Alabama, in 1878 "at the colored Baptist Church."[51]

Subsequently, the convention purchased property comprising about thirty-six acres with a building (formerly the agricultural fairground) at a cost of $3,000 located in the suburbs of Selma.[52] The school was initially named the Alabama Baptist Normal and Theological School, later called Selma University. In 1880, the school was adopted by the American Baptist Home Mission Society to receive support.

By 1881, the university had educated more than "one hundred students for the ministry, and about the same number of teachers"[53] to take on positions of responsibility in the state. Approximately eighty alumni of Selma University were teachers in the public schools of the state in 1881.

The year 1881 also witnessed the election of Rev. W. H. McAlpine to the presidency of the university. The new president was formerly a slave. Under his pioneer leadership, Selma University became one of the prominent institutions for the education of black leaders.

In 1895, the name of the school was changed to the Alabama Baptist Colored University, and in 1908 to Selma

University again. It struggled for several years to improve its academic standing. However, in 1919 the Alabama State Department of Education accredited the teacher's professional course in the junior college for the granting of teachers' certificates. As late as 1928, the university had not been formally accredited beyond this recognition by the state of Alabama.

Fortunately, the university experienced a significant growth in its enrollment and academic standards. It became affiliated with the State Department of Education and the Veterans Administration. By 1979, Selma University was organized into a coeducation four-year institution. Like other black Baptist colleges, Christian principles permeated the basic curriculum of the college.

## Arkansas Baptist College

Arkansas Baptist College, Little Rock, Arkansas, was originated by the black Baptists of the state in their annual convention at Hot Springs, Arkansas, August 1884. In November of the same year the school then known as The Baptist Institute was opened at the Mount Zion Baptist Church. It was operated until April 1885, under the direction of Rev. J. P. Lawson, a white Baptist minister of Joplin, Missouri, but was forced to close at that time because of insufficient funds. Later during the year 1885 the Mount Pleasant Baptist Church was secured, and Rev. Harry Woodsmall, a general missionary of the Baptist denomination for the states of Arkansas, Louisiana, and Mississippi, helped with the reorganization of the plans for the continuance of the school. Articles of the association were drawn up, and the institute was legally organized and incorporated under the laws of the state. The new corporate name was Arkansas Baptist College.

Subsequently, the black Baptists of Arkansas purchased a city block from Attorney Blake Turner for the sum of $5,000. The black Baptists of the state pooled their resources to construct a modern facility for the school upon this site.

Initially, the most prominent feature of the college was the "Pastors' Course" or theological department. The education of the clergy was the principal concern of black church leaders in the state. This interest was extended to include teacher education. Nevertheless, all preachers and student teachers were trained in moral questions, religious obligations, and spiritual work.

Currently, the Arkansas Baptist College serves as a basic Christian institution. It is committed to the theology of the Baptist denomination. Even the liberal arts program is under the influence of Christian principles.

## Butler College

In 1903, Butler College was established under the name of East Texas Baptist Industrial Academy and operated under that name for about twenty-three years. It was founded by the East Texas Baptist Association for the primary purpose of developing an educated black ministry and for providing Christian education for other black youth.

The structure of the new institution was developed by the East Texas Baptist Association. Under the plan of organization, the moderator of the association was to serve as president of the institution. Hence, Rev. C. M. Butler, who had been the moderator of the association for twenty-nine years, became the first president of Butler College. He served in this position for nineteen years until his death in 1924.

The leadership of the East Texas Baptist Association soon realized that the general black population of the area needed additional educational opportunities. This resulted in the academy being elevated to a junior college. In 1924, following the death of Rev. C. M. Butler, the grammar school was dropped, and the curriculum concentrated in a high school program, a liberal arts junior college, and a school of theology. With this change in the curriculum, the name of the school was changed to Butler College.

In 1931, the East Texas Baptist Association found it necessary to seek the cooperation of other Baptists to operate the school successfully. Hence, it extended an invitation to the Texas Baptist Convention to participate in a joint ownership of the property. The proposal was accepted by the Texas Baptist Convention, and the school was subsequently owned and operated by the East Texas Baptist Association and the Texas Baptist Convention.

In September 1947, the college added senior college work to its curriculum, and by February 1949, the college had been approved by the state of Texas as an accredited four-year liberal arts college.

The mission of Butler College was to be a feeder for Bishop College. It operated as a cooperative institution rather than as a competitor to Bishop College. The cooperative nature of Butler attracted the support of black Baptists throughout the state of Texas.

## American Baptist Theological Seminary

In 1913, black Baptists and Southern Baptists launched a new era of cooperation in the cause of black higher education. The Southern Baptist Convention appointed a committee of nine to "advise and confer with the colored brethren" regarding the establishment of a theological seminary for black Baptists.[54] This action was the real beginning of Southern Baptist activity for the establishment of the new school project.

Actually, the appointment of the committee or commission by the Southern Baptists was the culmination of much discussion within the Convention. As early as 1872, the Southern Baptist Convention expressed real interest in the religious education of black Baptists. Its Committee on the Colored Population recommended several activities in this direction: (1) white Baptist ministers were encouraged "to preach for them as frequently and regularly as they may have opportunity"; (2) local Southern Baptist churches were urged "to encourage the formation of Sunday Schools among them, and aid in the instruction of teachers for such schools," and (3) the Home Mission Board was to seek ways for "the establishment of an institution for the education of the colored preachers."[55] This set in motion a series of events. The year 1876 witnessed the beginning of ministerial institutes for black Baptist preachers. In 1899, the Home Mission Board encouraged white ministers to assist in the development of good libraries for black ministers. Many such activities preceeded the appointment of the commission on the establishment of the American Baptist Theological Seminary.

The National Baptist Convention, U.S.A., expressed a deep interest in the proposed project for a new theological school to enhance the professional training of black Baptist ministers. The leadership of the convention was always anxious to provide such opportunities. Prior to 1913, Dr. L. K. Williams, Dr. O. L. Bailey, and Dr. C. B. Bailey talked extensively regarding such a project. Out of these dialogues, the decision was made to bring the matter before both the Southern Baptist Convention and the National Baptist Convention, U.S.A. Both conventions appointed committees to work out plans for the establishment of the American Baptist Theological Seminary.[56]

The two committees or commissions worked out some rather minute plans for the seminary project. In 1926, Dr. L. K. Williams, president of the National Baptist Convention, U.S.A., reported to the convention that "the Southern Baptist Convention would build and equip the building necessary to the operation of the school if the National Baptist Convention would purchase and pay for the land."[57] The board of directors would be appointed by the two conventions. However, the National Baptist Convention was to hold the majority representation of "two-thirds of the total number of the membership" on the board.[58] The Southern Baptist Convention was given only "one-third of the total number of the membership of the Board."[59]

Apparently, the black Baptists were anxious to establish a controlling position in the school's administration. Dr. L. K. Williams specified that the "President of the Seminary must be a member of the National Baptist Convention."[60]

The long-time negotiations between the two conventions continued until the school was finally opened for its first session in Nashville, Tennessee, September 14, 1924. Among the pioneer presidents of the school were: Dr. Sutton E. Griggs, 1925-1926; Dr. W. T. Amiger, 1927-1929; Rev. Roy A. Mayfield, 1932-1934; and Dr. J.M. Nabrit, 1936-1943. The latter founded the National Baptist Missionary Training School on the campus of the American Baptist Theological Seminary.

In 1934, the National Baptist Convention, U.S.A., acquired the property formerly occupied by the Roger Williams University for the new site of the seminary. Plans were immediately developed to modernize the facility "for the operation of a Missionary Training School and a Home for Old Ministers."[61] Hence, the new site became a multipurpose center.

The school experienced substantial growth financially and physically. The Southern Baptist Convention contributed, however, the greater portion of the funds for the operation of the American Baptist Theological Seminary. In 1977, the Southern Baptist Convention established a scholarship program to provide "support for 100 church vocation students from National Baptist churches."[62]

Surely, the cooperative strides of black and white Baptists have been significant in black higher education. Many have been the ministers, theological teachers, and missionaries to benefit from the American Baptist Theological Seminary. Currently, the two conventions take pride in the historic mission of this institution.

## Virginia Baptist Theological Seminary

The Virginia Theological Seminary and College was founded by the Virginia Baptist State Convention during its annual session of May 1887, at Alexandria, Virginia. On February 24, 1888, the school was incorporated by an act of the General Assembly of Virginia. Under the provisions of the charter a committee was appointed to purchase suitable grounds. The committee purchased the present site in the city of Lynchburg, Virginia. The cornerstone was laid in July 1881. On January 13, 1890, the school was opened to give a thorough and practical education to black youths.[63] By 1896, the student enrollment numbered 200.

Rev. P. F. Morris was elected the first president of the school, but on account of failing health he resigned the position before the school had been completed. Hence, the real pioneer leader of the Virginia Theological Seminary and College was Gregory Willis Hayes, immediate successor of Rev. P. F. Morris. Initially, the new president started the work under many disadvantages, a depleted treasury on the part of the Virginia Baptist State Convention and with no available sources from which financial aid could be procured. By his zeal and enterprise a large building was constructed on a beautiful hill in the vicinity of the city of Lynchburg, Virginia.

A brief biographical sketch of Professor Gregory Willis

Hayes will reflect the strides of a great black Baptist in the educational progress of the race. He was born of slave parents in Amelia County, Virginia, September 8, 1862. He graduated from Oberlin College, one of the first institutions of learning in the state of Ohio, in the class of 1888 and was elected to the chair of pure mathematics in the Virginia Normal and Collegiate Institute. Also, he was the first president of the National Baptist Educational Convention of the United States and was commissioner in chief from Virginia for the Southern Inter-State Exposition.[64]

The Virginia Baptist Theological Seminary and College, under the leadership of Gregory Willis Hayes, made tremendous progress in the education of black Baptists in the state of Virginia. It was, however, open to students of all denominations. The free-spirited philosophy of Gregory Willis Hayes's "Self-help and Spiritual Independence" invigorated and inspired many of the great leaders of the race who passed through this unique institution.

Similarly, the school placed major emphasis on the value of teaching black culture and achievement in the various fields of human endeavor. This tendency caused the school to engage in a lively debate near the turn of the century. Two central issues of the debate have been noted by Dr. M. C. Allen:

> One of the questions which precipitated a wide-spread debate among Negro educators in Virginia in the early years of Virginia Theological Seminary and College was the advisability of including facts on Negro Baptists in text books on the Baptist denomination used in our seminaries. Another question around which much debate centered in those early years was that of the effect of outside control on Negro institutions supported financially by philanthropists from other groups. As the years passed, the thought of Negro responsibility for financial support and control of Negro institutions of higher learning began to crystalize until

educators and business groups interested in Virginia Theological Seminary and College were definitely committed to the idea of "self-help" and "self-direction."[65]

Moreover, the school has had a unique leadership style. The leadership has centered almost exclusively in the presidency. Each president left his unique style on the life of the school. Among the more noted presidents were Reverends R. C. Wood, W. H. R. Powell, Vernon Johns, and M. C. Allen.

During the administration of Dr. M. C. Allen, the school promoted a tremendous emphasis on black preaching and black power. He placed primary importance on the training of young black clergymen to excel in the pulpits of the nation. In 1952, Dr. Allen published a standard textbook entitled *Virginia Seminary Formula for Effective Preaching*. This little book was used by all theological students on both the college and seminary levels.

Equally important was the school's emphasis on black power. Dr. M. C. Allen was one of the earliest men in America to place major emphasis on black power. He preached and lectured on the subject a decade before the beginning of the modern black power movement of Stokely Carmichael and other leaders of the civil rights revolution. His was almost a lone voice in the struggle. However, many of his students became foremost leaders in the revolution.

## Early Black Education and Racial Progress

Racial progress was always the key factor motivating the evolution of the black press and the black school movements. Each institution played a significant role in the enormous progress black people made during the initial years of freedom. Collectively, the educational institutions surveyed in this chapter impacted the black man's struggles in the

Rev. M. C. Allen, founder and editor of *The Expected* and pioneer writer on the black power philosphy.

social, political, economic, and intellectual life of Western civilization. They provided the skills, optimistic attitudes, and general climate necessary for progress among a people of oppression.

The educational advancement of black Americans at the turn of the century was a great marvel. No other group of oppressed people ever advanced more rapidly in civilization. As we have seen, black Baptist educational institutions played a tremendous role in this progress.

One of the earliest challenges to the educational institutions was the issue of illiteracy. Black Baptist educational institutions, along with other black institutions, began early after the Civil War to launch a major attack on the problem of illiteracy among the race. Presumably, a brief sketch of the census reports between 1880 and 1915 will shed some light on racial progress.

In considering the data of illiteracy, it should be remembered that the percentage of illiteracy for black Americans as a whole, as for any other group, usually responds slowly to improvements in educational conditions. Strangely enough, however, black Americans seem to have excelled in this area of reducing the percentage of illiteracy. For example, while the total black population ten years of age and over increased from 5,328,972 in 1890 to 6,415,581 in 1900 and to 7,317,922 in 1910, the number of illiterates in this adult black population decreased from 3,042,668 in 1890 to 2,853,194 in 1900, and to 2,227,731 in 1910, or in terms of percentage from 57.1 percent in 1890 to 44.5 percent in 1900, and to 30.4 percent in 1910.[66] These data show a marked advancement in educational progress.

Not only were there advances in the problem of illiteracy, but black Americans showed also a marked increase in the attainment of quality education for participation in the life of the nation. Specifically, there were "hundreds of prominent men practicing law throughout the United

States"[67] by 1896; black businesses had increased significantly, and educated preachers and teachers were to be found throughout the nation.

Moreover, black Americans of the South began to diversify their economy in areas where black Baptist schools and other educational institutions strived. G. F. Richings remarked: "It is quite a common thing to find colored men engaged in large business enterprises in the South, where the colored population is large."[68] There was a direct relationship between the presence of black schools and the economic development of the race in those areas.

These developments were astonishing at the early period of freedom for most black Americans. They were able to advance into the state of upward mobility in the economic, cultural, and political life of the nation. Moreover, such progressiveness has continued under some of the most difficult circumstances to the present era of the black experience.

## Major Issues Facing Black Private Schools

Without question, the education of black folk claimed the early attention of black leaders. This often led to many controversies. Most of the early controversies were related directly to the social milieu of the United States. Black leaders and educators were given largely the awesome responsibility to develop a system of education to suit the unique needs of blacks. They attempted to meet this challenge in the context of extreme difficulties.

One immediate difficulty was the passionate conflicts of thought within the ranks of the black leadership. Black educational leaders differed strongly on the issues of quality and relevancy in black education. Each of the educators was aware of the need for something different from the general education of the majority race. However, the difficulty was: "How to reach a consensus on the nature of the difference?"

Unquestionably, the educational labors of Booker T. Washington were foremost among the issues in black education. He was the most esteemed educator ever produced in black Baptist circles. Born a slave in Virginia, Washington attained far more than his circumstances would normally allow. He graduated from Hampton Institute. Subsequently, he founded and developed the Tuskegee Normal and Industrial Institute, Tuskegee, Alabama.

At Tuskegee, Booker T. Washington advanced the concept of industrial education as a primary model for black education. In his fourth annual report to the trustees of the institute, Booker T. Washington affirmed:

> Greater attention has been given to the industrial department this year than ever before. Three things are accomplished by the industrial system: (1) The student is enabled to pay a part of his expenses of board, books, etc., in labor; (2) He learns how to work; (3) He is taught the dignity of labor. In all the industrial branches the students do the actual work, under the direction of competent instructors.[69]

Washington required each student at the institute to be involved in some actual work experiences in addition to taking studies in the academic department.

Initially, Booker T. Washington's attitude toward industrial education irritated some of the parents and local leaders in Alabama. Their irritation at him developed into a protest. During the first four years, Washington reminisced that "a large portion of the students brought either verbal or written messages from their parents that they wanted their children taught books, but did not want them taught work."[70] Fortunately, the protest did not last very long. Most parents and local leaders soon realized the wisdom of Washington's decision.[71] They were able to observe with a great sense of pride the building projects on the campus and other industrial products completed with student labor. Hence, the initial conflict over industrial education was resolved favorably.

Nevertheless, a conflict of major proportion soon developed in the national experience of blacks. In 1895, Booker T. Washington gave his world famous address on the centrality of industrial education. He was invited to deliver an address at the opening of the Cotton States' Exposition in Atlanta. In his attempt to facilitate racial harmony, he placated the whites of the nation by urging blacks to:

> Cast down your bucket where you are—cast it down in making friends in every manly way of the people of all races by whom we are surrounded.
> Cast it down in agriculture, mechanics, in commerce, in domestic service, and in the professions. . . . Our greatest danger is, that in the great leap from slavery to freedom we may overlook the fact that the masses of us are to live by the productions of our hands, and fail to keep in mind that we shall prosper in proportion as we learn to dignify and glorify common labor, and put brains and skill into the common occupations of life; shall prosper in proportion as we learn to draw the line between the superficial and the substantial, the ornamental gewgaws of life and the useful. No race can prosper till it learns that there is as much dignity in tilling a field as in writing a poem.[72]

Several black leaders fixed their minds on certain portions of the address and utilized a few pulpits and several black newspapers to denounce Washington's address. However, a vast majority of blacks and whites supported Washington's position. There were several strong leaders in the opposition.

The principle challenge to Booker T. Washington came from Dr. W. E. B. Dubois. Dr. Dubois, a graduate of Harvard University, raised the loudest voice of protest against the philosophy of industrial education in the educational experience of blacks. At the turn of the century, Dubois wrote his memorable essay entitled "The Talented Tenth," in which he argued that the future of black Americans depended more on quality education in the liberal arts and the professions than in industrial education. He argued further that the educated elite or "talented tenth" would lead the masses of their people to positions of productivity and respect in society.

Apparently, the critics of Booker T. Washington focused more on his social theories for race relations than on the actual concept of industrial education. Actually, he was misunderstood. Dubois and others were so fixed on Washington's social conservatism that they fail to see the broader implications of his educational emphasis. Washington was a pragmatist in his social and educational ideas. He related relevantly a broad approach to black education: "Each day convinces me that the salvation of the Negro in this country will be in his cultivation of habits of thrift, economy, honesty, the acquiring of education, Christian character, property and industrial skill."[73] Washington taught blacks necessary survival skills in an oppressive sociopolitical setting. This was relevant to the post reconstruction era in the South.

Similarly, strong was Booker T. Washington's emphasis on the development of Christian character in black educational experiences. He did not seek to develop sectarianism at Tuskegee Normal and Industrial Institute. The school was supported by the state of Alabama and private philanthropy. During the initial years of the school, Washington was able to boast that one years' graduating class was entirely Christian.[74]

In 1893, Booker T. Washinton organized the Phelps Hall Bible Training School of the Tuskegee Institute. The school was organized to meet the growing demands for an

educated clergy in the state. It was opened to all students
with a general interest in biblical studies. Its chief aim was
to give them a comprehensive knowledge of the entire
English Bible and to promote the Christianization of the
black population. Dr. Washington required all students of
the school to do missionary work in the various churches
and Sunday Schools in the vicinity of Tuskegee. This was
clear evidence of Booker T. Washington's concern beyond
his widely publicized industrial education emphasis.

Nevertheless, the publication of W. E. B. Dubois's
"The Talented Tenth" resulted in a persistent insurgence in
black education. A great polarization developed between
educators who sided with Booker T. Washington and the
Dubois faction. Unfortunately, the conflict extended into
the sociopolitical experiences of the race. Even the prestigious NAACP was later to experience repercussions from
the great clash of ideas among these educators.

The rise of secularism in America caused another issue
of major importance in black education. During the early
twentieth century, blacks became more and more influenced
by the secular changes in the general American society.
Secular humanism found a lodging place in the theology as
well as the general philosophy of education. The result was
a shift from the moral and spiritual foundations of historic
black education. This shift was more rapid at public black
colleges than at private ones.

More important, the real rationale for continual church
support to provide education has been the strong emphasis
on Christian and moral values at private church-related
schools. Such schools have been foremost in the resistance
of Christian educators and church leaders to the rise of
secularism. Hence, black Baptists and other Christian
churches have had to look more and more to church-related
schools for the moral and spiritual education of the race.

Finally, several other issues in black education have

been related more to the general administration of private schools.

In 1960, the Bureau of Educational Research of Howard University published a comprehensive study of black private and church-related colleges. Dr. John M. Ellison, chancellor of Virginia Union University, gave a detailed report on the status of those institutions related to black and white Baptists.

Dr. John M. Ellison pointed out that "the era of desegregation will raise new problems as it will remove barriers and will force our colleges to compete with other colleges of the country for students, faculty and funds."[75] The competitive environment of Baptist schools will also force them to upgrade their human and physical resources. Dr. Ellison observed that the "day of unaccredited colleges is rapidly vanishing."[76] Hence, he suggested in a summary manner five areas of necessary growth at black Baptist colleges.

1. Church leaders—lay and ministers—must reappraise available resources—human and material—and strive earnestly to achieve effective correspondence between projected programs and resources. . . .

2. Organization and planning must take place at the national level, for as the wave of migration continues the problem ceases to be local. Every section of the country must be concerned about the quality and preparation of all people. . . .

3. The planning must be long-ranged and comprehensive. It should include programming, curriculum, facilities, students, and finance. Serious consideration should be given to the possibility of regional institutions instead of state institutions. . . .

4. Vision and effort should include the preparation of our colleges for an integrated order. There is no future for educational institutions limited to serve only one ethnic group.

5. In any effort or planning to rebuild and redirect the

church-related College, leaders must be determined to maintain their distinctive witness to Christian faith. This means the enthronement of Christian principles in all of the programs of reorientation.[77]

The forecast made by Dr. Ellison is being manifested presently at all church-related schools. Each school is forced to reevaluate its mission in the light of relevancy in contemporary American culture. Strong indications seem to point out that some radical changes are in the air for black private education.

# 5

# The Sociopolitical Vitality of Black Baptist Tradition

Much has already been written on black theology. Among the most noted writers on the subject are such thinkers as Dr. James Cone, the pioneer black theologian and professor of theology at Union Theological Seminary in New York City; Dr. Joseph R. Washington, Jr., pioneer interpreter of black religion as a protest movement; Dr. Major J. Jones, pioneer interpreter of the ethical dimensions of black theology; Dr. Olin P. Moyd, pioneer interpreter of the redemptive nature of black theology in the context of black folk culture; and Dr. J. Deotis Roberts, proponent of black political theology. These scholars have done much to emphasize the distinctive role black church leaders and academicians have played in the advancement of Western civilization.

Generally speaking, most of the pioneer black theologians evolved their systems from the realms of theology and sociology. Limited consideration was given to role of black church history in the formation of black theology. Hence, the sociopolitical dimensions of such theology still must be extracted from the success strata of the historical experience of black American Christians. A strong argument may be offered to suggest that black Christians saw history differently from the general black man in American society. Therefore, a critical understanding of the unique role of history in the thought of black Christians, particularly Baptists, must be introduced into the debates in black theology.

Commencing with the old slave preachers progressively to the educated black Baptist ministry of the twentieth century, one discovers a theological tradition aimed at social reforms which resembles the better known Social Gospel of such figures as Walter Rauschenbusch and other white American theologians. It resembled the social ideas of white theologians but was not an imitation. The Social Gospel movement led by white theologians massed its attack upon a single, overriding cultural issue. This was the "industrial question" (Washington Gladden), the problem of "right distribution of property" (Josiah Strong), the unregenerate character of business life (Walter Rauschenbusch). Yet, black Christian thinkers were primarily interested in the broader issues of human rights, that is, justice, righteousness, humanity, and freedom. The fact is that this black Baptist "Social Gospel" predates the late nineteenth century. So it could not be a mere imitation of the Social Gospel movement. The social protest of black Baptists continues through the period under discussion in this chapter, roughly 1840 to the evening decades of the twentieth century.

The theological tradition of black Baptists was not initially eschatological in nature, as generally supposed, but largely committed to improve the quality of life for oppressed people in "this" world. One may see in the thought of such slave preachers as Rev. Lott Carey and Rev. John Jasper a practical concern for humanitarian issues in the Christian perspective. Hence, such black Baptist preachers were more concerned with the practical rather than the theoretical aspect of Christian theology.

Moreover, the black Baptist church grew up as the reflection of the thought of its preachers. It was therefore practical in all aspects of life and thought. This practicality caused the church to become largely political in nature. The voice of protest became a strong element in church life. Accordingly, black Baptists might be understood as the most authentic "protestant movement" in modern church history. One thing for certain, the black Baptist church emerged as a real proponent of democracy amidst the rugged power plays of conflicting political ideologies.

During the formative period of black church life, the black Baptist preachers, more specifically, had to come to grips with the pragmatic situation of life in America. They had to relate a relevant theology to slavery in the South and white racism throughout the nation. They had to keep in tune with the heartbeats of their brothers in black. With an unswerving commitment to justice and righteousness, black Baptists confronted the breakdown of slavery and reconstruction with its turmoil, violence, and unfulfilled promises. They had to cope with the brutality and poverty of southern agriculture in its years of decline and with further violence and discrimination of their fellow Southerners. They had to deal with migration out of the South, first to Kansas in the 1870s, then to the great industrial centers of the North. They had to face the challenge of the world wars and their impact on the social and economic life of black Americans. Through all this, black Baptists tried to preach, teach, and live their faith in ways that made the world itself better.

It is this lively tradition that we must attempt to extract from the successive strata of the historical experience. That much has escaped the pen of skillful black theologians and writers may be discovered through another careful "dig" into the old documents reflecting the process of theological maturation on the part of black church leaders.

In particular, the literary artifacts, consisting of association and convention minutes plus official addresses, of the early ministry reflect a unique development in black theology. The black Baptist preachers were, in a real sense, the political or social philosophers of the race. They were able and fearless advocates of truth, justice, and equal rights for an oppressed people. Often, they were required, of necessity, to communicate such a theological orientation in hidden songs and symbols during the slavery period. It has already been indicated by many previous writers that Negro spirituals, in particular, were songs of protest as much as of Christian faith.

The unique experience of oppression tended to force black Baptist leaders to extract from the faith committed to them a yen of hope in the social and political areas of their plight in America. They hoped and prayed for a day of liberation. Their historic cognizance synthesized with aspirations for liberation developed into a social gospel of tremendous impact. Accordingly, the slave preachers were compelled to draw logical inferences from the few remarks of Jesus Christ and the Old Testament prophets in areas of politics and sociology. In some mystical way, such inferences were interpreted in the light of extreme tension between the kingdom of God and the slave master's kingdom, American style. Hence, the slave preachers were among the earliest proponents of a social or applied gospel in American history. Therefore, the aim of this chapter is to survey how and why this social or applied gospel impacted the major movements of the nation.

## Black Baptists and the Abolitionist Movement

Roots of the abolitionist movement penetrated the young and fertile soil of the colonial period of American history. There were some early sounds from the colonial pulpits against the peculiar institution of slavery. However, the movement passed into a more aggressive stage during the labors of William Lloyd Garrison, Henry Clay, and other friends of oppressed people. On January 6, 1832, in the midst of stormy conditions, the New England Anti-Slavery Society was organized in the basement of the African Baptist meetinghouse on Belknap Street, Boston, Massachusetts. This society was the first association organized on the principal of immediate emancipation.

Though unnamed or noted in most historical documents, the fact that the New England Anti-Slavery Society was organized in the basement of a black Baptist church should be clear-cut proof to reasonable historians that black Baptists participated in the genesis of the abolitionist movement. They were not totally dependent on white abolitionists to carry the full responsibility of the great movement for the immediate emancipation of slaves. Though the twelve signatures affixed to the previously drafted declaration of principles of the society were those of white abolitionists, about one quarter of the seventy-two first signers of the constitution were blacks.

From its beginning, the New England Anti-Slavery Society entered upon an aggressive campaign of agitation to eliminate the institution of slavery in the United States. This society was probably responsible for more antislavery addresses and petitions throughout New England than had taken place during the preceding decades. So successful was the aggressiveness of the society that it became the prototype of similar societies which from that time forth sprang up in increasing numbers all over the North.

In 1843, the black Baptists of Ohio organized the first exclusively black antislavery society in the United States. As previously mentioned, the Union Anti-Slavery Baptist Association was organized to further the cause of the abolitionist movement. About the same time, the Providence Anti-Slavery Baptist Association and the Middlerun Anti-Slavery Baptist Association were organized in the state of Ohio. In 1837, black Baptist women in New York organized the Roger Williams Baptist Anti-Slavery Society as an auxiliary to the American Anti-Slavery Society. These associations were extremely significant in advancing the abolitionist strides of the era.

The life of all black abolitionists in general was rather precarious throughout America. As one might expect, however, the black leaders of the South faced extreme hardships. Most of these preachers were especially observed to see if they were entertaining abolitionist tendencies in their preaching. This was done with scrupulous scrutiny during the early stages of the Civil War.

A classic example of black Baptist preachers under

scrutiny was the case of Rev. William Thornton of Hampton, Virginia. In his testimony before the United States Congressional Committee on Reconstruction, Rev. William Thornton suggested that the whites of the area had been observing his ministry for a considerable period of time. He testified, February 3, 1866:

> I have a church once a month in Matthews County, Virginia, the other side of the bay. The last time I was over there an intelligent man told me that just below his house a lady and her husband, who had been at the meeting, received thirty-nine lashes for being there, according to the old law of Virginia, as if they had been slaves. This was simply because they were told not to go to hear a Yankee darkey talk. They said that he was not a Yankee, but was born in Virginia, in Hampton.[1]

Much of the antislavery and discrimination talk of black Baptist preachers was alluded to as "Yankee darkey talk," suggesting a tremendous exchange of ideas between northern and southern black abolitionists. Just how much of this sort of preaching was going on cannot be documented. Apparently, a significant number of these preachers were delivering messages which reflected a social gospel or "Yankee darkey talk."

Rev. William Thornton was questioned in more detail by the Honorable J. M. Howard who inquired about the general feeling of whites toward the blacks of Virginia. In reply to Howard's inquiry, Rev. William Thornton conversed freely:

> I was asked the other day if I did not know I was violating the law in celebrating marriages. I did not know that that was the case; and I went up to the clerk's office to inquire; I said nothing out of the way to the clerk of the court; I only asked him if there had been any provisions for colored people to be lawfully married. Said he, "I do not know whether

there is or not, and if there are granting licenses you can't have any; that is my business, not yours." After I found I was violating the law, I went to the Freedmen's Bureau and stated the case. A provision was afterwards made in the bureau granting licenses, and authorizing me to marry. Some days after that an old gentlemen named Houghton, a white man living in the neighborhood of my church, was in the church. In my sermon I mentioned the assassination of Mr. Lincoln. Next day I happened to meet Houghton, who said to me, "Sir, as soon as we get these Yankees off the ground and move that bureau, we will put you to rights; we will break up your church, and not one of you shall have a church here." Said I, "For what? I think it is for the safety of the county to have religious meetings, and for your safety as well as everybody's else's." "We will not have it sir," said he, and then he commenced talking about two classes of people whom they intended to put to rights, the colored people and the loyal white men. I asked him in what respect he was going to put them to rights; said he, "That is for myself."[2]

The testimony of Rev. Thornton reflects several major social issues that impacted the black church during slavery. First, the black church experienced a difficult time in interpreting the ethics of family life in the life and teachings of Jesus Christ in light of adverse civil laws. For the most part, most of the southern states prohibited the marriage between slaves and also slaves and free blacks. This legal denial of nupital rights to the black church was a major source of dehumanization and moral stress for black Americans. If any region of the nation supported such legislation, then a general atmosphere of dehumanization would be experienced by the whole race. Hence, the black church was caught in the tension between a situation of legal nupital denial and the higher law of God with reference to the nature of family life.

The struggle against all forces which tended to destroy the moral and spiritual basis of a Christian family life was one of the critical concerns of the black church during the slavery period. Many of the abolitionists used the issues of nupital rights and the solidarity of the black family as themes of their addresses and articles in the black press. For example, Rev. Noah Davis, though not referred to historically as an abolitionist, once referred to the nature of the Christian family in one of his sermons.

> But we will consider in the second place, "What is meant by providing for our own house?" House here means family. . . . It is the duty of all parents, to provide for their families every temporal good which adds to their own comfort or usefulness in life. And it is no less the duty of parents to provide for the spiritual necessities of their own families. And first—we shall consider the duty of parents, to provide suitable training for their children. This is a duty which God has enjoined and approves. . . . The duty of parents to train their children religiously, is clearly taught under the gospel dispensation.[3]

Rev. Noah Davis, pastor and founder of the Saratoga Street African Baptist Church of Baltimore, readily recognized the ethical demands of Jesus Christ and other New Testament writings relative to family life. His church, like other black churches, experienced the tension between such biblical teachings and the laws and practices in many states.

A second social issue of concern to the black church during slavery was the lack of response of civil authorities to inquiries about civil and human rights. In most southern states, the black church had no such rights to claim against any white person or institution. White men were not compelled by law or custom to recognize any civil or human rights claims of black Christians or any other black person. In fact, blacks were thought of as being in no respect equal in humanity to whites. Many whites never saw in the human flesh or spirit of black men or women anything like an authentic expression of the image of God. Hence, civil authorities and white Christians felt no compulsion to respond to the inquiries of black churches over such issues.

Similarly, implicit in the preaching of the black church during slavery was the broader issue of anthropology as applied to black Americans. This question was of such relevance that a survey of the social thought of the time may be enlightening. To be sure, there was a major difference between the anthropological thought of whites and blacks over the significance of the black man. An analysis of such thought will reflect just how radical such differences were.

A classic summary of the negative anthropology held by whites relative to black Americans was in the development of the constitution of the Confederate States of America. Generally speaking, the Constitution of the United States was adopted, with some alterations and additions. In those alterations and additions consisted all the objections that could be entertained to their previous form of government. Alexander H. Stephens, vice-president of the Confederacy, declared, in a speech delivered to the citizens of Savannah, Georgia, that:

> The new Constitution has put at rest forever all the agitating questions relating to our peculiar institutions—African slavery as it exists among us—the proper status of the negro in our form of civilization. . . . Jefferson, in his forecast, had anticipated this, as the "rock upon which the old Union would split." He was right. What was conjecture with him, is now a realized fact. . . . The prevailing ideas entertained by him and most of the leading statesmen at the time of the formation of the old Constitution were, that the enslavement of the African was in violation of the laws of nature; that it was wrong in principle, socially, morally, and politically. . . . Those ideas, however, were fundamentally wrong.

They rested upon the assumption of the equality of races. This was an error. It was a sandy foundation, and the idea of a Government built upon it was a wrong—when the "storm came and the wind blew, it fell."

Our new Government is founded upon exactly the opposite ideas; its foundations are laid, its corner-stone rests upon the great truth that the negro is not equal to the white man; that slavery, subordination to the superior race is his natural and moral condition. This, our new Government, is the first in the history of the world, based upon this great physical, philosophical, and moral truth.[4]

A critical analysis of this address by the vice-president of the Confederate States of America and the special provisions of that government will reflect the tremendous anthropological struggles of the black church during the abolitionist period.

It will be seen that the constitution of the Confederate States of America simply codified the prevailing sentiments of white America relative to racial relations. The constitution was simply an expression, in legal form, of the historic sociopolitical tradition of the nation. Therefore, the major issues of the black church during slavery may be understood in a comparative analysis of the two traditions: an anthropology of equality versus the tradition of racial inequality.

The black Baptist pulpit and press were the main forces at work to promote a social gospel of an emancipating anthropology. Though the artifacts of such tradition have been buried beneath the strata of dominant American theological and social tradition, the few artifacts that have been excavated clearly demonstrate the nature and vitality of an emancipating anthropology in the theological tradition of the black church movement. Black Baptists were participants in the evolution of such tradition.

A classic example of the evolution of an emancipating

anthropology in the tradition of the black church may be seen in what the slave preachers did with and to the theological tradition passed down to them from the white American churches. To be sure, the slave preachers and those free black preachers were not mere "imitators" who copied, without changes, the theological tradition of white America. There was, on the contrary, much originality in their doing of theology. They found ways and means of injecting an emancipating anthropology into the life of the black church which white America never taught. Charles S. Spivey correctly observed that the "preaching had a Christ-plus," which was a unique "creation carefully concealed in those doctrines and forms given him."[5] The genius of the slave preachers, in particular, was manifested in the way they took the theological tradition of white America, which was designed to make better slaves in the South and better second-class citizens in the North, and turned it into a mighty power for the ultimate liberation of oppressed people.

How did slave preachers and free blacks come to such intellectual awareness? First, we must examine the methodology of "doing theology" among preachers during the slavery period. Perhaps a little archaic, but they found in the Old Testament stories something radically different from the interpretations of the white American pulpit. In order to counter the tradition which held that "subordination to the superior race is his natural and moral condition" (mentioned earlier in the speech of Vice-president Alexander H. Stephens), the pulpit of the black church sought and found a new orientation for the liberation of the race. Specifically, they found in the Old Testament stories of the struggles of the Israelites a wealth of material for the development of an emancipating theology. From this storehouse of material, the black pulpit created symbols and enigmatic phases, understood only by the oppressed, which were "heavy loaded with the hidden dynamic of his new theology."[6] In this way, the categories and thought forms of white American tradition could be utilized as a secret codes for an emancipating theology.

One of the great discoveries of the black pulpit was the unity of humanity. The Old Testament gave the literary basis for the concept that all mankind came from the family of Adam. Consider, for example, a similar observation made by Charles S. Spivey.

> The Negro preacher made a discovery with far reaching consequences, when he arrived at the conclusion that all the sons of God are brothers. . . . "If I am God's son, and my master is His son, too, we have a common Father. . . . then we are brothers."[7]

Obviously, then, the black pulpit soon discovered the fatherhood of God and the brotherhood of man. If humanity has one Father, then brothers do not have the right to oppress a so-called weaker or inferior brother. The brotherhood of man implied, in the black tradition, the necessary equality of all men. This was the real beginning of the element of protest in the theology of black Baptists and other black denominations.

The institution of slavery then was the folly of one brother's attempt to oppress another brother. Conversely, the tradition of white superiority as an authentic anthropology was in direct tension with the new evolution of this social gospel of an emancipating anthropology. Behind such an attempt to dehumanize black Americans was a presupposition of some fallacy in the creative activity of God. Such tradition was repulsive to the mind and spirit of the black church. Moreover, the authenticity of the anthropology of white Americans was seen to be questionable. If the presuppositions of such an anthropology were questionable, then the whole tradition had to be reevaluated and a new one developed.

The task of developing an emancipating theology with a new anthropological orientation was not done systematically by the black church. To the contrary, individual preachers and thinkers slowly offered bits and pieces to the puzzle of anthropology in reference of black Americans. It was not until the closing decades of the slavery period that such an anthropology became evident. By the time of the Civil War, the black abolitionists had come close to the development of such an anthropology in speeches, sermons, and articles in the black press. This gave momentum to the struggle for liberation on the part of black Americans.

## Reconstruction Thought Among Black Baptists

The reconstruction period in American history was decisive to the widespread growth of the black Baptist churches. At the close of the Civil War, large numbers of blacks were attracted to the emerging black Baptist denomination because of its special appeal to expressions of personal freedom. It was easier for a man to become a prominent member in a local Baptist church than in the more hierarchical structured denominations. The democratic policy of Baptists was therefore especially appealing to the liberated blacks. They found in this denomination a greater freedom of expression than in other Christian movements.

Similarly, the liberated blacks found in the policy of the Baptist churches their desired control of an institution that was destined to play a preponderant role in the religious, social, and political future of the race. These churches soon became the training forum for black leaders to emerge and actively participate in the reconstruction of the Union. More specifically, they were schools in political activity.

The challenge of such reconstruction drew significantly on the energy and physical or human resources of the denomination. Many of the best qualified preachers were subsequently lured from exclusive pulpit ministries to enter reconstruction politics.

However, the leadership role of these black Baptist preachers who entered politics, as well as others from the different denominations, was a tremendous challenge to their energy, perseverance, and resourcefulness. They were often objects of criticism from both whites and blacks. Attitudes of stress and desperation on the part of the two races were the causes of such tremendous difficulties for black Baptist preachers.

Neither whites nor blacks were exempted from the tremendous upheavals of the Civil War. The reconstruction period was characterized by vast destruction of the Civil War, deep sectional and racial hatred, widespread desolation in southern homes, and disease. The white soldiers who returned from the Civil War often found their houses destroyed; blackened chimneys stood sentinel over cold ash heaps that once were houses. Throughout the South, fences were down, weeds had overrun the fields, windows were broken, livestock had disappeared. The assessed valuation of property drastically decreased in the decade after 1861.

More fundamental, from the white perspective, than the destruction of property and the paralysis of business was the disappearance of the South's basic economic institution. Slavery, so fundamental to the southern way of life, had ended as the advancing Union armies carried news of the Emancipation Proclamation and the confiscation acts into the deep South. The emancipation of slaves meant to whites not only the loss of property but loss of labor too. These economic and social problems enraged Southerers against practically all blacks, particularly the religious and political leaders of black Americans.

A brief survey of the rage of many southern whites against blacks will give some indication of the tremendous challenge of black Baptists in their quest for freedom and human dignity as defined by the American ideal. One will readily realize from the following attitudinal survey of whites that reconstruction was a formidable challenge to the black church. It took the best and strongest minds of the race to advance an emancipating anthropology adequate for the reconstruction challenge. The Civil War did not end the struggle for white supremacy but rather increased its intensity.

The question of reconstruction, that is, of readmitting the seceded states to their former position in the Union, was one which deeply agitated the country during 1866 and 1867. Major differences of opinion relative to the basic issues of federalism and freedmen's rights had divided the nation. Chief among these issues was racism. It was racism that prompted most of the debates and divided public opinion during the reconstruction period. A major difference of opinion existed between President Andrew Johnson and the Congress of the United States over the political technicalities of reconstruction. Each had specific plans of readmitting the seceded states to the Union. President Johnson recognized loyal governments as existing in Virginia, Tennessee, Arkansas, and Louisiana. In the case of the other states, he appointed provisional governors with authority to call conventions to establish permanent governments and restore the states to their former rights as soon as they should repeal their ordinances of secession, repudiate their Confederate debit, and ratify the amendment which Congress had proposed for the abolition of slavery.

With these conditions most of the states in question complied, but Congress would not recognize them as reconstructed without further guarantees. Accordingly, it proposed a fourteenth amendment to the Constitution which provided, among other things, that when the right of voting is denied by a state to any citizen, the basis of representation in such state shall be reduced in the proportion which the number thus excluded shall bear to the whole number of citizens in the state. This amendment became a part of the Constitution in 1868. Hence, a major challenge was advanced to those political leaders in the South who would limit the voting rights of black Americans.

The liberal stance of President Johnson toward the South was especially attacked in Congress by Senator Charles Sumner of Massachusetts. Referring to the president's address to the Congress, Senator Sumner said: "It is a direct appeal to the worst passions and worst prejudices of those rebels who, being subdued on the battlefield, still resist through the aid of the President of the United States."[8] Behind this charge was the idea that President Andrew Johnson shared the racist tendencies of the old Confederate States of America. Surely, the president would reestablish the old political leaders in the South without any requirement of a change in attitude over racial matters to be reflected in the legal codes of the states. Congress recognized that this would lead to the political victory of the South.

The Congress did not challenge the president's policy of reconstruction on mere opinions of general nature. Rather, it had done the necessary homework to determine racial attitudes reflected in public opinion in the South. On December 13, 1865, a joint committee of the two houses of Congress was appointed with direction "to inquire into the condition of the States which formed the so-called Confederate States of America, and report whether they or any of them are entitled to be represented in either house of Congress, with leave to report by bill or otherwise."[9] In 1866, the committee received testimonies from leaders throughout the South. Such testimonies proved to be a good sampling of the attitudes of southern whites toward the Union and a tremendous rage against black Americans.

On February 17, 1866, Robert E. Lee, the greatest military leader of the Confederacy, testified to Congress relative to the issue of suffrage for black Americans in the South. He affirmed: "I think it would recite unfriendly feelings between the two races. I cannot pretend to say to what extent it would go, but that would be the results."[10] He assured the committee that the southern political opinion was opposed to granting suffrage to black Americans in the South. There was a general feeling that to give black Americans suffrage was tantamount to the possibility of black rule over whites in certain parts of the South. This was especially repugnant to white racists.

A more detailed account of the attitude of the South toward politics of reconstruction was expressed by other men from various walks of life in the southern states. On February 1, 1866, J. J. Henshaw, a practicing physician in Lovettsville, Virginia, when asked if southern whites had the power would they reduce the blacks again to slavery, testified: "I do not think they would hesitate a moment in doing so."[11] Similarly, Josiah Millard of Alexandria, Virginia, testified regarding the attitude of white Virginians toward black emancipation:

> They did not like it at all. They protested against it to the very last, and some of them in the county now are trying their very best to make the colored man believe that they are still theirs; that they are not free. . . . They say they have raised the Negroes, and have fed them all their lives, and it is the Negro's duty to work for them.[12]

Yet more belligerent, George S. Smith, a farmer in Culpepper County, Virginia, testified on January 31, 1866, regarding the attitude of white Virginians toward black Americans: "They would entirely extirpate him from the

face of the earth. They would first commence with the
Union men, and then they would take the Negro."[13] In the
testimony of George S. Smith, the Congress could readily
recognize that the South had been beaten on the battlefields
but still persisted in its negative attitude toward the Union
and black Americans. They still desired the forced removal
of Union soldiers from southern soil and the oppression of
black Americans.

In the deep South, the attitude of some whites was
more extremist in nature and practice. D. E. Haynes, from
Rapides Parish, Louisiana, stated the opinion of many
whites in this region: "If there was not interference from a
superior power they would be in a worse condition than
they were when in a state of slavery."[14] Major General
Christopher C. Andrews agreed with D. E. Hayes that the
condition of the black Americans would be worse off than
when they were in slavery if Federal troops were removed.
He especially emphasized the economic plight of these liberated men.

> It was a common thing for the masters to say to the blacks,
> "Now, you are made free; you are free and can go wherever
> you please. Go, if you choose, immediately; but if you re-
> main with me you must remain and do just as you have done
> heretofore, and I will treat you just as I have hereto-
> fore. . . ." And I would further say, that there was an under-
> standing among those who had formerly been slave owners
> that the colored people should not be employed without the
> consent of their former masters.[15]

The general attitude of the deep South was not favorable toward the Union or black Americans. It was against
such attitudes that the black Baptist church had to cope
during the early days of reconstruction.

There were several black Baptist laymen who revealed
to the Joint Committee on Reconstruction just how severe

were the black man's problems in the South. They talked about the tremendous fears and apprehensions of black Americans. For example, Alexander Dunlop, a trustee of the First Baptist Church of Williamsburg, Virginia, testified, on February 3, 1866, relative to the lack of security for black people:

> My purpose was to let the government know our situation, and what we desire the government to do for us if it can do it. We feel down there without any protection. . . . We feel in danger of our lives, of our property, and of everything else. . . . I have suffered in the war; I was driven away from my place by Wise's raid; and so far as I, myself, am concerned, I do not feel safe; and if the military were removed from there I would not stay in Williamsburg one hour, although what little property I possess is there. . . . [In case of the removal of the military], "Nothing shorter than death"; that has been promised to me by the rebels.[16]

Due to the intensity of situation in Virginia, Alexander Dunlop saw the need for greater protection by the Federal troops and an increase in the operation of the Freedmen's Bureau. These were necessary because there was a general feeling of aggression against black Americans in the South. Their life was constantly in danger. Likewise, the southern whites had little or no respect for property rights on the part of black Americans. Hence, Dunlop realized that the only hope for him to lead a life of reasonable security depended on the presence of both the Freedmen's Bureau and Federal troops.

Similarly, Deacon Edmund Parson, a member of the First Baptist Church of Williamsburg, Virginia, testified on February 3, 1866:

> When the Union forces came there first a good many officers became attached to me and my wife, and we felt perfectly secure; but now the rebels use the officers that are

there "to pull the chestnuts out of the fire." . . . They threaten to do everything they can. My wife died about a year ago. I had a house, where I had been living for twenty years. A lawyer there went and got the provost marshal to send a guard and put me out of my house. They broke my things up and pitched them out, and stole a part of them.[17]

This black Baptist joined with others in expressing to the Congressional Committee on Reconstruction that the black man's situation in the South was grave. He suggested that black men were subjected to inhumane treatment from the majority white presence and even from the Union men on a few occasions. Some of the rebels soon found ways to utilize a few of the policies of the Federal government to work against black Americans.

To be sure, the general condition of black Americans during the early days of reconstruction was quite precarious. More specifically, it was pitiable. When the Civil War ended, what were the emancipated slaves to do? The cabins they lived in, the land they tilled, the tools they worked with all belonged to their former masters. They could only live in their own houses as renters or workers for wages. Of renting and wages they knew little or nothing. Hence, they were ready victims of extreme exploitation.

It was to this sort of situation that black Baptist leaders tried to assume the dangerous and uncomfortable role of reconcilers between the races. They saw this as an absolute necessity for the security and progress of the black race. Hence, much of the constructive energies of black Baptist preachers were exhausted simply in trying to maintain nominal independence for their congregations in particular and the race at large. Many members of their congregations were still in debt to the whites or dependent upon their former masters for jobs.

During the reconstruction period, the struggles of the

black Baptist churches in the South were linked with those of the North. The rise of cooperative church movements, Baptist schools, and the black press helped black Baptists to see the collective nature of oppression on the members of the race. In other words, the black man's problems in the South became the problem of all black men in the nation. So, the collective mentality of black Baptist leaders across the nation was utilized in the struggles of reconstruction.

Accordingly, black Baptist leaders sought to fulfill the vacuum in the life of the black community which had been caused by slavery, that is, the moral and social vacuum. This was partially done through an aggressive pulpit ministry designed to bring about additudinal changes among members of the race. Black Americans were taught to think like free men! Also, a tremendous socialization program developed within the churches. The rise of mutual aid societies and other church clubs led to a new social awareness among members of the local congregations. Social cohesion and economic development were primary objectives of the socialization.

More specifically, the churches provided opportunities for freedom, self-expression, and release from the social barriers faced by the race. When black people were forced to live in a segregated society, the churches provided for social expressions on the part of energetic youths and adults. Many social activities took the form of church suppers, lectures, musical recitals, debates, and religious plays. Increasingly, the churches facilitated the cultural homogeneity of black Christians.

These progressive developments in the experiences of black Baptists and other Christians were summarized in a "Report to the Triennial Meeting" of the Consolidated American Baptist Convention which convened in 1877. The report stated the following:

Nearly 500,000 souls are embraced within our denominational limits. Owing to the many detrimental lines of distinction drawn between white and colored citizens in this
country, the thousands of children and youth within our
denominational boundaries will have to depend, in a large
measure, for years to come upon our churches for their
intellectual, moral and social development. . . . Then let us
so deliberate, and resolve, and do, as that heaven and earth
shall be made to rejoice.[18]

Basic to these attitudinal developments among black
Baptists was a strong emphasis on economic cooperation.
The pooling of resources and cooperative construction work
on the new church buildings that went up throughout the
nation at the end of the Civil War tended to foster economic
cooperation. These construction projects gave black Baptists the opportunity to learn to work cooperatively in an
atmosphere of trust. Hence, they developed a new philosophy of industry with an air of dignity noting that "the eyes
of the civilized world are upon us." This was an important
step toward the economic improvements of black Americans in general.

## Black Baptists and the Temperance Movement

The experience of slavery was a tremendous challenge
to the moral development of black Americans. The family
as the basic unit of society had been seriously disrupted,
and the morals of the race had been accordingly lowered.
Nevertheless, the black church had also been laboriously
involved in the elevation of morals along the lines of Christian ethics. The leaders of the churches were generally concerned over the issues of marriage and family life, honesty
and mutual respect for all men.

A basic moral issue of considerable concern to the black
church at the end of the Civil War was the matter of overin-

dulgence in alcoholic beverages. Prior to the Civil War, alcoholism had been a rare phenomenon among black Americans. Overindulgence was primarily a weekend affair. However, the problems and uncertainties of the new freedom led an increasing number of black Americans to indulge excessively in alcoholic beverages. This problem even manifested itself among black Baptists.

After the first decade to the post-Civil War era, the black Baptist national leaders decided to align themselves with the national Prohibition movement at least in spirit. In 1869, the National Prohibition Party was organized in Chicago. The effects of the movement were rapid. Thirty-two states had, after the 1870s, adopted statewide prohibition. In other states great sections were made "dry" by what was known as "local option", that is, towns and counties by a popular vote decided whether or not to close saloons. As early as 1869, the Consolidated American Baptist Convention adopted a standing resolution: "That the use of intoxicating drinks is injurious and most destructive to morals, and we recommend all, over whom we have influence, to immediately abandon their use."[19] This resolution was published annually in the convention's publications.

In 1872, the convention took even stronger measures to encourage temperance among its members. J. H. Magee, chairman of the Temperance Committee, offered a report which led the convention in a discussion of far reaching significance.

> We, your Committee on Temperance, beg leave to submit the following as our report:
> Whereas, The sale and use of intoxicating liquors as a beverage, including wine, beer, and everything that produces intoxication, is of itself a gross immorality and sin against God and humanity.
> 1. Resolved, That it is the duty of every friend of God who is for the advancement of the Redeemer's kingdom, to ab-

stain from the use of such articles as will intoxicate, and also
to discourage the distribution of the same by sale or otherwise, and do all in their power for the suppression of this
worst of oppressors of mankind.

2. Resolved, That the members of this Convention, the
pastors and deacons of our Churches, the superintendents of
Sabbath Schools, teachers, and parents, are requested to totally abstain from the use of those articles, and use their
influence against this great curse among our people.

3. Resolved, That we recommend the reading of this report in all of our Churches and Sabbath Schools once a
quarter at least.[20]

Baptists were among the few church movements to clearly
reflect the temperance movement in the church covenant.

The use of alcohol as a beverage was deemed a moral
wrong, and total abstinence was a moral position of the
Baptist church. This was reflected in the church covenants.
It was the duty of black Baptists who believed total abstinence a Christian duty to persuade others to this belief and
practice. Some churches, like First Baptist of Baltimore, organized local temperance societies. Hence, black Baptists
made a strong appeal to men's conscience and moral judgement relative to the temperance movement.

## Black Baptist Strides Against the Overthrow
## of Reconstruction Progress

There were many forces at work to militate the social,
political, and moral advancements of black Americans during the reconstruction era. The white attitudes of extremism
were not altered altogether by the general strides of reconstruction. The liberal congressional policies, presence of
Federal troups and the overidentification of black leaders
with the carpetbaggers were destined to ignite the latent
extreme violence of southern whites. Even during the suc-

cessful strides of reconstruction when blacks were given a significant political role, these latent forces were surfacing in various places in the South.

The Fourteenth Amendment to the Constitution which had given manhood suffrage to blacks was soon to be challenged by local state laws. Some of the southern states had been forced to ratify the amendment in order to get back into the Union. Once these states regained their status in the Union, they gradually worked against black suffrage and civil rights. One major strategy was to blame black politicians, church leaders, and carpetbaggers for some of the so-called failures of the reconstruction in the light of the southern ethos.

This ethos was expressed in the writings of Charles H. Otken, a southern white historian. He claimed that black Americans were "destitute of the rudiments of political knowledge" and therefore lacked the necessary skills for political leadership in the South. He maintained that those blacks holding political offices were merely figureheads for northern white politicians.[21]

In spite of the Fourteenth Amendment to the Constitution, the whites of the South did everything they could to keep black Americans away from the polls and limit the political ascendancy of black Republicans. The Federal government responded by the passage of the Fifteenth Amendment in which it was expressly declared that the states and the United States should never take the vote away from any citizen on the account of "race, color, or previous condition of servitude." This amendment was duly ratified and proclaimed law in 1870.

Southern Democrats viewed with great alarm the end of their friend's administration in the person of President Andrew Johnson, the success of Congress's so-called "radical" reconstruction program, and the ascendancy of solidarity between President Grant and Congress on reconstruction. They reacted violently to these new political developments. They felt driven to the point of desperation. The agency of violence that came to their hands was the Ku Klux Klan (originally formed in Pulaski, Tennessee, by a group of young men for their own amusement). Dressed in ghostly costumes, they frightened the superstitious black Americans by appearing as the spirits of dead Confederate soldiers. The movement soon developed violent strategies throughout the South to destroy the social, political, and economic progress of black Americans. They were joined by other white extremist and violent organizations, such as the Knights of the White Camelia, White League, White Line, the Pale Faces, and the Order of the White Rose. These organizations struck such terror in the hearts of black Americans in the South that thousands of them gave up on politics. This led to the overthrow of reconstruction progress and the ascendancy of the southern white power political machine, that is the Democratic Party.

At that critical time, black Baptists reacted against such attempts to overthrow reconstruction progress; and perhaps the greatest literary and legal offensive in the history of black Americans was precipitated. Nevertheless, the persistence of white supremacy, in terms of cumulative tradition, was destined to necessitate the offensive of black Baptists to spread over decades, maybe a century, of American history. Black Baptists labored with unquenchable love of justice and the resolve that all men should be free to realize the fullest of their true humanity.

## The Texas Movement

The response of black Baptists to the rise of violence and white racist control of politics was varied. Some believed in the inevitable triumph of justice and righteousness in American democracy. Others were more pessimistic. An example of the pessimistic group was Rev. Harvey Johnson, pastor of the Union Baptist Church of Baltimore, who believed it was hopeless to suppose that white attitudes would improve regarding black Americans. Rev. Johnson was known widely for his sociopolitical views on the progress of black Americans. He was a strong advocate self-help programs and freedom for black Americans in the National Baptist Convention, U.S.A., Inc., as well as in local Maryland state politics.

In the early 1890s, Rev. Harvey Johnson proposed a plan of separation between the races in America. Accordingly, he organized the "Texas Movement" which advocated setting aside the entire state of Texas for a sort of reservation or black separatist nation for black Americans. He was one of the foremost social thinkers and proponents of a social gospel among black Baptists. His views were usually welcomed and highly respected by the black Baptist leadership. Nevertheless, most black Baptists were generally not disposed to accept a plan with any tendency toward escapism, and the Texas Movement died out within a short period of its inception.

The failure of the Texas Movement idea did not stop Rev. Harvey Johnson from attempting a visible approach to the racial situation in America. He preached and delivered many addresses that were saturated with sociopolitical thoughts. Locally, he led the fight that changed the constitution of Maryland so that black doctors and lawyers could practice medicine and law, and black teachers could teach in the public schools of the state. He also led the movement among black Baptists churches in Maryland to declare their autonomy from white Baptists, resulting in the organization of the first black Baptist convention in the state, the Colored Baptist Convention of Maryland. Subsequently, Rev. Harvey Johnson helped to establish the Clayton Williams Academy in Baltimore for the training of black preachers.

As early as 1897, Rev. Johnson delivered an address before the Seventeenth Annual Meeting of the National Baptist Convention held in Boston, Massachusetts, entitled "A Plea for Our Work as Colored Baptists, Apart From the Whites." He echoed potent sociopolitical ideas to the convention's delegation.

> Yes, the white man is in a crisis and a panic in nearly every management confined to time, and still he is considered by us, and he considers himself, a manager and leader most sagacious, and yet so reckless, so unfaithful and unsuccessful has been his leadership in every capacity that confidence is destroyed everywhere. . . . We have leaders of our own, and the sooner we lay out plans and learn to follow them the better it will be for the colored Baptist demonination.[22]

In the early 1900s, Rev. Harvey Johnson delivered another sermon with tremendous sociopolitical overtones. His clear and powerful intellect was evidenced in this message entitled "The Hamite—The Only Historical Nation." Some of Rev. Johnson's succint observations were:

> We again assert that the Bible shows that neither Shem nor Japheth ever settled a country, or built a town or city. Of three sons of Noah, Ham, and he alone, is accredited with settling countries, and building cities. . . . The white man boasts of his color, yet he does not know how, or when he became white, or when he became known, even to romantic history, as a white race or tribe. Then why should we, the colored race, have such craving to be like them? He has been, and still is, a failure in government, wherever found; and since we have our own leaders both great and grand, let us follow them, and be content to do so.[23]

Strangely enough, Rev. Harvey Johnson was accused by many black Americans as well as whites of being too extreme in his racial views. To be sure, his views were "radical" enough to challenge the white supremacy ideologies of the nineteenth and twentieth centuries. He was a potent force in the development of a positive anthropology for black Americans. Even more significantly, he contributed a tremendous body of literary thought designed to correct the white man's views of white and black anthropology and ultimately to the future elimination of racism in America.

## Early Civil Rights Struggles of the Twentieth Century

The turn of the century witnessed the emergence of a large group of black Baptists with the determination to participate in the evolution of an intellectual offensive against racism and discrimination in the United States of America. In 1902, Miss N. H. Burrough, a distinguished lay leader in the National Baptist Convention, U.S.A., Inc., issued "An Appeal to the Christian White Women of the Southland" to move their conscience on behalf of the black man's struggle for equal treatment on the public transportation facilities of the nation. This pioneer black Baptist woman stated:

> We wish to appeal to you in behalf of the thousands of mothers in this land who have suffered in silence the unchristian humiliation to which they have been subjected in the Southland since the introduction of the separate-coach law. . . .
>
> The separate-coach law in the Southland is not only a reflection upon our advancement, but a stigma upon us, and the better class of whites throughout the country consider it a stigma upon American civilization, and would join heartily in its removal.[24]

She appealed directly to the heartbeat of white Christian women to join blacks in their struggle for fair treatment in the South. Miss Nannie Helen Burrough believed that all

Americans should have equal access to public transportation. This could only be accomplished through active and
cooperative efforts of southern Christians. Moreover, Miss
Burrough recognized the powerful influence of white Christian women in southern politics. They were able, if only
willing, to exert tremendous pressures to change public
opinion. Potentially, white Christian women held the key
to public transportation facilities being made available to
blacks.

Unfortunately, the appeal to white Christian women in
the South was not generally effective. Some few made small
gestures, but the vast majority supported the status quo in
the sociopolitical life of the South. Then too, most southern
Christians, Baptists in particular, were not inclined to utilize
the power of the church to bear on political issues. They
held, as previously mentioned, tenaciously to the separation
of church and state. This constituted the major obstruction
to the utilization of the sociopolitical potential of Southern
Baptists.

Nevertheless, Miss N. H. Burrough remained for many
years a strong fighter for the cause which was so dear to her
heart. She labored through the Women's Auxiliary of the
National Baptist Convention, U.S.A., Inc., to use its influence and resources to aid the cause. Several women's groups
subsequently led movements to petition the legislatures of
Tennessee and Louisiana to repeal the obnoxious Jim Crow
car laws. These brave women, like Miss Burrough and many
others, played a major role in the early civil rights struggles
of the twentieth century.

In the case of *Plessy* versus *Ferguson*, the "Jim Crow"
laws, segregating blacks and whites on railroads were
upheld "where there has been provision for substantially
equivalent accommodations for each race, on the grounds of
promoting the public comfort and preserving peace." Nevertheless, black Baptist leaders continued to sound their

voices against such discrimination against American citizens. In 1908, Rev. William B. Reed, pastor of the First Baptist Church, Madison, New Jersey, issued some strong sociopolitical statements in his "Echoes of the Emancipation Proclamation Relative to the 'Jim Crow' Laws."

> The condonation of the President [Taft] to the savage wrongs of the South has done the colored race an inestimable injury. His failure to ask for legislation, on the investigation of disfranchisement laws, or reduction of Southern representation, has embroidered negro-haters and made them excessive in their mistreatment of the colored man. His announcement that there was no law against Jim Crow cars was a hard blow to a people whose hearts went out to him.
>
> The colored race will no more submit to Jim Crow law than disfranchisement, its elder brother. And the operation of this inhumane rule will be an imposition, and not an accepted law with the entire race.
>
> It is not the principle of the Republican Party to impose on the colored man. If the President knew how respectable people of our race are treated, on trains and steamboats, etc., I believe he would have remained silent rather than fostered this unholy cause. . . . In the South we are not privileged to dining cars, railroad restaurants, sleeping cars, decent coaches or waiting rooms.[25]

There were many tremendous sociopolitical developments taking place in America which overshadowed the appeals of black leaders for justice and civil rights. The agrarian movement in the South and Southwest, the industrial revolution, and the conflicts between major industries and labor unions held the attention of national political leaders. The North was too engrossed in its major industrial concerns to be responsive to the so-called "Negro problem." The South acted toward black Americans as if the Fourteenth and Fifteenth Amendments did not exist.

What black Baptists leaders had to deal with at the

dawn of the twentieth century was the battle of public issues to gain a significant hearing on the part of the economic and political systems of the expanding and developing Republic. The first decade of the century was so dominated with issues that basic human rights for black Americans were forced from the focus of public opinion in America. To be sure, the rise of "big business," industrialization, and expansionism overshadowed the "Negro problem."

Accordingly, President William H. Taft was not really concerned about Rev. William B. Reed's issues raised in his "Echoes of the Emancipation Proclamation Relative to the 'Jim Crow' Laws." In fact, the President, though essentially judicial and liberal in his political and social outlook, was not significantly sympathetic with the "Negro problem" in America. He was so preoccupied with the issue of how to relate to the tremendous influence of Theodore Roosevelt that many of the important national issues escaped him. The administration of President William B. Taft passed down in history as one of the worst failures in office in the whole presidential list.

During the administration of President Woodrow Wilson, black Americans experienced some signs of relief. His administration was far more stable than that of former President William H. Taft. Under this administration, Rev. W. B. Reed was able to note some progress in the legal status of black Americans in the civil rights struggles.

> On the 21st of last June when the Supreme Court overthrew the Oklahoma Grandfather Clause and the Maryland election vote, there was handed down another decision of far-reaching significance. This decision overruled a sleeping car law passed by the legislature of Wisconsin. This law provided that the occupant of a lower berth could have the upper berth closed so long as it was not sold. . . .
> This decision is in accord with our contention in our 1913

Report that when a man buys one ticket he has one space, one privilege—and has nothing to do with other space sold or unsold. We believe the time will soon come when these foolish train passengers will be sufficiently educated in matters of public decorum to know that they have nothing to do with the sold or unsold upper berth or the other seat occupied or unoccupied, which they did not pay for. . . .

The freedom of unrestricted travel is a right in this country of every law abiding citizen. We recognize no legality in the sign "white" and "colored," nailed in trains; and when political tyranny of those thirteen Democratic States is overthrown these signs will be done away with.[26]

Rev. W. B. Reed looked with tremendous disdain to the farthest significance of the southern Democratic machine that was "schemingly getting the power they had before the Rebellion."[27] He realized that any political or legal gains made by black Americans would be null and void in the "solid South" without the intervention of the Federal government. The South had insisted on a "let us alone" policy in relations to the Federal government, especially in matters dealing with the "Negro problem." At the same time, he noted that the thirteen Democratic states of the South were in the position to dominate the great committees of the House and Senate which originate tariff bills, internal revenue, corporation taxes, individual income tax, special or excise, war, or Democratic deficit tax, all the sources of government revenue, all the appropriations carrying the great supply bills, civil and military, and so forth. Hence, the only way to break up that undue political power of these southern states and assure black Americans of their civil rights was to promote federal supervision of the elections in the South. Rev. W. B. Reed believed that it was absolutely necessary for black Americans to share some of the tremendous political power of the "solid South." Only under such conditions would the proper balance of power in American politics be assured. Otherwise the South would reestablish "slavery" under new names.

## The Anti-Lynching Movement

"Lynching is the black spot on America's soil," remarked Rev. L. B. Brooks in his 1922 state of the country address before the New England Baptist Missionary Convention.[28] Rev. L. B. Brooks went on to say: "So long as America holds the record for its illegal taking of life, so long as the headlines of foreign papers carry in large letters 'America burns another Negro,' just so long will her shame be world-wide."[29]

Lynching was one of the most inhumane practices in the history of the American Republic. Hundreds of black Americans were lynched "to protect white womanhood from what they call Negro Male Coon or Brute,"[30] while southern whites, at the same time, used as common-law wives the daughters, sisters, and cousins of the same so-called Negro brutes. To be sure, lynching was a widespread practice throughout the South. Rev. L. B. Brooks pointed out the following statistics on lynching.

> If you read the *Crisis Magazine*, the April number, the following facts are found on the question of lynching, that our proud Government had allowed to go on without remedy:
> From the year 1889 there have been 3,443 known mob murders, 54 of them the victims being women. American mobs murdered 54 persons in 1921, four of whom were publicly burned at the stake. In only a few instances has prosecution of lynchers been attempted.[31]

Rev. L. B. Brooks was a very strong participant in the antilynching movement. He constantly utilized the pulpit of the Mount Ararat Baptist Church of Rutherford, New Jersey, where he served as pastor, to advance the cause for freedom and protection for black Americans. His was also a very strong pen in the sociopolitical climate of the New England Baptist Convention. He was perhaps the first black Baptist to lay the blame on the southern white clergy for the lynchings. He protested:

> The white preachers of America can break up lynching, clean up the debauching evils of destructive prejudice, injustice and civil robbery in all parts of our land; if the true dispensation of the Gospel is preached and practiced! . . . But we find thousands of white preachers who hold the pulpits of the churches where lynchers are members, there men and women sit in the pews each Lord's Day who are members of State Legislature, where corrupt laws have been enacted, lawyers, judges of the courts, and jurors who are vile and unjust to men because of their color or race; and are too cowardly to raise their voices against these criminals in high places. God cannot use these preachers because they are slaves of wicked man.[32]

The NAACP began the legal battle to terminate lynching in the United States in the 1910s. Many petitions and protests were sent to the House and Senate relative to the lynching problem. In 1921, one congressman named Lemidas Dyer, Republican from Missouri, decided to introduce a bill (H.R. 13) "to assure persons within the jurisdiction of every state the equal protection of the laws and to punish the crime of lynching." The bill would inflict a heavy fine upon any county in which a lynching occurred, requiring part of the money to be given to the victim's relatives. The measure was referred to the Judiciary Committee and reported out favorably on October 20, 1921.[33]

The Dyer Anti-Lynching Law created a considerable amount of interest in the American black communities. Much hopeful discussions centered on the absolute necessity of this bill's passage. The bill was hailed throughout the country, among black Americans and liberal whites, as a major step forward in the civil rights struggles of the nation.

Unfortunately, the initial excitement over the bill was short lived. The "solid South" with its powerful political machine was able to block the passage of the bill in the Senate through an extensive filibuster. Consequently, the Republican leaders agreed to withdraw the bill on December 2, 1921. The fight over the Dyer Anti-Lynching Bill in Congress did result in an improvement in race relations in the United States.[34]

The black Baptists of America were not willing to accept the bill's failure in the Congress. Rev. W. J. Winston, a distinguished pastor and educator from Baltimore, offered a resolution on the Dyer Anti-Lynching Bill to the National Baptist Convention, U.S.A., Inc., urging:

> Whereas, the Dyer Antilynching Bill is fresh in the minds of our people, and by all indications will be re-offered in the coming Congress, a bill which should engage the mind and attract the attention of every Colored patriotic American who believes in a square and fair deal to all, and especially should this bill be supported, since it has for its objective the destruction of the unholy and nefarious system of lynching which is a disgrace to American civilization, and enacting an adequate legislation for the amelioration of our condition and the respect for even handed justice and sympathy for the oppressed and persecuted.
>
> Resolved, That we urge our people to rally to the support of the candidates for election and re-election for Congress and the United States Senate who will solemnly pledge to vote for the passage of the Dyer Antilynching Bill and that each delegate be and is hereby requested to either write or interview his representative in Congress and the United States Senate, asking his assistance in the passage of the bill, thereby helping to correct the many wrongs having been perpetrated upon our people, and to protect a people who

have stood loyal and heroic by this country in time of war and have never been traitors to the flag.[35]

The convention readily offered its support to the resolution, and black Baptists across America worked for the passage of the bill. The struggle was destined to be long and lacking in hope. As late as 1936, the New England Baptist Missionary Convention was still lamenting the failure of the bill in Congress.

No Party seems willing to pass a lynch law to stop Mob violence in the South. The Republicans refused to do so in the Senate, and the Democrats with the largest majority of America's history has left the question for their successors to settle.[36]

## Enforcement of Black Suffrage

The early 1920s witnessed a tremendous surge in the Law Enforcement Movement in the nation. Many of the nation's most distinguished and influential civil workers lined up behind the movement and constantly encouraged the national government to get more involved. The movement urged the enforcement of every law in the Constitution of the United States. The Women's Auxiliary of the National Baptist Convention, U.S.A., Inc., went on record to encourage the movement: "The Negroes of this country want to see the law obeyed—including the Fourteenth and Fifteenth Amendments. We have been asked to call your attention to the Law Enforcement Movement and distribute printed matter."[37] The Baptist women also suggested that the movement would be strengthened through greater participation in politics on the part of black women.

Negro women are in politics to make a new name for themselves and a new place for their race. . . . With Mrs. George S. Williams of Georgia, and Mrs. Mary Booze of

Mississippi, as our spokesmen in the National Council of the Republican Party, we have the "understanding"—a foundation on which to stand—something to stand on and somebody who will stand on it. . . . We did not "get in" until last June when for the first time in American politics, two Negro women were put on the National Committee of the most powerful political party.[38]

Perhaps, the strongest stand on the whole area of law enforcement and the political liberation of black Americans was delivered by Rev. W. J. Winston who was the former president of Northern University, Long Branch, New Jersey, and pastor of the New Metropolitan Baptist Church of Baltimore, Maryland. His address was entitled "Disfranchisement Makes Subject-Citizens Targets of the Mob and Disarms Them in the Courts." The central points of the address of protest include:

1. The disfranchisement of black Americans deprived them of their rights of citizenship and "chartered immunities."

2. It made them victims of mob violence and exposed them to the "sham court trials" in the South.

3. Black economic development was hindered by disfranchisement.

4. Blacks were denied active participation in the judicial process.

5. The rise of racism would go unchecked by the black vote.[39]

To be sure, Rev. Winston recognized the great danger posed by disfranchisement to the actual survival of black Americans living in the South. Significantly enough, the majority still lived in that region of the nation.

Consequently, the rise of organized crime, the resurgence of the KKK, and the failure of white America to enforce the federal laws weighed especially heavy upon black Americans. Black Americans were caught in the vicious wave of crime without the basic protection of law enforcement officers guaranteed to all citizens of the nation. To compound the problem, the courts of the nation were generally unfavorable to justice for black Americans. Hence, the leadership of the black Baptist church readily recognized that the Law Enforcement Movement must be high on the priority list for the church's agenda. Black pulpits across America began to echo the clarion call for law enforcement, order, and justice for all Americans. Many presidential addresses on the local, state, and national levels were uniquely concerned with these basic issues in American democracy.

## Black Migration

The migration of black Americans, beginning in the 1890s, has been a phenomenon of far-reaching significance to the growth and development of the black Baptist church movement. The changing economic and political situations in rural areas, especially in the South, were primarily responsible for the mass migration of black Americans from rural to urban areas. There was an attraction to the expanding opportunities of urban life. Urban life was seen as the center of economic freedom, culture, and progress for all aggressive and free-spirited Americans. To understand such appeals, a survey of the situation in the rural South must be related.

Initially, black Baptists were principally concentrated in the rural south with all of its negative experiences. They were poor, largely illiterate, and dependent upon the soil of the South for subsistence. Unfortunately, the southern rural economy worked adversely to the subsistence of black Americans in general. There were several specific developments during and after reconstruction that forced blacks from rural areas and drained the membership of rural churches.

First, there was the development of the credit system in the rural south aimed at improving the general plight of the farming communities. The credit system encouraged the development of two types of farmers: the merchant farmers and the resident farmers. The merchant farmers were the wealthiest class who usually resided in towns and upon whom the resident farmers depended for money and supplies to operate their farms. Invariably, blacks were of the latter class and subject to tremendous exploitation. They were not granted bills for their credit nor receipts for payments of debts. Hence, they were at the mercy of merchant farmers' honesty or sense of fair play. For the most part, however, the merchant farmers were not honest in their dealing with blacks. The system was often a blueprint for bankruptcy for most blacks. Often, blacks became so poor that they lost the little property which had been accumulated after the Civil War.

Second, blacks were often caught in the middle of the struggle between the white merchant farmers and resident farmers. Both classes depended largely on black labor. They became competitors for such labor, and bitter rivalry developed. Generally speaking, blacks were more inclined to work for merchant farmers as sharecroppers for two specific reasons.

(1) The share plan was a favorite with blacks because it allowed them to be their own managers. The employer furnished the land, the mule, and necessary farm tools. Blacks were primarily responsible for the labor. The merchant farmer generally received half the cotton and corn produced by the black sharecropper.

(2) The share plan with the merchant farmer allowed certain blacks to enjoy a favorable social status in comparison to those who worked for the resident farmers. They had

the social distinction of being identified with the wealthy class of farmers who lived away in the towns or small cities.

Gradually, some of these blacks were able to experience a degree of prosperity and purchased their own land and houses. This group became especially strong and influential in the local black Baptist churches in the rural south.

Blacks who were identified primarily with the resident farmers were poor and more inclined to migrate to urban areas in search for a better life. They were often humiliated by these white farmers because of their complete "slave-like" dependence. The resident farmers could come to the house of a black man and demand the labor of the family on any given day. Not only was this demoralizing, but the system kept many of the youth from school and other social experiences. These major disadvantages forced black Americans to look to the urban areas of the North and Northwest for a better way of life.

By the turn of the century, a large number of blacks had migrated from the South. Black youth and young adult migration especially affected the rural Baptist churches. This left these churches with only a few youth and young adults to participate in the programs of the rural churches. Rural church leaders were faced with the problem of educating a group of people who would not return to the local churches to demonstrate their talents. The only time these youths could be expected to return was on the "homecoming days." Surely, these developments caused some weariness on the part of rural clergy. They saw their once striving and progressive churches diminish to centers of the very young and older adults.

Similarly, the black Baptist churches of the urban centers were affected by the influx of large numbers of black Americans from the rural areas of the South. One major problem was the cultural shock experienced by most rural blacks with their initial encounter with the city. The fact that they were transplanted culturally had tremendous significance to the mental, emotional, and spiritual development of these migrants. Hence, the crucial task of the urban black Baptist churches was to help these migrants get over the cultural shock of their new environment and become adjusted and accepted in urban life. In a report to the Women's Convention, Auxiliary to the National Baptist Convention, U.S.A., Inc., the following observations were made relative to black migration to urban areas.

> Northern Negroes, as a group, look down with scorn on southern migrants. They are afraid that Jim Crow is coming North to live and move and have his being; that southern Negroes will southernize the North, instead of the North northernizing them. . . .
>
> What we need in the North to work out this new social problem is not turned up noses but rolled up sleeves, and Everybody working Everybody until we get in enough leaven to leaven the whole lump. Finding fault and talking superiority is the game of fools and snobs. Finding a way out is the method of wise men with great souls.
>
> Only great souls can work side by side with and for their ignorant brothers—undaunted and unafraid. The task in the North is for big Negroes—spiritual Hercules—who will put their whole souls to the task. Negroes who are not afraid of losing their northern prestige by lifting their southern brethers.[40]

In order to address these problems, the black Baptist churches of the North developed a unique cultural program. One part of this program was the transplantation of southern church music to urban churches. Another part was the introduction of rural black preachers to the leadership of urban churches. Summer camps, retreats, and prayer bands were also developed to help alleviate the cultural shock experience caused by black migration.

Rev. L. K. Williams, president of the National Baptist Convention, U.S.A., Inc., remarked:

> The migration of Negroes from the South to the North is a striking phenomenon of race friction and no movement since the Emancipation of the Negro has had so many potential eventualities as this one, yet concerning which some otherwise loquacious leaders have been tempted to maintain an unbroken silence.[41]

He had an early fear that the Baptist churches of the North were not completely ready for black migration. His prediction was later proven to be correct. Urban churches were able to meet many of the needs of the black migrants as long as they were residing in well defined "black neighborhoods." However, the racial situation in urban areas seriously hindered the effectiveness of these churches in urban areas to meet the needs of the migrants. With the process of a decentralization of "black neighborhoods," the urban churches slowly lost a great deal of influence over black migrants, and consequently the population grew much faster than church membership. Actually, the significant number of black migrants became secularized in their attempt to adjust to the urban cultural shock. Their value system, largely nurtured by Southern mores and folkways, was radically altered by the emerging secular culture of northern cities.

## Black Baptists and a New Cosmopolitan Outlook

The intellectual movement for equal rights and freedom for black Americans assumed a new stance when World War I commenced. Historians have readily seen this great war as a critical turning point in modern history. This was the visible end of an era of stability in national politics and economics, followed by social upheavals, economic changes, and international tensions on a global scale. The result was a significant and distinctive transition in the Western mind. There was a rather sudden widening of the emotional and intellectual outlook of most Americans.

Black Baptists were not unaffected by the general transition in the Western mind. The sociopolitical thought among these great men and women assimilated the new world view of the Western mind. The world war forced them to see racial problems of American culture in the light of world movements. The parochialism of postreconstruction thought gave way to make room for a new intellectual approach to the racial problem with an expanding horizon. The world war brought black Americans in close contact with the various sociopolitical problems around the world and their apparent interrelationships. Black leaders came to realize that the mob violence of the Ku Klux Klan and disfranchisement could now be viewed in the cosmopolitan milieu of dehumanizing political systems around the world designed to quench the human spirit of freedom, equality, and justice. Deprived minorities and other ethnic groups around the world were viewed by black Baptists as part of their general struggle for human dignity.

One crucial development precipitated by World War I was the attempt of white American proponents of racial supremacy to transplant their theories internationally. Rev. E. C. Morris, long-time president of the National Baptist Convention, U.S.A., Inc., was well apprised of the new international offensive of American proponents of white supremacy. He alluded to this in his last presidential address.

What country would welcome the Turks in wholesale numbers among them? If the many false statements sent abroad about the morals of the Negro are allowed to go unchallenged, it will not be long before the doors of all great countries of the world will be shut in our faces, and we will be forced to eke out an existence in the land of the lynchers. The Negro does not desire to leave the United States, not even the South. But the South must change, or the Negroes will seek homes in a more congenial clime.[42]

These words were designed to have a twofold effect. On the one hand, Rev. E. C. Morris wanted to counter the charges of American proponents of white supremacy on the international front. White American soldiers were reporting to Europeans that blacks were deprived in morals and deficient in intellect. Rev. Morris believed in the moral and intellectual equality of the races. On the other hand, he sought to advise black Baptists to keep their options open. If the attitudes of white Americans, particularly in the South, did not radically change, then black Americans might determine that their interests might necessitate a migration to another part of the world away from the land of the lynchers.

Rev. W. G. Park, who suceeded Rev. E. C. Morris to the presidency of the National Baptist Convention, U.S.A., Inc., remarked the same year:

As a race we have made rapid strides of progress, notwithstanding the many oppositions which have confronted us. The door of opportunity has been shut against us, the industrial mills have denied us, the factories have rejected us, prejudice and race hatred have met us in all the avenues of life. We, so to speak, have been forced to make brick without straw, but we are not discouraged. We have been loyal and patient in tribulations. We have fought and will still fight to protect the flag under whose folds many of the members of our race unjustly bled and died. . . . As a race, we have answered every call to arms from the Revolutionary War to the World War and have never insulted the flag. Search the record of 1812, the Civil War, the war with Spain, and the war with Mexico and you will find that the Negro soldier has done his bit in each and that his record for bravery and heroism cannot be questioned. In times of war, he has been a hero, and in times of peace he has never been charged with harming a single chief magistrate, nor throwing a single bomb.[43]

Similarly, the black Baptist leadership of the New England Baptist Missionary Convention joined the ranks of other black church leaders in the call for "a square deal" in American life. That leadership also recognized the immense importance of the recent world war to the so-called "Negro Problem." As early as 1919, Rev. W. B. Reed told the convention:

> The guns of the mighty have ceased their roaring, their forts are silenced, their navies gone, armies disorganized, and the people waiting for orders. . . . The armies of our allies with untold hardships, backed up with a willing sacrifice of the people got the victory, and from pools of mingled blood triumph has been written in history. We, in this, the forty-fifth annual session of our convention, rejoice with the rest of mankind over the victory of our armies and the triumph of a sacred cause. Any cause charged with complete liberties and rights of the weak is sacred. . . .
>
> Victory has been won on the battlefields; the defeated enemy had made a most humiliating surrender; the last of our soldiers will soon tread upon home soil with the nation's acknowledgement of well done. But world or home democracy is not yet.[44]

## World War II

The rise to power of Adolph Hitler and his political theories were perhaps the most radical international challenge to the progress of black Americans. The racial myth was given a potent international thrust with the development of Nazism, as an ideology in Germany. While the Jews were the primary objects of this myth, black Americans realized that the world with an ideology of Nazism was not safe for their progress. They saw the fantastic potency of sheer mythology was part of the racist attitudes of many white Americans. Therefore, black Americans watched with grave concern the rise of Adolph Hitler and the advance of World War II.

As early as 1938, Rev. J. H. Jackson, corresponding secretary of the Foreign Mission Board of the National Baptist Convention, U.S.A., Inc., recognized the threat of Hitler. He realized that the foreign mission program of the convention was related to world movements. Hence, Rev. J. H. Jackson remarked:

> As we look across the world today, we behold many discouraging signs and must admit the presence of many stalwart enemies of the Cross of Jesus Christ. These may be found in the form of materialistic philosophies, the secular mind and political states. . . .
>
> Fascism and Nazism are demanding the loyalty and, in many instances, the sacrifice of the human personality to the orders and dictates of the State. In such political organizations man is not evaluated as an end in himself but he is a means to an end. . . . The totalitarian idea of man runs counter to the Christian concept of human personality and negates the sacred truths uttered by Jesus of Nazareth. Along with this development of the cult of the State there has risen the doctrine of the supremacy of race. To follow such a theory or view of life to its logical conclusion will naturally divide the world into many hostile camps where each race will be pitted against the other.[45]

Similarly, Rev. J. C. Jackson, president of the New England Baptist Missionary Convention stated in his address to the convention, June 18, 1942:

> To begin with, I want it thoroughly understood that I want and hope the allies will win the War and destroy

forever the spirit of dictatorship, but to do this the monster prejudice must be obliterated from the face of the whole earth. Prejudice is the most costly thing in the world today, and person or nation that possesses it nurtures and seeks to keep alive this monster, is to be pitied.[46]

Rev. J. C. Jackson clearly understood the affinity between American racism and the ideologies of Fascism and Nazism. He was anxious to warn black Americans to keep a critical eye on world developments.

Among the major concerns of black Baptists relative to the world wars was the issue of the abuse of black soldiers. It was ironic that the military and civil leaders of America were not willing to deal justly with black soldiers on the battlefield to defend the American flag. The abuse of black soldiers was so severe that the National Baptist Convention deemed it necessary to issue a "Resolution on Abuse of Colored Soldiers."

WHEREAS, There is much concrete evidence that native born colored American soldiers now in training in Army camps in the South have been in hundreds of instances subject of humiliations, discrimination, brutalities, and, in at least one case, a trainee was murdered, even when clothed in the uniform of the United States Army. And,

WHEREAS, We are not only segregated but have been deprived of a fair proportion of officers and men, although there are thousands of patriotic and loyal men well qualified, and those taken in have been restricted to a few of the many regular services.

WHEREAS, We seek not to take Negro soldiers from the South, for geography does not count in a democracy. We do ask that the War Department armed with power and authority use drastic measures to protect them from un-American practices of individuals and brutal mobs, just as would be done if Nazis, Communists, Ku Klux or Night Riders attempted to humiliate, abuse, intimidate white sol-

diers in the U.S. Army. Colored Americans are super patri-
ots, 100 per cent Americans by birth and love of country,
who are being trained to fight, and if need be to die for their
native land and for democracy, although they do not fully
share equally in its beneficences. Democracy is needed in the
army.[47]

Black soldiers were also "barred from enlisting in the
U.S. Navy, except as messmen, flunkies and valets with no
hope of promotion to the higher ranks."[48]

Black Baptist women were also apprised of the tremendous significance of world events on the racial problem in
America. In 1944, Miss Nannie H. Burroughs, a national
leader mentioned earlier, gave a broad survey of the plight
of black Americans in the national and international arena.
She remarked:

We sincerely hope that Negro and white soldiers in
Europe have been getting along better fighting together than
Negroes and whites over here have been getting along work-
ing together.

The first stark reality the Negro will face in the post-war
world will be that while he helped to beat Hitler into complete surrender that Hitler's kind of race prejudice is still
unliked, and abroad in the world.

It is against this background that the Negro will have to
fight his economic battle. He will have to compete with the
very people whom he fought to help liberate. America will
give aliens jobs and give Negroes their walking papers.

Let nobody fool you—We are in for a long, hard uphill
battle on the American front. The pressure of the European
war emergency will be gone. The army will be on world
fronts. The home front battle will have to be fought by
civilians—Negro and white—who want to free America
from her home-made Hitlers.[49]

The astute observations of Miss N. H. Burroughs were
prophetic because successive decades were to witness many

"home front battles." Black Americans were later called upon to fight in the Korean and Vietnam wars while at home the battles remained unsettled. To be sure, the "homemade Hitlers" were more formidable than any international threat to the progress of the race. The unsettled issues on the American front were to summon a cadre of sociopolitical minded preachers of the black Baptist church to champion the greatest civil rights movement in world history.

## The Civil Rights Movement of the Middle Twentieth Century

The civil rights movement of the decades of the 1950s and 1960s has been described as the most remarkable revolution in the history of the nation. Slowly, events in the long struggle for civil and human rights took on the appearance of a movement designed to bring about the greatest change in the social fabric of American life since the Civil War. From half-hidden depths of impatience and mental aggression, black Americans pressed forward their revolution to a crescendo of protest in the middle of the twentieth century. Curiously enough, the revolution began long before it was recognized as such by white America. To be sure, the civil rights movement of the middle of the twentieth century, revolutionary in intent and momemtum, was a continuation of the struggles of the century. There was no period of the twentieth century wherein black Americans did not protest the injustices and inconsistencies of American democracy. Significantly, black Baptists were foremost in the new revolution. Hence, the civil rights movement of the middle of the twentieth century may be spotlighted in the thoughts and actions of several black Baptist leaders.

## The Harlem Politician: Adam Clayton Powell, Jr.

The greatest link between the civil rights movement of the turn of the century and the revolutionary civil rights movement of the 1950s and 1960s was in the person of Rev. Adam Clayton Powell, Jr. He grew up in Harlem and was nurtured in the best sociopolitical tradition of the race and the Baptist demonination. In the early 1920s Harlem became the center for the social and political development of black Americans. The black world looked to Harlem for inspiration and leadership.

Nieuw Haarlem was founded by Peter Stuyvesant more than a century before the revolutionary war and was a farming community until the last century was well under way. In the 1900s Harlem was joined to New York City, and when the elevated railway was extended there after the Civil War, it became a fashionable place in which to live. The original white population prevented black Americans from enjoying the social prestige of Harlem residency until the turn of the century. However, it was not until World War I that Harlem became the center of the cultural, intellectual, and political development of black Americans. The apex of Harlem's development in black life and culture has been described as "the Harlem Renaissance."[50]

It was during the Harlem renaissance that Rev. Adam Clayton Powell, Jr., received his nurture at the Abyssinian Baptist Church under the pastorate of his father, Rev. Adam Clayton Powell, Sr. To be sure, he was exposed to the most favorable tradition of black Americans in general. During his period of nurture, Adam Clayton Powell, Jr., studied Marcus Garvey and became intrigued over the racial consciousness and pan-Africanism of Garvey's movement. Subsequently, he helped pioneer the tactics of mass action against racial discrimination. In 1931, Powell, age twenty-two, led 6,000 marchers to New York's City Hall to protest the barring of five black physicians from the staff of Harlem Hospital. Subsequently, he led innumerable demonstrations that focused public attention and black energy on campaigns to open up jobs for black Americans in New York City. As director of relief efforts in Harlem during the depression, Adam Clayton Powell, Jr., helped feed 1,000 persons a week and later led rent strikes to protest evictions and slum conditions.[51]

After he inherited the pastorate of Abyssinian Baptist Church, Rev. Adam Clayton Powell, Jr., became a typical embodiment of the social gospel tradition of the black church. In concomitance to his regular pastoral duties, Rev. Adam Clayton Powell, Jr., operated a day nursery for working mothers, a grocery store, and other services all with a staff of twenty workers. He got jobs in 125th Street by demands, marchers, and selective buying campaigns.[52] All this was done during the early 1930s.

The paramount contributions of Rev. Adam Clayton Powell, Jr., to the civil rights movement were rendered after his election to Congress. On November 7, 1944, he was elected to the Seventy-Ninth Congress of the United States of America—Harlem's first black congressman. The congressional position paved the way for him to succeed Booker T. Washington and W. E. B. Dubois as the single most powerful black American. From the outset of his political career, Rev. Powell led a persistent fight for civil rights with a cosmopolitan outlook. During the Eighty-Eighth Congress, he reminisced:

> Mr. Speaker, much has been said in recent months regarding the necessity of passing an effective civil rights bill. The urgency has been recognized as essential for America's proof to the world that she believes in democracy.
>
> The question of civil rights is no longer the problem of Negro people—it is the problem of all the people of the United States of America. Many fear that the United States

may be finished as a great power in the eyes of the world unless it solves this problem and solves it now.

However, on November 7, 1944, when I was elected to the 79th Congress of the United States of America, I pledged myself to dedicate my efforts to the task of making democracy work.[53]

These remarks reflected the quality of Rev. Adam Clayton Powell's commitment to the strength of the American Republic. He was faithful to the patriotic spirit of earlier black Baptists. Generally, they did not want to destroy the Republic but to aid and inspire it on its march to justice, equality, and quality life for all citizens.

Accordingly, Rev. Adam Clayton Powell, Jr., expressed an interest in a broad spectrum of issues affecting the life of black Americans who were struggling for a truer democracy. He initiated a major challenge to racism in American society and tangled relentlessly on the floor of Congress with southern racists. His addresses were designed to advance the civil rights struggle in the highest chambers of government. A sheaf of civil rights bills was introduced by the Harlem congressman.

*At the outset of Powell's congressional career, he expressed a specific interest in the way black Americans were treated in the armed forces of the United States.* Practices of discrimination were long standing through the nation. In 1944, Powell introduced H.R. 2708: "A bill to prohibit race segregation in the Armed Forces of the United States after the termination of hostilities in the present war and the beginning of the demobilization."[54] The bill failed in the Seventy-Ninth Congress but was reintroduced in the Eightieth Congress. This time Powell was more specific in his request to end segregation in the armed forces:

H.R. 495 (Mr. Powell): To prohibit racial segregation in the Armed Forces of the United States:

I make no excuse, when I present this amendment, for the patriotism of my people, the Negro people. Back in the beginning of this Republic, the first blood that was shed that America might be free was shed on March 5, 1773, on Boston Common by a black man, Crispus Attucks. From the days of then until the days of now Negro people have been the most loyal minority in this democracy. The Negro people will stand ready at all times to defend this Nation, but they are saying, "We want some of the democracy here now at home that you are trying to sell abroad to other people that you ask us to go ahead and fight for. We have proven our loyalty. We are asking for democracy now.[55]

It was not until 1948 that some progress was made in the area of racial equality in the armed forces. Powell testified in the Eighty-First Congress:

Six years ago when I first came to this body I was the first to introduce legislation to abolish discrimination and segregation in the Armed Forces. At that time discrimination and segregation were rampant and rife in all branches of our military service. I have consistently kept up the fight. When this particular bill came before us in 1948 I led the movement that kept the House in session over 1 week. During the past 6 years we have seen considerable progress and today in our armed services, in the Coast Guard—which, of course, is really not a part of the Armed Forces but in time of war is a part of the Navy—and in the Navy, and to a certain extent in the Air Corps, there is but little discrimination and little segregation. In our Army, however, the President of our Nation and the committee which he appointed, have come up against some stubborn opposition. The time has come now for the Congress to act.

When we had the battle of the Belgian Bulge, Negro men who had been restricted to certain menial capacities were called up out of transportation and out of porter's work and given guns. Black and white stood together and fought for democracy. When victory came the Negroes were left in

Europe and the whites paraded on Fifth Avenue. Is that democracy? Now, in peacetime, I ask that we here will do that which at least we owe to the citizens of this Nation, to our conscience, and to the world, give men the right to serve side by side with their fellow citizens in all branches of our services.[56]

None of Powell's bills and amendments on the cessation of discrimination and segregation in the armed forces passed the Congress and Senate of the United States. General relief in these areas came primarily from programs initiated by the executive branch of the government. By the Eighty-Second Congress, Powell was able to note significant progress. One factor which influenced the progress was the intensity of the Korean conflict. It was this conflict that caused Powell to adopt a more temperate position. He tried to appeal more to the sensibleness of white moderate politicians. He sought to accomplish this by linking real democracy for black Americans to the national security interests.[57]

The influence of Rev. Adam Clayton Powell, Jr., in the Congress of the United States did more than any other person or movement to end racial segregation and discrimination in the Armed Forces of the nation. His bills were not passed, but they did influence the executive branch of government to bring some changes. Hence, Powell must be recognized for his tremendous strides in the improvement of the plight of black Americans in the military establishments of this Nation.

*The next area of major concern on the part of Rev. Adam Clayton Powell, Jr., was the violence experienced by black Americans.* As noted earlier, black Americans were constantly victims of mob violence and other acts of crime in American life. White America was very slow in its strides to afford black Americans due protection as citizens of the nation. Rev. Adam Clayton Powell, Jr., was especially forceful in his claims that

America had a special responsibility to protect its citizens from violence at home as well as abroad. During the Seventy-Ninth Congress, Powell introduced "H.R. 1747 (Mr. Powell): A bill for the better assurance of the protection of persons within the several States from mob violence and lynching."[58] Like the Dyer Anti-Lynching Bill, Powell's bill fell on deaf ears. Nevertheless, he assumed a persistent stance, introducing bill after bill to the Congress to assure the safety of black Americans in all parts of the nation. By 1963, Rev. Adam Clayton Powell, Jr., had become weary of the failure of the Congress to pass protective legislation for black Americans. That year he made reference to his most detailed piece of legislation relative to the issues of lynching and mob violence:

H.R. 546 (Mr. Powell): Federal Anti-Lynching Act.— Defines lynching as a assemblage of two or more persons which shall, without authority of law, (1) commit violence upon the person of any citizen because of race, creed, color, national origin, ancestry, language, or religion, or (2) exercise by physical violence any power of correction over any person in the custody of a peace officer or charged with any criminal offense for the purpose of preventing the trial or punishment not authorized by law. Sets the maximum penalty for lynching at $10,000 fine and/or 20 years imprisonment. A State or local officer failing through neglect to prevent a lynching or to apprehend or prosecute any member of a lynching mob, shall be punished by a $5,000 fine and/or 5 years imprisonment. Any governmental subdivision failing through neglect to prevent a lynching or an abduction followed elsewhere by a lynching shall be liable for $2,000 to $10,000 in damages recoverable in a civil action. The interstate transportation of persons with a view to lynching is made subject to the penalties provided in the Lindbergh kidnapping law [death or life imprisonment].[59]

Powell's bill H.R. 546 was the most comprehensive

piece of legislation ever introduced in Congress for the protection of black Americans from lynching and mob violence. It was so comprehensive that all minorities were protected by the special provisions of the bill. Hence, the legal thought behind the famous Civil Rights Bill of the 1960s was fashioned by Rev. Adam Clayton Powell, Jr.

*The next area of major concern on the part of the Powell's tenure in the United States Congress was the issue of voting rights.* Rev. Adam Clayton Powell, Jr., was especially critical of all tactics used by southern whites to prevent black Americans from voting. In the Seventy-Ninth Congress, he introduced a bill relative to "Poll tax and voting."

> H.R. 2183 (Mr. Powell): A bill making unlawful the requirement for the payment of a poll tax as a prerequisite to voting in a primary or other election for national officers.
>
> This Nation will never achieve full stature until the whole South is free. The South can never start the upward march to political freedom until the chains of poll taxes are broken. Two dollars is a lot of money to 6 million sharecroppers in the Southern States who average less than 6 cents per day. Two dollars is a lot of money to men who at the end of a year's work are told that they still were the planter's money.[60]

Like other civil rights bills, Powell found it necessary to introduce the same piece of legislation over and over in the Congress of the United States. During the Eighty-Fifth Congress, he modified the proposal to include a "Voter Registration Commission":

> H.R. 7957 (Mr. Powell): To provide for the establishment of a Federal Voter Registration Commission to provide, in certain instances, for the registration of citizens of the United States for the purpose of voting in Federal and State elections, and for other purposes.[61]

A brief survey of other civil rights bills proposed by

Rev. Adam Clayton Powell, Jr., will reflect the depth and breadth of the Harlem politician's sociopolitical thought. During the Seventy-Ninth Congress, he introduced a House joint resolution "proposing an amendment to the Constitution of the United States empowering Congress to grant representation in the Congress and among the electors of President and Vice-President to the people of the District of Columbia"[62]; a public accommodations bill "to assure to all persons within the jurisdiction of the United States full and equal privileges with respect to public conveyances and places of public accommodations, resort, entertainment, amusement, assemblage, and institutions"[63]; and the school lunch programs amendment to "see that minority races have the same opportunity in the free-lunch program as do those of the majority race."[64]

The following sessions of Congress were characterized by an avalanche of civil rights legislation from the pen of Rev. Adam Clayton Powell, Jr. Included among these were:

Interstate Transportation Bill H.R. 22: "To amend the Interstate Commerce Act so as to prohibit the segregation of passengers on account of race or color."[65]

Antisegregation Day H.R. 3016: "Making May 17 in each year a legal holiday to be known as Antisegregation Day."[66]

Federal assistance for school construction H.R. 7535: An amendment that "school facilities of the States are open to all children without regard to race, in conformity with the requirements of the U.S. Supreme Court decisions"[67]

Housing H.R. 12538: "To provide that Federal funds shall not be used for loans, grants, or other financial assistance to provide housing with respect to which there is any discrimination against occupancy on account of race, religion, color, ancestry, or national origin."[68]

Fair labor standards H.R. 6887: "Extends protection of Fair Labor Standards Act to employees of large hotels, motels, restaurants and laundries with gross sales of $1 million annually."[69]

Immigration H.R. 543: "Grants natives of British Guiana, British Honduras, the British Virgin Islands, and the West Indies Federation unlimited access to the immigration quota for Great Britain."[70]

Manpower resources J.R. 7396: "Provides for a program of occupational training of the Nation's labor force. . . . Provides for on- and off-the-job training and vocational training for the unemployed."[71]

Equal pay for women H.R. 11677: "To prohibit discrimination on account of sex in the payment of wages by certain employers engaged in commerce or in the production of goods for commerce and to provide for the restitution of wages lost by employees by reason of any such discrimination."[72]

In 1963, Rev. Adam Clayton Powell, Jr., summarized the importance of this avalanche of civil rights bills in rather suggestive language: "Civil rights to me is what Israel is to the Jew or as sacred as Ireland is to an Irishman or Catholicism is to a Catholic."[73]

Unfortunately, the vitality of Rev. Adam Clayton Powell's civil rights career in the United States Congress was overshadowed by a political scandal. His personal standard of public morality left a lot to be desired: "As a member of Congress, I have done nothing more than any other member and, by the grace of God, I intend to do not one bit less."[74] This philosophy of public morality was unacceptable to both his black constituency and the members of the House of Representatives of the United States. He openly rebelled against many rules set down by whites, drove expensive foreign cars, dined at exclusive restaurants, and made regular trips abroad. The big blow to Rev. Adam Clayton Powell's political career came on March 1, 1967, when 307 legislators voted to exclude him from the Ninetieth Congress. He became the first congressman in modern times to be excluded by a vote of the House.

Specifically, the grounds for Powell's exclusion from the Ninetieth Congress were misuse of public funds and defying the courts (for months Powell had stayed away from New York to avoid arrest in a complicated libel suit begun after he called a Harlem widow a "bag woman" for corrupt police officials). Significantly, he was reelected twice during this scandal. In 1969, the Supreme Court reversed his expulsion from Congress, but by then Powell was suffering from cancer and spending most of the time in his Bahamian Eden on Bimini. In 1970, Rev. Adam Clayton Powell, Jr., in a Harlem primary, lost by 150 votes.[75] Powell was defeated by State Assemblyman Charles B. Rangel. After his defeat, he retired permanently to his island home. Shortly thereafter, he died. The death of Rev. Adam Clayton Powell, Jr., ended a great era of social activism wherein one man became an institution reflecting the basic thought of an emerging social revolution.

## The Black Social Revolution: 1956-1970

The civil rights movement of the decade of the 1960s was a continuum of the sociopolitical struggles of previous decades. There were many forces at work which prepared the way for the new black revolution. Momentum was gained through the political activity of Adam Clayton Powell, Jr., Presidents Roosevelt, Truman, and the US Supreme Court. Specifically, the United States Commission on Civil Rights provided a tremendous body of research data for a legal and political approach to the problem of race in the United States. It was created by the Civil Rights Act of 1957 as a bipartisan agency to study civil rights problems and report to the president and Congress. More specifically, the commission's function was to advise the President and

Congress on conditions that may deprive American citizens of equal treatment under the law because of race, color, religion, or national origin.

Black leaders across the nation voiced their intimate knowledge of the data reflected in the commission's report. It was clear that the nation began with an obvious inconsistency between its precepts of liberty and the actual sociopolitical experiences of black Americans. The majority race saw the nation and its Constitution as a nation of the white, by the white man, and for the white man. The social revolution which emerged was designed to bring a radical change in the very structure of life in the nation.

On December 1, 1955, the match was struck to ignite the dynamo of the greatest social revolution of the historic American experience. Nothing less than an explosive revolution began when Rosa Mae Parks boarded the Cleveland Avenue bus in Montgomery, Alabama. She sat down in the "whites only" section and decided to say no to the bus driver's demand that she get up and let a white man have her seat. News reports of Rosa Mae Park's arrest swept the black community and proved to be the catalyst for a different styled protest movement.

Shortly after the bus incident, the clergy leadership of Montgomery, Alabama, met to consider the significance of the new development. The clergy decided to call on the black community to stage a bus boycott for the following Monday morning. They utilized their pulpits on Sunday to set the stage for the boycott. Rev. Martin Luther King, Jr., a local Baptist pastor of the Dexter Avenue Baptist Church, accepted the monumental task of mimeographing and distributing printed material to be distributed in the black community. Significantly enough, the bus boycott was almost 100 percent successful.

A tremendous community organization grew out of the initial bus boycott in Montgomery. Under the leadership of

Rev. Ralph David Abernathy, pastor of
West Hunter Street Baptist Church,
Atlanta, Georgia, and cofounder with Dr.
Martin Luther King, Jr., of the S.C.L.C.

two Baptist clergymen—Rev. Martin Luther King., Jr., and Rev. Ralph David Abernathy—Montgomery blacks formed the Montgomery Improvement Association, boycotted the bus lines, and referred their case to the state court and then to the US Supreme Court. The Montgomery Improvement Association demanded courteous treatment to blacks on public transportation facilities and the hiring of black bus drivers. Both the district court and the Supreme Court ruled that segregated busing was unconstitutional.

Throughout the initial days of the movement, the black leadership looked to Rev. Martin Luther King., Jr., as their supreme spokesman. This was part of a strategy developed by Rev. Ralph David Abernathy and several other clergy, and other powerful community leaders were able to maintain their solidarity behind Rev. Martin Luther King, Jr., when confronted by deliberate attempts on the part of the white leadership to fragment the movement.

The initial victory of the Montgomery Improvement Association propelled Rev. Martin Luther King, Jr., into a position of national and international prominence and led to the organization of a regional civil rights group called the Southern Christian Leadership Conference (SCLC). The new regional organization consisted of approximately one hundred southern clergymen who believed that civil rights leadership must be revitalized by churches and church leaders. This new organization, with several affiliate groups, became active in the area of voter registration, protests, and citizenship training. From the beginning of the Southern Christian Leadership Conference, Rev. Martin Luther King, Jr., inspired the movement to be guided by the principle of nonviolence.

Rev. Martin Luther King, Jr., the famous leader of the black revolution, was raised in the Baptist tradition of the South and later educated in liberal theology at Boston University where he received a doctorate in theology. During his academic career, King was highly influenced by the social ethics of Christianity and the philosophy of Mahatma Gandhi of India. He was able to synthesize the thought of Gandhi with the Social Gospel of Christianity. A third ingredient was later introduced into King's synthesis—the sociopolitical theories of Henry David Thoreau. From this synthesis emerged King's commitment to passive resistance and nonviolent protest. With such a commitment, he was able to meet the challenge of the black revolution and provide for Americans—both black and white—a leader and a focus on the civil rights movement in the 1960s.

To be sure, the new black revolution provided a tremendous challenge to the intellectual, moral, and psychological development of Rev. Martin Luther King, Jr. He worked out the pragmatic significance of social Christianity in the context of the black revolution. The revolution became the testing grounds of King's synthesis.

Several years after the Montgomery bus boycott, Dr. King left Montgomery and returned to Atlanta where he became associate pastor, along with his father, of Ebenezer Baptist Church. However, King realized that it was impossible for him to leave behind or drop out of the black revolution that had begun in Montgomery, Alabama. In Atlanta, he settled down as the executive head of the Southern Christian Leadership Conference. This position afforded King the opportunity to specialize in the leadership of the revolution.

One very potent characteristic of King's sociopolitical thought for the revolution was an emphasis on the significance of history to the plight of black Americans. He once remarked:

> Whenever I am asked my opinion of the current state of the civil rights movement, I am forced to pause; it is not easy to describe a crisis so profound that it has caused the most

powerful nation in the world to stagger in confusion and bewilderment. Today's problems are so acute because the tragic evasions and defaults of several centuries have accumulated to disaster proportions. . . . What might once have been a series of separate problems now merge into a social crisis of almost stupefying complexity.

I am not sad that black Americans are rebelling; this was not only inevitable but eminently desirable. Without this magnificent ferment among Negroes, the old evasions and procrastinations would have continued indefinitely. Black men have slammed the door shut on a past of deadening passivity. Except for the Reconstruction years, they have never in their long history on American soil, struggled with such creativity and courage for their freedom.[76]

Rev. Martin Luther King, Jr., was able to identify the tremendous power of black Americans in the "magnificent ferment" and plan an appropriate strategy to utilize that power for the black revolution of liberation from oppression. He recognized that black Americans were wide awake to the struggles of the revolution. One strategy was to harness the tremendous voting power of black Americans. King advised:

The constructive program ahead must include a campaign to get Negroes to register and vote. . . . Even where the polls are open to all, Negroes have shown themselves too slow to exercise their voting privileges. There must be a concerted effort on the part of Negro leaders to arouse their people from apathetic indifference to this obligation of citizenship. In the past, apathy was a moral failure. Today, it is a form of moral and political suicide.[77]

Another strategy, as previously mentioned, was the utilization of the Social Gospel in the civil rights struggles of the 1960s. The Social Gospel provided King a means of dialogue with liberal white Americans to recruit their support for the black revolution. He viewed the necessity of such a gospel approach with unconditional seriousness. He observed: "The social gospel is as important as the gospel of personal salvation. Any religion that professes to be concerned about the souls of men and ignores social and economic conditions that cripple the soul is a spiritually moribund and dead religion, and it is only waiting for the day to be buried."[78] King saw in the Social Gospel "one of the most potent weapons available to oppressed people in their struggle for freedom."[79]

King was largely responsible for the march on Washington for Jobs and Freedom in August 1963. The march was attended by the top echelon of the civil rights movement. This was the largest assembly of black and white Americans in the history of the nation. Americans from all walks of life gathered in the Capital City to ask President John F. Kennedy and the US Congress for a federal fair employment practices commission and the power for the Justice Department to step into civil rights disputes on state and local levels.

Already pending was a proposal by the President to enact a Civil Rights Bill. On June 19, 1963, President Kennedy asked Congress to enact the most comprehensive legislation on civil rights since Reconstruction. This proposal represented a shift in Kennedy's civil rights policies from executive action (executive orders and persuasion directed toward voluntary elimination of racial discrimination) to legislative means for the solution of America's greatest social problem. This shift was motivated partly by the influence of Rev. Martin Luther King, Jr., and the resurgent militancy of the South.

The march on Washington was the apex of the revolutionary struggle. Rev. Martin Luther King, Jr., witnessed the highest moment of his career when he uttered the world famous "I have a dream" speech. King talked forcibly about the future of the black American Revolution. He affirmed a vision of hope for an America free of racism.

I have a dream that one day on the red hills of Georgia, sons of former slaves and sons of former slaveowners will be able to sit down together at the table of brotherhood.

I have a dream, that one day, even the state of Mississippi, a state sweltering with the heat of injustice, sweltering with the heat of oppression, will be transformed into an oasis of freedom and justice.

I have a dream that my four little children will one day live in a nation where they will not be judged by the color of their skin but by the content of their character. . . .

This is our hope. This is the faith that I go back to the South with. With this faith we will be able to hew out of the mountains of despair a stone of hope.

This speech projected in capsule form King's religious and social philosophy for the civil rights movement.

The response of white America to King's speech was twofold: on the one hand, more whites joined the ranks of the freedom movement; but, on the other, some white racists strengthened their resolve to maintain segregation and white supremacy. The former recognized in King a strong commitment to fundamental American values. Others, however, were even more blatant in their attempt to brand King as a communist—a strategic maneuver to destroy his influence on public opinion and policy. The "communist brand" had long served such purposes in twentieth-century American politics.

A critical analysis of King's "I have a dream" speech and other documents reflecting his thought tend to demonstrate a profound respect for the American political process. Nowhere does one find any "un-American" thought or activity in Rev. Martin Luther King, Jr. Although King was influenced by the social thought of Karl Marx and Mahatma Gandhi, he, nevertheless, remained loyal to America and American idealism. King remarked:

My reading of Marx also convinced me that truth is found

neither in Marxism nor in traditional capitalism. Each represents a partial truth. Historically capitalism failed to see the
truth in collective enterprise and Marxism failed to see the
truth in individual enterprise. Nineteenth-century capitalism failed and still fails to see that life is social and Marxism
failed and still fails to see that life is individual and personal.
The Kingdom of God is neither the thesis of individual
enterprise nor the antithesis of collective enterprise, but a
synthesis which reconciles the truths of both.[80]

Similarly, Coretta Scott King recalled that Martin Luther King, Jr., stated emphatically that he could never be a
communist.[81] King stood for an America of freedom, justice,
and righteousness. Hence, all of his criticism of America was
for that end.

Increasingly, the South and its racist sympathizers in
the North and West resorted to militant activities to stop
the civil rights revolution. Strong forces in many forms of
government life tried to check King's strides toward freedom and to block passage of President Kennedy's Civil
Rights Bill in Congress. About three weeks after King's
speech, a white racist (or racists?) put a bomb in the Sixteenth Street Baptist Church in Birmingham, Alabama, that
resulted in the death of four little black girls attending Sunday School. This incident shocked Rev. Martin Luther King,
Jr., profoundly. In his eulogy for the little girls, King called
them "Heroines of a holy crusade for freedom and human
dignity."[82] He concluded that their death should give even
greater momentum to the stride to make the American
dream a reality. Still a few weeks later, King had to endure
on November 22, 1963, along with other Americans, the
shocking assasination of President John F. Kennedy.

Nevertheless, the net result of these and other acts of
violence only inspired the new President Lyndon B. Johnson to continue Kennedy's policies. On November 28, 1963,
President Johnson, in a special address to Congress, stated

his support of Kennedy's civil rights program. The new President's actions signaled a direct challenge to his fellow southerners. Consequently, the Civil Rights Bill was debated with great emotions in Congress. In fact, the legislative battle in Congress over the President's civil rights proposals was no less bitter than the racial battle outside of Congress.[83] On February 10, 1964, the Civil Rights Act was passed by Congress. To be sure, King was greatly elated when President Johnson signed the Bill into law. He was invited and attended the ceremony at the White House.

King's influence in civil liberties or human rights issues gained the attention of the world. In December 1964, Rev. Martin Luther King, Jr., received the Nobel Peace Prize Award and was congratulated by King Olav of Norway along with other world leaders. This event established King as one of the greatest Baptist leaders in world history.

Between 1964 and 1968, King expanded his moral and political vision to include the peace movement against the war in Vietnam and liberation movements in Southern Africa. Significantly enough, his stand against the Vietnam War resulted in sharp criticism on the part of many white liberals and black Americans. The Vietnam War issue, coupled with the rise of a militant black power movement, gradually undermined the popularity of Martin Luther King, Jr. Nevertheless, King remained until his assasination on April 4, 1968, the soul of the black revolution in America. He challenged the consciousness of the free world to come to grips with the biblical principles of peace, brotherhood, love, and goodwill to all men.

## The Post-Revolutionary Period: 1970-1984

The death of Rev. Martin Luther King, Jr., signaled the beginning of the end of the black revolution in America. Black Americans lost faith in King's strategies for the revolution. The rise of the black power advocates completely overshadowed the nonviolence and passive resistance. Violence broke out in many of the major metropolitan areas of the nation. The result of the race riots was a virtual breakup of the cohesive forces of the black revolution. A struggle, largely unsuccessful, emerged for the leadership of the revolution. To make matters even worse, black Americans no longer saw the need for a black leader in the struggles for civil rights. They became apathetic because the "Great Society" of President Johnson had dawned upon the American experience. Furthermore, the liberal whites gradually withdrew from the movement because they were reluctant to be linked with a violent movement in the nation. Hence, the close of the 1960s set the stage for a gradual decline in the black revolution.

A large number of the leaders of the black revolution were later to be found in prominent positions within the "system." They became convinced that the "Great Society" was finally ready to be inclusive of all Americans. A significant amount of upward mobility did result in the experiences of a select group of black Americans. But the masses were still very much estranged from the mainstream of American life. The decade of the seventies witnessed high black unemployment, street violence, drug addiction, and a gradual decline of the black church and family. Some of these problems resulted from the general rise of secularism and the new morality in American culture. Blacks were largely caught up in the general spirit of the age.

Just before the close of the decade, black leaders began to realize that a major threat to the gains of the black revolution had surfaced in the American experience. On the economic front, Rev. Leon Sullivan began to urge black Americans to involve themselves in "black capitalism." He urged:

Ultimately, I think, the black man will require a fair share of ownership in the American economy. And that will come in large part through his own efforts. Thus he will gain self-respect through self-help.

A man is not free until he owns something and has self-pride. This is not to say that riots and disruption may not be productive of gains in their own peculiar way. Many of my people are locked up in a box of deep prejudice and segregation and ignorance, and they can't get out. The only way they can let you know they are there is just to pound on the box and even knock down the sides.[84]

Rev. Sullivan organized the Opportunities Industrialization Centers to advance black capitalism. This was one of the greatest movements among blacks in the 1970s. The movement spread throughout the United States and parts of Africa. Rev. Leon Sullivan, pastor of Zion Baptist Church of Philadelphia, was one of the greatest among the black Baptist leaders of the 1970s. He made a tremendous impact on the economic development of blacks around the world. Millions of dollars and other resources were utilized by this leader's creative genius to improve the quality of life for a large number of people.

The voice of Rev. Ralph David Abernathy was also heard aloud at the close of the decade of the 1970s, warning black Americans not to allow the gains of the revolution to be lost. He made many forceful attempts to remind black Americans of the civil rights struggles and urged them to continue in the struggle. It was Rev. Ralph David Abernathy and other black churchmen who helped make possible the election of President Jimmy Carter. They were highly impressed with Carter's stand on civil and human rights issues. Perhaps the linkage of black Baptists in the politics of "human rights" was the most significant achievement of the post revolutionary decade.

The post-revolutionary period witnessed also the rise

to power of Rev. Jesse Louis Jackson from the ranks of the young confidants of Rev. Martin Luther King, Jr. He rivaled the leadership of Rev. Ralph David Abernathy and the old regime of civil rights workers in the popular sentiment of black Americans. Significantly enough, the focus of the American press was more on Rev. Jackson than Rev. Abernathy. Presumably, this may have contributed partly to Abernathy's inability to be very effective in the leadership of SCLC. Despite the fact that Rev. Abernathy worked hard, the SCLC lost the momentum it once had under the leadership of Rev. Martin Luther King, Jr. Rev. Jesse Louis Jackson, following the death of Rev. King, was careful to remain before the American people as a vibrant leader of the civil rights struggle of black Americans.

The primary organization which served as a basis for Rev. Jesse Jackson's (as he was popularly called) new leadership role was Operation PUSH (People United to Save Humanity). He organized this movement three years after the death of Rev. Martin Luther King, Jr. The purpose of PUSH was to promote the economic progress of black Americans and other minorites. Initially, Rev. Jesse Jackson's PUSH facilitated agreements with major American companies to hire and do business with minorities. Also, PUSH's "Project Excel" inspired many young black Americans to stay in school and achieve academically. Subsequently, Rev. Jesse Jackson emerged as a symbol of upward mobility to a large number of the nation's black youth.

In 1980, Rev. Jesse Jackson came to Baltimore to meet with the Ministerial Alliance to encourage their participation in the "Pilgrimage March for Jobs," May 17, 1980. He was very critical of national politics, suggesting that neither blacks nor the poor could be satisfied with the balanced budget. The impact of a balanced budget meant for Rev. Jackson a drastic loss of jobs for minority Americans. Accordingly, he traveled throughout the nation to encourage black church leaders to challenge the direction of national politics.

By the end of 1982, Rev. Jesse Jackson had experienced some significant success in his attempts to improve the economic life of minority Americans. Five of the six major companies targeted by PUSH since 1981 actually signed trade agreements totaling approximately $1.5 billion. Consequently, Rev. Jesse Jackson launched a national movement designed to force the compliance of the sixth company.

Rev. Milton A. Reid, owner and managing editor of the *Journal and Guide,* Norfolk, Virginia, was reluctant to support Rev. Jesse Jackson in this struggle. He criticized some of Rev. Jackson's dealings within the black community.[85] Challenges such as this one signaled a growing opposition on the part of many black church leaders to the leadership role of Rev. Jesse Jackson. Slowly, negative feelings on the part of the old civil rights regime surfaced to hinder his aggressive leadership. He never completely recovered from this plague.

On November 3, 1983, Rev. Jesse Jackson added a new dimension to his leadership role in the struggles of black Americans. He shocked the nation when he announced his candidacy for the presidency of the United States of America. Initially, Jackson's announcement was not taken seriously. Slowly, he was able to put together his "rainbow coalition" behind the theme, "Run, Jesse, run." This theme was chanted even in some parts of Africa.

The presidential campaign caused Jackson to enter some new areas in the struggle for human rights and freedom. One of the high points in his quest for the presidency was his attempt to secure the release of captured US Navy airman Lt. Robert Goodman, Jr. This event gave Jackson nationwide media attention. He planned a "moral appeal" to President Hafez Assad of Syria to release Lt. Goodman as "a humanitarian gesture." News of the success of this mission was heard around the world. Black Americans and the so-called "Third World" peoples were especially excited over Rev. Jesse Jackson's success. Hence, Rev. Jackson was able to endear himself in the popular sentiment of the black world community; and, consequently, a few of the old civil rights regime began to side with him. By and large, Rev. Jackson's primary support came from the black community generally rather than from the black leadership of the church and community.

Slowly, Rev. Jesse Jackson broadened his focus to some very sensitive issues in American politics. He challenged the presence of US Marines in Beirut, suggesting that the multinational force should be withdrawn and replaced by United Nations troops or other neutral forces. Like the experience of Rev. Martin Luther King, Jr., Rev. Jackson's shift in focus to very sensitive political issues resulted in a loss of popularity and increased hostility toward him from other national leaders.

As an ordained Baptist minister and associate pastor of the Fellowship Missionary Baptist Church in Chicago, Rev. Jackson viewed his quest for the presidency as a special mission. He remarked: "I want to inspire hope in our young people and let them know that America can offer them more than unemployment, dope, jails and the military."[86] Hence, he has taken a strong and unequivocal stance against nuclear proliferation and has discussed other issues especially sensitive to the political leadership of the United States.[87]

The presidential candidacy of Rev. Jesse Jackson apexed at the 1984 Democratic National Convention. He made a major address to the convention and world community. This was the first time that a black church leader attained such a unique opportunity to address such an audience on some of the great issues of the age. The full import of this event is yet to be realized in the life and vitality of the black church.

In summary, the role of Rev. Jesse Jackson and the earlier civil rights leaders of the black church tend to reflect a political sensitivity and involvement on the part of black church leaders in the practical issues of American life. They were not afraid to criticize the political leadership of the nation and the failure of such leadership to live up to basic American idealism. The concepts of freedom, justice, and humanity were foremost in the thought of these great and talented black church leaders. From among them came some of America's great statesmen. Seen in this light, the black church has been far more than just another religious institution. It has never really shied away from politics. Born in the political and social institution of slavery, the black church responded to and participated actively in the great political and social issues affecting black Americans.

# 6

# New Trends in
# Black Baptist Life

The most characteristic description of contemporary black Baptist life is *transition.* Everywhere in the life of the church, transition is the order of the day. This transition is resulting from tremendous changes in the religious, social, and political life of America. Black Baptists are caught in the tidal wave of unprecedented changes. In order to understand these mighty forces, a critical analysis of the causative factors precipitating the transition in black Baptist life is necessary.

One very significant stimulus of transition in black Baptist life is the impact of the civil rights revolution. One particular result is the change in the old southern ethos. The racism ethos of the South that once permeated the region, as well as other parts of America, is slowly changing under the pressure of new civil rights legislation, educational philosophy, and new styles of social intercourse between black and white Americans. To be sure, the old southern ethos is rapidly cracking, and its debris is seen falling slowly from the old walls of segregation and racial discrimination. New opportunities for black participation in the evolution of a new ethos for southern life and the broader American experience are apparent in most localities. This is seen as the fulfillment of prayers and dreams in black Baptist life.

On the political scene, black Baptists occupy some strategic positions in both local and national life. For example, Rev. Benjamin Hooks, former pastor of two Progressive National Baptist Convention churches, was elected in 1977 to serve as the executive director of the NAACP, following the retirement of Roy Wilkens. Previously, he served as a Federal Communication Commissioner (1972), banker, lawyer, judge, and civil rights activist. Reverend Hooks was the first black lawyer to be appointed by the governor to serve as a criminal judge in the state of Tennessee. Currently, Rev. Benjamin Hooks is one of the most influential black men in America. His expertise and strong personality are major factors in the vitality of the civil rights struggle. Under his leadership, the NAACP is increasing its momentum as a catalyst of social change.

Two other black Baptists need to be mentioned. They are Rev. Noel C. Taylor, mayor of Roanoke, Virginia, and Rev. Walter E. Fauntroy, delegate to Congress, House of Representatives, from the District of Columbia. The latter is head of the US Congressional Black Caucus. These men are good examples of black Baptists direct involvement in local and national politics. There are others in our national political life but these representative men stand out for their commitment to the improvement of the quality of life for all Americans. It is no wonder then that black Baptists throughout the nation take great pride in the contributions of these great preachers to the evolution of new life-styles in American civilization.

Moreover, the new open-minded spirit of regional and national life is resulting in new mobility trends in black Baptist life. One trend is the slow reversal of the historic migration of black Baptists to the North. Currently, blacks in general are taking a fresh look at opportunities the South offers to all creative and industrious-minded people. New industry is moving to the South, opening up opportunity for upward mobility in the economic life of the region. Concomitantly, the adverse impact of black migration on the life-style of black Baptist churches is slowly in transition.

Large numbers of black Baptists have decided to invest their future in the new southern ethos. They are taking a fresh look at themselves, their life-styles, and the new possibilities of Christian ministry. The result is twofold: new ministries within traditional black Baptist churches and a greater degree of cooperation and involvement in the life of white Baptist groups.

## Black American Baptist Churches, U.S.A.

Currently, there is a significant movement on the part of black Baptist churches to join white Baptist organizations. One clear example of this is the growth and development of the American Baptist Churches, U.S.A., in the South as well as in other parts of the nation. Black Baptist churches are developing a trend toward dual alignment with American Baptists and one of the traditional black Baptist national conventions.

The evolution of black American Baptists is of tremendous significance historically. To be sure, there has always been a significant number of black Baptist churches connected with the white Baptists of the North. The exodus of black Baptists from white churches in the North was not as radical as that of the southern ones. The color line was not so clearly drawn in the North. Hence, many of the northern churches chose to maintain a close affinity with white Baptists and, at the same time, relate to their own black church organizations. The number of such churches increased slowly well into the twentieth century. The statistical data in the minutes of the Northern Baptist Convention for 1926 reflects that there were 410 black Baptist churches with 116,137 members in the convention in 1925 and 627 black Baptist churches with 97,246 members in 1926.[1] These churches were located in twenty-three of the northern and northwestern states of the nation. In 1926, 323 of the 627 black Baptist churches aligned with the Northern Baptist Convention were located in the major cities of the North and the Northwest.[2]

By the middle of the twentieth century, the American Baptist Churches, U.S.A., experienced a gradual decline in white membership. Partly to offset such a decline in numbers, the convention launched a more aggressive program to increase its membership. The convention looked to the

South for new members. It also sought to attract more black Baptists from all regions of the nation.

The aggressive nature of the program for new members among American Baptists was successful. In 1977, the American Baptist Churches, U.S.A., had more blacks than any other denomination. The denomination's 1.6 million members included 200,000 blacks, or about 2 percent of the total.[3]

Recent statistical data of black Baptist membership in the American Baptist Churches, U.S.A., reflected a tremendous growth. There are about 800 black Baptist churches in the convention with a membership of approximately 400,-000. In the southern region, there are 200 black Baptist churches in the convention distributed in 17 states of the South and Southwest. This reflects a growth of 173 new black American Baptist Churches since 1926.

The most significant new trend has been the apparent success of American Baptists in the South. During the decade of the 1970s, the convention began a massive attempt to bring black Baptist churches into the American Baptist Churches, U.S.A. A committee of the Southern Caucus at the American Baptist Convention was appointed to organize the work of the American Baptist Churches in the South. This committee laid the groundwork for a new trend. For the first time, black Baptists and white Baptists in the South united to form a new regional structure within the American Baptist Convention (subsequently called American Baptist Churches, U.S.A.). By 1970, nearly one hundred black Baptist and white Baptist churches entered organic relationships with the convention. These churches came from a broad area of the South.

The American Baptist Convention took great strides to reflect the new southern life-style in the racial composition of the Committee on the Organization of the New Southern Region. Among the more influential black members of the committee were Rev. Kelly Miller Smith, pastor of the First Baptist Church, Capitol Hill, Nashville, Tennessee; Rev. Barry Hopkins of Richmond, Virginia; Rev. Marcus Garvey Wood, pastor of Providence Baptist Church, Baltimore, Maryland; and, Rev. LeRoy Jordan, pastor of the First Baptist Church, Tulsa, Oklahoma. The actual organizational meeting took place at the Myers Park Baptist Church, Charlotte, North Carolina.

The pioneer black Baptist appointed to steer the new regional experiment in black and white Baptists organic relationships was Rev. E. B. Hicks. He became the first executive minister of the American Baptist Churches of the South. Rev. E. B. Hicks brought to the region a new emphasis on the paramount importance of Christian education in the life of black Baptist churches. He, along with Rev. J. B. Henderson, the region's first president, developed workshops, stewardship programs, and mission projects of great vitality which were later to rival those of the traditional black Baptist organizations.

Rev. E. B. Hicks and other black American Baptists sought desperately to chart a course of complete cooperation between the races for this great experiment. Never before were white Baptists so richly challenged to share power at all levels of church life with their brothers and sisters in black. For some this was a welcomed trend, while others were forced psychologically to adjust to a new order of things in race relations. Initially, the task was made easier by the election of the first black man ever to head the national body of American Baptists. Rev. Thomas Kilgore, Jr., pastor of the Second Baptist Church, Los Angeles, California, was elected in 1971 to the presidency of the American Baptist Churches, U.S.A. He brought to the convention one of the most innovative programs ever attempted by black and white Baptists. This was the Fund of Renewal project—a joint effort with the Progressive National Baptist

Convention to raise seven million dollars to revive America's financially troubled black colleges. The new project was received enthusiastically by both black and white American Baptists. Similarly, the members of the Progressive National Baptist Convention responded favorably.

The southern region of the convention represents the most significant new trend in Baptist life. This region, as previously mentioned, is the real test of a noble experiment in black and white Baptist relationships. To be sure, progress has been made. But one of the most challenging developments to continual progress in the racial situation is the apparent tendency on the part of white American Baptists in the South to decrease their personal participation in the local and regional meetings. There is a conspicuous absence of white American Baptists. Several black American Baptists have become significantly critical of this new development. They realize that the southern region is slowly becoming another all-black movement. There is hope, however, that this new trend is only temporary. To a large degree, the future of the southern region may rest on the ability of black and white American Baptists to accomplish an authentic model of genuine racial cooperation and mutual respect for the person of the other human being.

## Black Southern Baptists

The rise of the "New South" ushered in a new day for black Baptist participation in the life of the Southern Baptist Convention. Beginning with the decade of the 1970s, black Baptists discovered some new doors of opportunity opened to them by the Convention. They were given a new status radically different from that of their forefathers of the antebellum South. Indeed, the "New South" has come to represent a radical departure from the segregation, discrimination, and violence of the "Old South." Fortunately, the

Southern Baptist Convention opened itself to the winds of change. The quality of participation on the part of black Baptists in the life of the Convention developed into unprecedented racial relationships in southern Christianity. This new precedent centered in the rapid transition from the radical paternalism of historic southern white Baptists toward blacks to the new trend of equality of participation in Southern Baptist life.

To be sure, the new trend in black and white relations in Southern Baptist life resulted largely in reaction to the civil rights revolution of the 1960s. Slowly, black Baptists made the transformation in racial awareness from "Negroes" to "black people." This new racial consciousness forced the Convention to rethink its work with black Baptists. Similarly, the ethical cries of Dr. Martin Luther King, Jr., and other black Christian social thinkers were particularly potent catalysts of change in Southern Baptist life. Consequently, Southern Baptists slowly transformed their Convention to meet the challenges of the post-civil rights revolution era.

A slow breeze of change was seen in the Southern Baptist Convention as early as 1956. That year, the Convention began drifting slowly from some of its old paternalism. This was seen in the change of name from the Convention's "Department of Negro Work" to the "Department of Work with National Baptists." The new name was designed to make Southern Baptists more aware of the need to cooperate "with" black Baptists of the three national bodies, each using the title "National Baptist." Baptists affiliated with each of these bodies were living in areas directly influenced by the Southern Baptist Convention. The decade of the 1950s also witnessed the entrance of the first black Baptist church in this century into Southern Baptist life.[4] Washington E. Boyce led the Community Baptist Church of Santa Rosa, California, to affiliate with the Redwood Empire As-

sociation, thereby becoming the first black Southern Baptist
church of this century in the United States.[5] Other churches
slowly followed the path of the Community Baptist
Church.

During the decade of the 1960s, Southern Baptists
made the bold step to elect the first black Southern Baptist
moderator of an association. Rev. William T. Vernon, a
black Southern Baptist, was elected moderator of a Southern Baptist association in Oakland County, Michigan. The
association consisted of thirty-nine churches, six of which
were black. During the crises of the civil rights revolution,
Rev. William T. Vernon as moderator of the local association, was able to unite several black and white Southern
Baptist pastors with other clergymen to become visible in
Pontiac, Michigan, to curb the riots. It was believed that
such visibility would tend to lessen racial tensions.

In 1973, the Home Mission Board of the Southern Baptist Convention assumed the bold stance of eliminating the
vestigial paternal perspectives by changing the name of the
Department of Work with National Baptists to the Department of Cooperative Ministries with National Baptists.

The emphasis became that of cooperation rather than
mere "unilateral" Christian philanthrophy from white Baptists to black Baptists. This trend recognized the quality of
black institutional potentials for mutual ministries. Consequently, this transition in philosophy opened the way for
black Baptists to be in mutual ministry with whites rather
than being recipients only. Black Baptists welcomed the
new style of ministry with Southern Baptists.

To be sure, the philosophical changes in Southern Baptist life were met with deep appreciation on the part of
many black Baptists. Historically, black Baptists experienced a strange tension in their relationships with
Southern Baptists. On the one hand, blacks, particularly
those in the South and Southwest, felt a close affinity to the

conservative theological stance of most Southern Baptists in the so-called "Bible Belt." But, on the other hand, they were estranged from Southern Baptists due to racism and paternalism. This constituted a dichotomous order of existence.

With the dawn of the new philosophy of "mutual Ministries," the relationships between black Baptists and Southern Baptists experienced a tremendous transition. The decade of the 1970s witnessed a significant increase of black Baptist participation in Southern Baptist life. The Convention witnessed a steady increase in black membership. By the latter part of the decade, Southern Baptists were able to report among their *95 Shocking Facts* the presence of "over 500 Southern Baptist black churches in the Southern Baptist Convention, and they are growing fast."[6]

Much of the pioneer work for this new trend in black Baptist and Southern Baptist relationships was done by Rev. Emmanual McCall. Rev. McCall, a native of Sharon, Pennsylvania, came to work initially with the Southern Baptist Convention as an associate secretary of the Home Mission Board's Department of Work with National Baptists. This position brought him into a new relationship with The Southern Baptist Theological Seminary, Louisville, Kentucky, where he became a visiting professor and coordinator of Black Church Studies. By 1975, Rev. Emmanual McCall had ascended to the prestigious position of director of the Department of Cooperative Ministries with National Baptists. He brought to this position a keen and penetrating mind on the historic relationships between blacks and Southern Baptists.

Rev. Emmanuel McCall and Rev. Edward Lorenzo Wheeler have brought a new vitality to the unique relationship of blacks and Southern Baptists. Rev. McCall articulated the three facets of the program of the Department of Cooperative Ministries with National Baptists in terms of cooperative ministry efforts with the three Black National

Baptist bodies, black church activities to help develop churches which are both Southern Baptist and black, and programs for racial reconciliation. These facets of the program have witnessed significant progress.

For example, the cooperative work through Southern Baptist agencies aides black Baptists in the fields of evangelism, Christian education, stewardship, and Christian citizenship. Specifically, the Convention provides scholarships for theological students; makes gifts to the American Baptist Theological Seminary for library development; cooperates with the National Baptist director of Baptist Student Union programs for college students; publishes literature especially relevant to black Baptists; promotes conferences, institutes, clinics, and workshops on evangelism in cooperation with state directors of cooperative ministries with National Baptists; employs black Baptist college students in Student Summer Mission Programs; and shares with state conventions and associations in providing missionaries for developing a Christian education program among rural black Baptist churches. These are some of the more successful ministries of cooperation between black Baptists and Southern Baptists.

These ministries of the Southern Baptist Convention are both the outgrowth and stimulus of growth in statistics among the Convention's black Baptists. Currently, there are black Southern Baptists in more than 3,500 Southern Baptist churches. There are approximately 200,000 black Southern Baptists in more than 500 predominantly black churches and an additional 50,000 in predominantly white churches.[7]

Moreover, the increased presence of black Southern Baptists bring some additional changes in the life of the Southern Baptist Convention. During the decade of the 1970s, black Southern Baptists assumed some strategic positions within the Convention. The state convention of Alaska elected two black Southern Baptist presidents.

California, Texas, Michigan, Kentucky, and Colorado elected several black Southern Baptists to the vice-presidency of their state conventions. In 1974, the Southern Baptist Convention elected a black Southern Baptist to the vice-presidency of the national body.[8] Currently, there are approximately two hundred black Southern Baptists serving various agencies of the Convention.[9]

Perhaps the key issue for the future of quality relationships between the racial groups will be the extent of progress in understanding and reconciliation rooted in the biblical concept of man "in Christ." There must emerge out of the encounter of black and white Southern Baptists a new anthropology free of the racial overtones of recent decades in the American religious experience. Rev. Edward L. Wheeler has cogently expressed the crucial nature for such a transition.

Racial reconciliation is not an option for the believing Christian; it is an obligation. As long as we are alienated we deny God's accomplished reconciliation in Christ and our professions of Christianity serve only to condemn us.[10]

Rev. Emmanuel McCall summarized the present state of relationships between black Baptists and Southern Baptists in words of a cautious optimism.

I think that we have come a long way. I definitely think we have made progress. We are a long ways from where we were, but we still have quite a ways to go.[11]

## Black Women in Ministry

Unremittingly, the winds of change or transition are pressing hard on the doors of all aspects of the institutional life among black Baptists. This is nowhere truer than in the response of black Baptists to the women's liberation movement. Pressed hard by the preponderance of women in local churches, black Baptists leaders are generally forced to take a fresh look at the role of women in ministry—both lay and clergy. Then, probably, the very fact that black Christians are generally interested in liberation movements around the world may also contribute to their response to the women's movement in America.

One of the most shocking signs of changes in the role of women in black Baptist life came in 1979 when the seventy-one-year-old Baptist Ministers Conference of Baltimore and Vicinity admitted, under the leadership of its President Rev. Vernon Dobson, women preachers for the first time to its membership. Admitted to the conference were Rev. Lydia Starks, pastor of the Fellowship Baptist Church of Baltimore, Rev. Minnie Robinson, associate pastor of Mount Lebanon Baptist Church of Baltimore, and Rev. Agnes M. Alston, associate minister of Gillis Memorial Christian Community Church of Baltimore. The shock signals were felt far and near in black Baptist life. Specifically, the Baptist Ministers Conference of Washington, D.C., and Vicinity severed its longtime relationship with the Baltimore conference in protest of the action of the latter. They believed that the Baltimore conference had made a radical departure from black Baptist faith and practice. The new trend in black Baptist life will inevitably affect other regions of the nation. Rev. Pettaway of the New England Baptist Convention admitted recently, while visiting the Baltimore conference, that the decision to admit women preachers "will be of assistance to him as his Conference is faced with the question of whether or not to ordain women."[12]

Once the initial door was open, women preachers readily applied for membership in the Baltimore conference. Presently, they are actively involved in the total life of the conference. The trend also expanded to the local churches. Black Baptist churches throughout the city of Baltimore began licensing and ordaining women in the ministry. Increasingly, these women are invited to do "women's day" services and other important worship experiences in the life of local churches.

Equally radical, the Saint John Baptist Church of Columbia, Maryland, announced in 1981 the ordination of women deacons. Rev. Hubert Eaton, pastor of the Saint John Baptist Church, led the congregation to ordain Ms. Gertrude J. Frank and Ms. Ester S. Vine to serve as the first women deacons in any black Baptist church. In a recent interview, Rev. Hubert Eaton offered his theological rationale for this action. He expressed that the call of God in Jesus Christ for persons to serve in the church is not a sexist call. Eaton went on to argue that all persons are called to the ministry and sexual gender has nothing to do with serving tables and nurturing people. Also, Rev. Eaton pointed out that the American Baptist Churches, U.S.A., were influential in helping the Saint John Baptist Church to make its decision to ordain women deacons.

The rise of Mrs. Gladys Williams Patterson to the presidency of the American Baptist Churches of the South was another high point in the response of black Baptists to the women's liberation movement. As a young adult, Mrs. Gladys Williams Patterson worked as president of the Matrons of First Baptist Church, Baltimore, Maryland, under the pastorate of her father. Soon her talents were recognized throughout the state and she became president of the statewide Matron's organization of the United Missionary Baptist Convention of Maryland. This was just the beginning of more extensive involvement in black Baptist life. The Maryland Area of the American Baptist Churches of the South bestowed upon her the rank of its highest offices, vice-president and president respectively. Subsequently, Rev. E. B. Hicks, executive minister of the region, influenced her to become the first woman president of the American Baptist Churches of the South.

During the presidency of Mrs. Patterson, the strides of the women's liberation movement were moderately felt. In a recent interview, she affirmed an allegiance to many of the traditional values of family life and role of women in society. She believes, however, that all women ought to receive equal rewards for equal work done with men in the general industrial life of the nation. Furthermore, she thinks that the overwhelming presence of women in black Baptist churches signals a greater involvement in congregational life.

Not quite so radical perhaps is the new trend toward programs of Christian education among black Baptists. There is a widespread tendency in many churches to organize boards of Christian education to facilitate new and creative ministries of Christian education. These boards are responsible for such ministries beyond the general scope of the traditional Sunday Schools and training programs. To be sure, the new educational trend is significantly affecting the life-style of black Baptist churches.

One further issue that necessitates changes in the institutional life of the black Baptists is the rise of middle-class black Christians. This is a matter of great concern on the part of many church leaders. Ms. Monzella Mitchel, writing for the *Journal and Guide* of Norfolk, Virginia, suggested that there is already a tremendous conflict between black clergymen in general and the middle class. She believes further that the real conflict begins beyond institutional lines. The initial arena of conflict is the struggle for leadership in the black community, a role traditionally monopolized by the clergy. Today, the middle-class blacks want to share this role with the clergy. Hence, they are conspicuous in such areas as political caucuses, black sociologists, doctors, and dentists organizations, and other activist and scholarly movements.

Again, Ms. Mitchell feels that the effectiveness of

clergy and black middle-class Christians lies largely in how well the "black church" will be able to absorb this emerging new class and utilize freely and responsibly their expertise and skills for the betterment of the black society and the world, while at the same time ministering to the spiritual needs of all its communicants, including the middle class, at a mature intellectual level.[13] As may be seen, some churches, particularly large urban churches, have displayed a remarkable creativity for integrating the black middle class into their total life-style. One particular joint ministry of the black clergy and their middle-class parishioners is the development of relevant programs to heal the black community of its tremendous social problems, that is, black-on-black crime, drug abuse, child abuse, and increased suicide rates. The clergy realize the valuable assistance of middle-class blacks in such action and educational ministries targeted at specific social problems. Such cooperative ministries hold tremendous potentials for the renewal of vitality in the life of the churches.

## The Ecumenical Movement

The pluralistic context of American culture and its encounter with blacks affords another potent challenge to traditional black Baptist life. More and more, we are facing new forms of Christian witness as well as the rise of other world religions in American culture. Everywhere there are new cults, denominations, and new faith movements encountering the life of blacks. Many of these movements tend to prey particularly on black Baptists. Black Baptist laymen seem especially vulnerable to these religionists because of their historic failure to be equipped educationally for meaningful dialogue with such groups.

In its more positive sense, the ecumenical movement is designed to facilitate greater unity or solidarity in Christian life and work throughout the world. The term *ecumenical* (from the Greek *oikoumene,* meaning "the inhabited earth") in recent Christian thought has been used as a synonym for "universal." Hence, the ecumenical church is the universal church. This may mean simply interdenominational cooperation or it may mean working toward the merging of all Christian bodies in a single world church. Especially for black Baptist leaders, the latter is not a tenable option. To be sure, Baptists in general tend to reject any organic unity with other denominations.

At the root of the ecumenical movement is the sharp contrast between the actual state of the church and the affirmation of all Christians that the church is in some sense "one" in Christ. Loyalty to Christ, according to the New Testament, means self-sacrificing love for one another and the transcending of those barriers which divide. Understood in this manner, the racial experiences of black Baptists in America tend to cause them to be more open to ecumenical winds than their white counterparts. The ecumenical movement is often viewed as another liberation movement and thus related to the goal of black liberation theology. On the other hand, white Baptists (Southern Baptists, in particular) are less inclined to respond to the ecumenical movement.

Nevertheless, the ecumenical movement is affecting northern black Baptists more readily than those of the South. The urban areas of the North are more characterized by religious pluralism. Baptists from these urban centers are in frequent contact with the institutional life, religious beliefs, and practices that are different from their own. Nevertheless, the migration of some of these black Baptists back to the South will greatly influence the spread of the ecumenical movement to southern churches. Already there are signs of such influence through southern contacts with the national bodies of black Baptists. All of the national church bodies of black Baptists are related directly or indirectly to those church movements which foster the ecumenical spirit: the Baptist World Alliance, the National Council of Churches, and the World Council of Churches.

In short, the social gospel emphasis of black Baptists tends to play a positive role in the spread of the ecumenical spirit in the life of the churches. One classic example is the recent National Black Pastors Conference held in Detroit, Michigan. This conference consisted of pastors from the major black denominations. They came together for the purpose of drafting a common agenda for the "black church" in the context of changing social and political winds in America and the world. Another factor affecting the spread of the ecumenical movement is the purchase of edifices from white Christians of other denominations. Obviously, the architectual styles of these edifices and the rich variety of artwork tend to influence the worship and thought of black Baptists. It is evident, then, that the ecumenical movement will increasingly affect the life-style of black Baptists in the future.

## Radical Religious Tradition

The evolution of the ecumenical movement and the turbulent transition of social and political values are forcing unprecedented changes in the life of black Baptists. To an alarming degree, the stability of a simple theological tradition that once permeated the life of an oppressed people no longer is as operative in the black Church experience. That rich theological tradition is almost gone with the winds of change. Accordingly, black Baptists find themselves pressed with the responsibility to redefine Christian theology in a changing cultural milieu.

Obviously, the church gradually came to the realization that it faces an age of unparalleled breadth, depth, and speed of change in science, economics, politics, and modes of living. The first signs of an awakening to these wordly issues came when black church leaders aligned themselves with liberal movements in American culture. This relationship gradually exposed the black church to vigorous debate and theological ferment of twentieth century white Christianity. All of these forces have gradually challenged the vitality of black Christian leadership.

Generally speaking, black Baptists are more readily affected by liberal movements in American culture because of their leadership role in the historic civil rights struggles. By and large, black Baptist leaders think of themselves as being the conscience or soul of the nation. The fact is, however, that they are slowly losing that elevated status to a spirit of accommodation to secular culture.

The signs of accommodation to secular culture are seen almost everywhere in the life of black Baptists. More and more, sermons and literary productions in the church's life tend to reflect little more than social treatises with religious overtones. In other words, the new theological emphases of black Baptists reflect a movement from the center of the gospel tradition to a social philosophy far beyond the religious thinking of the biblical prophets of God. Such sociopolitical issues as individual liberties, fair business practices, and equality before the law are emphasized with religious overtones.

Conversely, a large number of black Baptists are reacting against the trend toward secular religious tradition in their religious experience. They are becoming uncomfortable with the liberal leadership of some black theologians and church leaders. The radical announcement made by Thomas J. J. Altizer and William Hamilton that God has died in our time, in our history, in our existence, sent shock waves throughout black Baptist life. For the first time, some black leaders of liberal persuasion came to realize the danger of radical theology. Consequently, black theologians gradually came to realize that a new theology from the black perspective was necessary. Subsequently, a positive theological trend is slowly emerging which emphasizes the Living Lord of the church and His kingdom. This trend is gradually permeating black preaching, music, and prayers!

Moreover, black theologians such as Joseph R. Washington and James H. Cone, as previously mentioned, formulated an academic scheme for the development of "black theology." They believed that Christian theology must address itself to the unique black experience in American society. Specifically, the new theological orientation challenged two trends: secular religious tradition and racism in society at large.

But even so, many black Baptist leaders rejected black theology as another secular or worldly religious movement. They felt that it became a victim of the racism it sought to destroy. So viewed, Rev. J. H. Jackson, president of the National Baptist Convention, U.S.A., remarked:

> Our conception of the Christian Church and our idea of God must not be taken from the segregated and segregating policies of any white church; neither must we anchor our faith in blackness that has not enough virtue to save or redeem the lost among people of all classes and kinds, be they black or white, brown or red. I fear that religion which is so motivated by anti-white sentiment that it would make a god out of blackness and a savior out of the tenets and symbols of one's race.
>
> This is no time to develop a second-rate religion or a Christianity without Christ or a theology without a living God. It matters not how eloquent it might sound, a theology that substitutes pigmentation for divine principle is not sufficient to save any race or nation from sin. Our faith in ourselves as first-class citizens must be further established and proved by the deeds we perform, by the lives that we live, and by the notion of God that we proclaim.[14]

Judging from these remarks, Rev. J. H. Jackson tends to reject completely the relevancy of black theology in the life of black Christians. It might be justly argued that he fails to understand the nature and purpose of black theology.

In order to understand the nature and scope of black theology, it is necessary to view such a new trend in Christian theology as a transitional phenomenon. Black theology must address a particular era in Western religious life. It is immediately confronted by a dilemma: the current need for black Christians to accept a positive black consciousness for liberation from white racism and, at the same time, meet the higher need to go beyond pigmentation theology to a colorless and authentic concept of Deity. If black theology ties itself too closely with the worldly concerns of human pigmentation, then it runs the risk of devaluation into secular humanism. To be sure, pigmentation has nothing to do with how God relates to man in terms of ultimate reality.

The crucial task of black theology is, accordingly, the necessary attempt to separate pigmentation theologically from ontology. Rev. William A. Jones, pastor of Bethany Baptist Church of Brooklyn, New York, comes very close to such an emphasis in his recent book entitled *God in the Ghetto.* He affirmed:

> A simple, surface diagnosis of "The System" reveals a sick sociology based on a faulty anthropology, which emanates from a false theology. A man's attitude toward other men reflects the nature of his ultimate values.[15]

Actually, Rev. William A. Jones comes just a little short of drawing the theological implications of his assertions. He moves quickly to the sociopolitical significance of "color" in ghetto life. Again, this is the apparent failure of most black theologians. They tend to accommodate theology to culture.

Black theology has also the task of relating itself relevantly to ontology. This task may be partly reflected in the significance of apologetics in the black experience. There are some very pointed questions that must be raised by black theologians and church leaders before Christianity can be rightly understood by blacks. Do black people understand reality differently from whites? Is there a black revelation separate and distinct from a white revelation? Does pigmentation affect man's reason, wisdom, or methods of knowledge? Black theology must reject all such notions as perverted understandings of the nature and destiny of man. Yet, racism in American culture is saturated with such absurd beliefs. Hence, black theology must help all Americans to cross the bridge between absurdity in their theological orientation to an authentic ground or state of reality.

The liberation of men from racism is a task almost equal in importance to that of the salvation of the soul. For, indeed, there may be a slight relationship between the salvation of the "soul of black folk" and their liberation from the negative powers of color consciousness. It is always fallacious to relate color to the question of one's humanness. To the extent that black theology performs this task, it will ultimately overcome racial walls in the American religious experience. The credibility of the Christian religion will accordingly be established with a degree of finality.

## Creative Black Baptist Holistic Ministries

Significantly enough, black Baptists were pioneers among Protestant Americans in the development of holistic ministries. Long before the term *holistic* became popular in professional circles, black Baptists expressed a real concern for the total needs of black Americans. This was largely due to the unique significance of the social gospel in the life of the churches. As previously mentioned, black Baptist churches served as the neighborhood community centers for many black communities.

A rich variety of ministries consequently has emerged among black Baptists throughout the nation. Progressively, black Baptists came to realize that Christian ministry must reflect the full gamut of the human experience. This has developed into a holistic approach to ministry in some of the leading or model churches. Such areas as medical care, recreation, housing, counseling, problems of the aging, youth centers, business enterprises, food co-ops, credit unions, and other social ministries have found central positions in the scope of ministry among black Baptists. To be sure, black Baptists have concretized the social gospel rhetoric of the Christian church. A brief survey of such ministries may serve as models for other Christian groups.

One of the earliest pastors to develop a holistic ministry was Rev. William Homes Borders. The creative spirit of this black Baptist pastor was a powerful influence in the life of the late Dr. Martin Luther King, Jr. Serving as pastor of the Wheat Street Baptist Church of Atlanta, Georgia, he became one of the most noteworthy pastors of the denomination. He became widely known as "the Prophet of Wheat Street." This was a title given to him by his close friends in honor of the outstanding nature of his ministry.

Rev. Borders led the Wheat Street Baptist Church to develop a $12.5 million conglomerate: church buildings, housing project, retirement homes, and multiple services for his congregation.

The Wheat Street Baptist Church conglomerate now represents one of the most extensive and imaginative ministries in the Christian world. Specifically, the church operates a job placement center, a credit union with approximately a half million dollars on deposit, an Alcoholics Anonymous program, a $5.5 million dollar housing project (the first of its kind in the nation), voter registration drives, and encourages the operation of a black-owned shopping center in Atlanta. The black-owned shopping center is the direct result of the organizational mind of Rev. William Homes Borders.[16]

As early as 1953, the Second Baptist Church of Los Angeles, California, began the development of a holistic ministry under the creative leadership of Rev. J. Raymond Henderson. At that time, the church's ministry consisted of the Henderson Community Center with a day nursery, home for the aged, two dormitories for working girls, and a recreational building. Under the current leadership of Rev. Thomas Kilgore, Jr., the church has expanded its social ministries. A holistic ministry has indeed permeated the style of Rev. Thomas Kilgore, Jr., at Second Baptist Church.

In 1964, the Good Street Baptist Church of Dallas, Texas, one of the largest churches in the city, initiated its holistic ministry under the leadership of Rev. Caesar Clark. He was quite concerned about the housing needs of blacks in the city. Consequently, Rev. Caesar Clark led the church to purchase the Good Haven Apartments. The complex was completely renovated to include central air conditioning for 332 apartments. The project was financed under the 221 (d-3) program.[17] Significantly, the leadership of the church was not reluctant to utilize government funds for the development of its holistic ministry. Later, this became the acceptable trend in the creative ministries of other black Baptist churches.

The holistic ministries of black Baptists extended to reach the handicapped. One pioneer in this movement was Rev. William Thomas Ward. He led the Philadelphia Baptist Church of Los Angeles, California, to operate the first deaf and hearing church in the National Baptist Convention, U.S.A. Many of the handicapped of the city found their needs met through the creative ministry of the Philadelphia Baptist Church.[18]

The Calvary Baptist Church of Paterson, New Jersey, has developed a holistic ministry under the leadership of

Rev. Albert P. Rowe. The ministry of the church includes: Calvary Baptist Mini-Varsity, Calvary Baptist Federal Credit Union, Calvary Baptist Early Childhood Development Program, Calvary Baptist Creative Learning Center, Calvary Baptist Vocational Exploration Center, and other smaller social ministries.[19]

In 1974, the Friendship Baptist Church of Detroit, Michigan, dedicated a six-story nursing home. It was named the Friendship Manor Nursing Home. This creative ministry was developed under the leadership of Rev. Louis Johnson.

Currently, the Friendship Manor Nursing Home is a skilled nursing care facility designed to minister to 170 patients of any race, creed, or color. It also provides for a small number of children.[20]

In 1974, the Tabernacle Missionary Baptist Church of Chicago, Illinois, opened the Tabernacle Community Hospital and Health Center on the south side of the city. It was formerly the Evangelical Hospital of Chicago founded by the Evangelical Church. The Tabernacle Community Hospital and Health Center was the first all black, church-owned hospital in America. This ministry was developed under the leadership of Rev. Lewis Rawls. In 1974, the Standard Oil of Indiana Foundation contributed $60,000 to Rev. Lewis Rawls for the hospital.[21]

The Allen Temple Baptist Church of Oakland, California, has developed a significant holistic ministry under the leadership of Rev. J. Alfred Smith. The church has a Federal Credit Union, a Blood Bank, Counseling Center, Adult Day School, Big Brothers Program, an all-year Tutorial Program, Mini-Market for Senior Citizens, Senior Activity Center, Athletic Department, Spanish-Speaking Ministries, and the Allen Temple Housing Corporation. It has constructed on the East 14th Street of Oakland an apartment complex of seventy-five units for the elderly and eight apartments for the handicapped persons of the city.

Similarly, the Calvary Baptist Church of Jamaica, New York, has developed an extensive ministry to impact the economic development of blacks in the city. The Calvary Baptist Federal Credit Union earned a National Credit Union Association (NCUA) Thrift Honor Award for its success in stimulating savings among small savers. The credit union attained a monthly growth rate of 3.0 percent in share accounts. On June 30, 1977, the credit union has 752 members with total savings of $600,849. It was chartered in 1955 to serve the members of the Calvary Baptist Church and their immediate families.[22]

In 1979, Rev. Joy J. Johnson, pastor of the First Baptist Church of Fairmont, North Carolina, organized an Inter Racial Co-op. The new enterprise developed a program with authority to own, operate, manage, market, manufacture, lease, sell, or construct the following components: clergy apparel; church furniture, equipment, supplies, instruments, literature, and religious books; purchasing and leasing of clergy and church vehicles; insurance and real estate; construction of low and moderate income housing; professional church fund raising; speech research and writing; and group purchasing.[23]

In the decade of the 1970s, the First Baptist Church of Saint Louis, Missouri, organized the First Baptist Church Alcoholic Drop-In Center. The center was developed under the leadership of Rev. Benjamin Carroll, Sr. On Friday, July 30, 1976, the center received certification from the state of Missouri as a bona fide institution for helping those with alcoholic problems. This marked the first time in history that a church was certified in Missouri for such a program.[24]

Currently, the center is the only one of its kind. The prime purpose of the Alcoholic Drop-In Center is to help those who cannot help themselves. The clients receive counseling and alcohol education. The center is staffed by experts in the field and operates twenty-four hours Mondays through Fridays. Its program is varied to include: referrals, individual counseling, outreach, group counseling, tutoring, aftercare, outpatient, teenage care, and housing.

The ministry of Ebenezer Baptist Church of Atlanta, Georgia, is known internationally. Much of this world fame is due to the ministry of the late Dr. Martin Luther King, Jr., and the church's involvement in the civil rights revolution. The church attracts more national and international visitors than any other black church in America.

Ebenezer Baptist Church is a national shrine. Located near the Martin Luther King, Jr., Center for Social Change, the church has a special place in the religious and social life of Atlanta. This prestigious status helps to shape the ministerial style of the church. Under the leadership of Rev. Joseph L. Roberts, Jr., Ebenezer Baptist Church operates a Television Ministry, Ministry to International Students, Voter Registration Drive, and The Ebenezer Golden Age Resource Center (Adult Day Rehabilitation).[25] Also, the church sponsors political forums and supports other social ministries throughout the nation.

Finally, the largest and fastest growing church in Nashville, Tennessee, is the Temple Baptist Church. The church was organized by Rev. Michael Lee Graves in 1977 at American Baptist Theological Seminary in Nashville. Beginning with only two members, the church currently has over one thousand members with a budget of $265,000. The church owns twenty-eight and one-half acres of land in the city to be developed into a "new church campus."[26] It has the largest black Sunday School in Nashville. To be sure, the ministry of the church is creative and varied: an electronic church ministry, Temple Child Development Center, Temple Academy, and a singles ministry. Plans are being developed for cottages on the church campus for visiting guests and to provide emergency shelter for the needy.

## Black Baptists and the Moral Majority

Another significant trend in American life confronting black Baptist leaders is the moral majority movement. It has tremendous relevance to the historic role of black Baptists in the social and political life of America. Moral Majority leaders have captivated a similar role of involvement in American culture and developed a religious strategy of tremendous sociopolitical impact. This similarity of involvement is what constitutes a dilemma for most black Baptist leaders. They are aware that there may be elements in the movement that are positive on the one hand, and on the other there is a fear of potential racial overtones running through the mainstream of the movement.

The cardinal principles and strategies of the Moral Majority movement have been outlined by Rev. Jerry Falwell, president of Moral Majority, Inc. Each of these principles and strategies should be exposed to the test of reason in the context of the black experience in America.

The first basic principle of the movement as defined by Rev. Jerry Falwell affirmed:

We believe in the separation of church and state. Moral Majority, Inc., is a political organization providing a platform for religious and non-religious Americans, who share moral values, to address their concerns in these areas. Members of the Moral Majority, Inc., have no common theological premise. We are Americans who are proud to be conservatives in our approach to moral, social, and political concerns.[27]

America has had a long history of the doctrine of the separation of church and state. For the most part, all Baptists share in this basic concept of church and state relationships. However, black Baptists have been forced not to draw a radical line of separation between such basic institutions in American life. Black Baptists have developed a policy of direct involvement in all forces affecting the well-being of black peoples in the world.

So, there is a definite point of departure between the Moral Majority, Inc., and black Baptists relative to the separation of church and state. Black Baptists necessarily cannot accept any theory of a radical separation. It is for this reason that they do not see any contradiction in cooperating with federal and state agencies in the development of antipoverty programs. Involvement in such programs might be in the form of the operation of federal or state funded day-care centers, head start programs, or housing projects. Literally millions of dollars flow through church sponsored programs in the black community. Black Baptists view such ministries as both valid and desirable in their attempt to develop holistic ministries.

Conversely, there is a point of agreement in the first principle of the Moral Majority and black Baptists. Both agree that the conservation of moral values in American life is a basic concern and ministry of Christians. One valid criticism of black Baptist church life is its unbalanced concern with sociopolitical issues at the expense of some basic principles of biblical morality. For instance, black Baptists seem at times to be too involved in attempts to legislate morality. To be sure, laws are helpful but the primary law of the church must be that of love. Such must regain primacy in the preaching and teaching of black Baptists.

Equally important is the necessity of black Baptists to remind the Moral Majority of the significance of conservatism in American life. Conservatism as a sociopolitical concept has come to mean the preservation of the *status quo* of the "System" of materialism and oppression. At such point, black Baptists face the challenge of helping the Moral Majority to understand the inherent dangers of such concepts of conservatism. Conservatism so understood may very well involve the Moral Majority in the immorality they set out to oppose! If conservatism is understood, on the other hand, as the conservation or preservation of American values designed to enhance the quality of life for all of its citizens, then black Baptists may rightly join in the struggle for conservatism. The necessity for a fresh understanding of conservatism is urgent in all phases of life in America: religious, political, and social.

To some extent, the second basic principle of the Moral Majority surpasses the practical theological development of black Baptist life. Rev. Jerry Falwell again affirmed:

> We are pro-life. We believe that life begins at fertilization. We strongly oppose the massive "biological holocaust" which is resulting in the abortion of 1 1/2 million babies each year in America.[28]

The prolife stand of the Moral Majority is basic to the biblical understanding of life. Black Baptists should realize the centrality of life in the gospel tradition of the historic church. The church has a ministry of life!

Unfortunately, black Baptist leaders, for the most part, are not thinking through the tremendous moral issue involved in abortion. They are more concerned with the relationship between the population explosion and poverty in America. Hence, several church leaders have come out in favor of government-sponsored abortions for welfare recipients solely on economic grounds. They fail to come to grips with the tremendous moral issue of abortions. Even black theology fails to offer black medical professionals a moral frame of reference for decisions relative to human life. To this extent, it fails to serve the special needs of blacks who face such issues daily. As a matter of fact, it seems quite paradoxical for black theology to address so forcefully the issue of liberation yet fail to promote "the human and civil rights of millions of unborn babies."

To be sure, there are some authentic moral questions relative to the issue of abortions that are not at all simplistic. For instance, medical professionals are faced with a variety of valid questions: At what point does human life begin? What should be done when the life of the mother is at stake if the pregnancy should continue? or, Should the life of predetermined medical deficiencies in the unborn be allowed birth especially when such are irreversible? Such questions must be addressed by black theology. Black theologians and church leaders are challenged to apprise themselves with some of these medical variables and draw from them some moral implications. To be sure, this may be pioneer territory for all theologians and church leaders but a very necessary task of doing theology.

Perhaps the most significant principle of the Moral Majority is their "protraditional family" emphasis. If there is any issue of concern to blacks and their survival, it is the issue of the "black family." Several secular books by black sociologists occupy important places in American libraries. Yet the black Baptist churches are all but too slow in relating to the contemporary problems of black family life. There is a critical need for guidance from church leaders.

For instance, the Moral Majority movement has moved ahead of black Baptists in taking a stand on the moral implications or homosexual marriages and common-law marriages. Rev. Jerry Falwell argued:

> We believe that the only acceptable family form begins with the legal marriage of a man to a woman. We feel that homosexual marriages and common-law marriages should not be accepted as traditional family units.[29]

Both the issues of homosexuality and common-law

marriages affect the black community. These alternate life-styles are very visible within and without black Baptist churches. Black pastors tend to overlook quietly their prevalence in the life of congregations. Nevertheless, such issues are of tremendous moral significance and threaten both the moral and spiritual life of black Baptist churches.

Similarly, black Baptists are challenged to share with the Moral Majority a concern about pornography and the drug traffic in American culture. These two moral issues are pressing hard at the doors of blacks, especially those in urban areas. The negative impact of obscenity and vulgarity is especially acute in the socialization of black youth. Black churches everywhere are experiencing tremendous difficulties in holding youth. Pornography is one significant factor in turning young minds from the traditional moral and spiritual values of the church to the characteristic secularism of this age. The industry of pornography is contending with black churches for the minds of their youth. Hence, the leaders of black Baptist churches are challenged to develop a counterstrategy to ward off this attack on the minds of youth.

Perhaps, one of the most controversial issues in the dialogue between the Moral Majority and black Baptists is that of support to the state of Israel and the Jewish people internationally. There are some blacks who share with the Jewish people a common sense of struggle in the broader world community. They see Jews as a vital part of the world liberation movement. However, there are other black leaders who view the Jews as a part of their economic plight in American society. Hence, the existence of any anti-Semitism in the black community might be attributed to economic factors. But even so, black Baptists are challenged to learn more about the industrious spirit of Jews and apply some of the wisdom of the Jewish community to the economic development of blacks in urban areas. There is no legitimate place for anti-Semitism in the thought of black Baptists, but there is a place for mutual cooperation with Jewish people in liberation movements throughout the world.

Many black leaders have serious questions with reference to the Moral Majority's support of the military establishment in the United States. For the most part, blacks generally believe that military expenditures deprive them of essential antipoverty programs and government services.

In summary, there are some significant points of agreement on moral issues and radical difference on others between the leadership of black Baptist churches and the Moral Majority. They tend to agree only on those issues that do not reflect racial overtones. However, issues of sociopolitical significance to the unique needs or concerns of blacks are viewed differently between black Baptists and the Moral Majority. Nevertheless, there seems to be a valid need for dialogue between these two special interest groups in American life. To be sure, some of the tactics for social reform are similar in the life of the two groups. Each can learn from the other. For instance, black Baptists are well experienced in nonviolent revolutionary tactics. The challenge, then, is for both groups to utilize such tactics to fight revolutionary battles for moral values and sanity in this nation. It is therefore incumbent upon black Baptists to take on responsible leadership positions within any movement designed to call America to basic moral values of Christianity. Perhaps it might even be necessary for black Baptists to organize their own independent "moral majority" movement in America.

Black Baptists are a distinct part of the development of Christianity in America. A rich history and heritage are filled with stories of advance and decline, joys and sorrows, and growth toward denominational maturity. What will the future bring? I believe that details of the future will escape one who seeks to predict what will happen. Nevertheless, I am confident that black Baptists will continue to be involved in and make major contributions to the continuing growth and development of American Christianity.

# Notes

## Chapter 1

1. Daniel I. Rupp, *An Original History of the Religious Denominations at Present Existing in the United States* (Philadelphia: J. Y. Humphreys, 1844), pp. 42-43.

2. Ibid., p. 45.

3. Ibid., p. 47.

4. E. M. Brawley, *The Negro Baptist Pulpit: A Collection of Sermons and Papers on Baptist Doctrine and Missionary and Educational Work* (Philadelphia: American Baptist Publication Society, 1890), p. 11.

5. Davis Collier Woolley and others, eds., *Baptist Advance: The Achievements of the Baptists of North America for a Century and a Half* (Nashville: Broadman Press, 1964), p. 1.

6. Rupp, p. 49.

7. Ibid., p. 50.

8. W. D. Weatherford, *American Churches and the Negro: An Historical Study from Early Slave Days to the Present* (Boston: The Christopher Publishing House, 1957), p. 119.

9. Ibid.

10. Ibid., p. 121.

11. Ibid.

12. Ibid., p. 125.

13. Mary Burnham Putnam, *The Baptists and Slavery 1840-1845* (Ann Arbor: George Wahr, Publishers, 1913), p. 7.

14. Ibid.

15. Ibid., pp. 9-10.

16. Ibid., pp. 13-14.

17. Ibid., p. 16.

18. Ibid.

19. Ibid., p. 24.

20. Ibid., p. 17.

21. Richard Fuller and Francis Wayland, *Domestic Slavery Considered as a Scriptural Institution* (New York: Published by Lewis Colby, 1845), pp. 116-117.

22. Ibid., p. 119.

23. Weatherford, p. 131.

24. James M. Simms, *The First Colored Baptist Church in North America* (Philadelphia: Printed by J. B. Lippincott Company, 1888), p. 21.

25. Ibid., p. 22.

26. Weatherford, p. 117.

27. Ibid.

28. Ibid., p. 120.

29. Miles Mark Fisher, *A Short History of the Baptist Denomination* (Nashville: Sunday School Publishing Board, 1933), pp. 37-38.

## Chapter 2

1. Fisher, *A Short History of the Baptist Demonination* (Nashville: Sunday School Publishing Board, 1933), p. 39.

2. Carter G. Woodson, *The History of the Negro Church* (Washington, D.C.: The Associated Publishers, 1921), p. 85.

3. Souvenir Program of the 50th or the Golden Anniversary Celebration of the First African Baptist Church, Richmond, Virginia, April 29, 1928, p. 1.

4. Ibid., p. 5.

5. Charles H. Brooks, *Official History of the First African Baptist Church, Philadelphia, Pa.* (Philadelphia: Charles H. Brooks, 1923), p. 11.

6. James M. Simms, *The First Colored Baptist Church of North America* (Philadelphia: Printed by J. B. Lippincott Company, 1888), p. 59.

7. William B. Hesseltine, *The South in American History* (New York: Prentice-Hall, Inc., 1943), p. 163.

8. *The Negro Church in New Jersey,* comp. by James A. Pawley and Staff, supervisor of Social Problem Unit, 1938, p. 41.

9. Fisher, p. 40.

10. Ibid., p. 47.

11. J. F. Weishampel, *A History of Baptist Churches in Maryland Connected with the Maryland Baptist Union Association* (Baltimore: Printed and Published by J.F. Weishampel, Jr., 1885), p. 87.

12. Ibid., p. 87.

13. Charles Octavia Boothe, *The Cyclopedia of the Colored Baptists of Ala-*

# Notes

*bama: Their Leaders and Their Works* (Birmingham: Alabama Company, 1895), pp. 22-23.

14. Ibid., p. 28.

15. Jesse Laney Boyd, *A Popular History of the Baptists in Missi* son: The Baptist Press, 1930), p. 70.

16. Ibid.

17. Ibid.

18. Ibid.

19. Ibid., p. 112.

20. T. O. Fuller, *History of the Negro Baptists of Tennessee* (Memphis: Haskins Print-Roger Williams College, 1936), p. 27.

21. A. W. Pegues, *Our Ministers and Schools* (Springfield, Mass.: Willey and Company, 1892), pp. 48-51.

22. E. Franklin Fraizer, *The Negro in the United States* (New York: The Macmillan Company, 1957), p. 89.

23. *Inventory of the Church Archives of Virginia,* "The Negro Baptist Church In Richmond," (Richmond, Virginia: The Historical Records Survey of Virginia, June 1940), pp. 4-5.

24. Jeffrey R. Brackett, *The Negro in Maryland: A Study of the Institution of Slavery* (Baltimore: Johns Hopkins University, 1889), p. 177.

25. W. D. Weatherford, pp. 123-24.

26. "The Baptist and Slavery", *Social Science Quarterly,* December 1968, Volume 49, No. 3., p. 667.

27. The Ninth Annual Report of *The Historian,* National Baptist Convention, U.S.A., by L. G. Jordan, September 5, 1934., p. 18.

28. Ibid.

29. N. H. Pius, *An Outline of Baptist History* (Nashville: National Baptist Publishing Board, 1911), p. 64.

30. Ibid., p. 65.

31. L. G. Jordan, *Negro Baptist History, U.S.A.* (Nashville: The Sunday School Publishing Board, 1930), pp. 84-85.

32. Report of The Consolidated American Baptist Convention, 1872., p. 12.

33. Ibid., p. 19.

34. Ibid., p. 12.

35. Theodore S. Boone, *Negro Baptist Chief Executives in National Places* (Detroit: A. P. Publishing Company, 1948), p. 15.

36. Woolley and others, p. 202.

37. Pius, pp. 68-69.

38. Ibid., p. 73.

39. J. A. Whitted, *A History of the Negro Baptists of North Carolina* (Raleigh: Presses of Edward and Broughton Printing Company, 1908), p. 35.

40. Ibid., pp. 24-25.

41. *Minutes of The National Baptist Convention, U.S.A., Inc.,* 1922, p. 273.

42. *Minutes of The National Baptist Convention, U.S.A., Inc.,* 1933, p. 9.

43. Ibid., p. 273.

44. The Eighth Annual Report of the Historian made at The Fifty-Eighth Session of The National Baptist Convention, U.S.A., by L. G. Jordan, historian and general missionary, 1933., p. 9.

45. *Minutes of The National Baptist Convention, U.S.A., Inc.,* 1956., p. 64.

46. Ibid., p. 65.

47. *Minutes of the Progressive National Baptist Convention, U.S.A., Inc.,* 1975., p. 9.

48. Ibid.

### Chapter 3

1. Report of The Fifth Annual Meeting of The Consolidated American Baptist Convention, September 1871, pp. 14-15.

2. The Triennial Report or Thirty-Seventh Annual Report of the Consolidated American Baptist Missionary Convention, 1877, pp. 30-31.

3. Ibid., pp. 8-9.

4. Edward A. Freeman, *The Epoch of Negro Baptists and the Foreign Mission Board, National Baptist Convention, U.S.A., Inc.* (Kansas City, Kans.: The Central University Press, 1953), p. 110.

5. The Ninth Annual Report of the Historian, National Baptist Convention, U.S.A., Inc., by L. G. Jordan, 1934., p. 28.

6. H. F. Kletzing and W. H. Crogman, *Progress of a Race: Or the Remarkable Advancement of the Afro-American Negro* (Atlanta: J. L. Nichols and Co., 1898), p. 32.

7. G. I. Penn, *The United Negro: His Problems and His Progress* (Atlanta: The Lutheran Publishing Company, 1902), p. 310.

8. Freeman, p. 109.

9. Forty-Fifth Annual Report of the Foreign Mission Board of the National Baptist Convention, Inc., by J. E. East, September 9-14, 1925, p. 6.

10. Ibid., p. 8.

11. Kletzing and Crogman, pp. 380-81.

12. *The Mission Herald,* Vol. 12, No. 19, Louisville, Kentucky, October 1909, p. 3.

13. *The Mission Herald,* Vol. 23, No. 1, Philadelphia, Pennsylvania, March 1919, p. 1.

14. *The Mission Herald,* Vol. 37, No. 5., Philadelphia, Pennsylvania, September-October 1934, p. 7.

15. *The Mission Herald,* Vol. 73, No. 7., Philadelphia, Pennsylvania, Convention Issue 1970, p. 11.

16. Francis B. Watson, *The Native Liberian Missionary Field* (Washington, DC: Courant Press, Inc., 1956), p. 19.

17. Ibid., p. 1.

18. Ibid., p. 11.

19. Ibid., p. 19.

20. C. C. Adams and Marshall A. Talley, *Negro Baptists and Foreign Missions* (Philadelphia: The Foreign Mission Board of The National Baptist Convention, U.S.A., Inc., 1952), p. 49.

21. Maude J. Brockway, *Manual for Woman's Missionary Societies* (Nashville: The Sunday School Publishing Board, 1947), p. 72.

22. George Shepperson and Thomas Price, *Independent African: John Chilembwe and the Origins, Setting and Significance of the Nyasaland Native Rising of 1915* (Edingburgh: The University Press, printed in Great Britain by R. and R. Clark, L.T.D., 1958), p. 37.

23. *The Mission Herald,* Vol. 11, No. 12, Louisville, Kentucky, February, 1907, p. 4.

24. Ibid.

25. Shepperson and Price, p. 37.

26. Shepperson and Price, p. 116.

27. Ibid., p. 140.

28. Robert W. July, *A History of the African People* (New York: Charles Scribner's Sons, 1974), p. 446.

29. Shepperson and Price, p. 367.

30. C. C. Adams and Marshall A. Talley, *Negro Baptists and Foreign Missions* (Philadelphia: The Foreign Mission Board of The National Baptist Convention, U.S.A., Inc., 1952), p. 56.

31. *The Mission Herald,* Vol. 11, No. 12, February 1907, p. 4.

32. Ibid., p. 1

33. *The Mission Herald,* Vol. 15, No. 8, Louisville, Kentucky, October 1910., p. 4.

34. Forty-Sixth Annual Report of the Foreign Mission Board of the National Baptist Convention, U.S.A., Inc., by James E. East, 1926, p. 26.

35. Ibid.

36. Ibid.

37. Ibid., pp. 21-22.

38. Ibid., p. 22.

39. Ibid.

40. Robin W. Winks, *The Blacks in Canada: A History* (New Haven: Yale University Press, 1971), p. 1.

41. Ibid., p. 23.

42. Ibid., p. 31.

43. Fisher, p. 103.

44. James K. Lewis, *Religious Life of Fugitive Slaves and Rise of Colored Baptist Churches, 1820-1865, in What Is Now Known as Ontario* (New York: Arno Press, 1980), pp. 27-28.

45. Ibid., pp. 28-29.

46. Ibid., pp. 31-32.

47. Ibid., p. 39.

48. Winks, p. 340.

49. Ibid., pp. 345-46.

50. Ibid., p. 341.

51. Ibid., pp. 341-42.

## Chapter 4

1. Abraham Chapman, *Steal Away: Stories of the Runaway Slaves* (New York: Praeger Publishers, 1971), pp. 15-16.

2. Ibid., p. 17.

3. Ibid., p. 24.

4. I. Garland Penn, *The Afro-American Press and Its Editors* (Springfield, Mass.: Willey and Co., Publishers, 1891), p. 26.

5. Ibid., pp. 26-27.

6. Frederick G. Detweiler, *The Negro Press in the United States* (Chicago: The University of Chicago Press, 1922), p. 39.

7. Ibid., p. 45.

8. Penn, p. 108.

9. Ibid., p. 120.

10. Ibid., p. 142.

11. Ibid.

12. Ibid., p. 144.

13. Ibid., p. 164.

14. Ibid., pp. 194-96.

15. Ibid., p. 196.

16. Ibid., p. 218

17. Ibid., p. 258.

18. Detweiler, p. 18.

19. *Negro Population 1790-1915.* Department of Commerce Bureau of the Census (Washington, DC: Government Printing Office, 1918), p. 405.

20. *Journal of Negro Education,* Vol. 111, 1934, published by The College of Education, Howard University, Washington, DC, p. 174.

21. Ibid., p. 175.

22. Ibid., pp. 175-76.

23. *Baptist Home Missions in North America, Including a Full Report of the Proceedings and Addresses of the Jubilee Meeting, and A Historical Sketch of the American Baptist Home Mission Society 1832-1882* (New York: The American Baptist Home Mission Society, 1883), p. 402.

24. Ibid., p. 402.

25. Ibid., p. 403.

26. Ibid.

27. Ibid., p. 439.

28. Ibid.

29. Bonnie V. Winston, "Missionaries Began VUU to Educate Former Slaves," *Richmond Times-Dispatch,* Richmond, Virginia, Sunday, January 24, 1982, p. 5.

30. Ibid., p. 5.

31. G. F. Richings, *Evidences of Progress Among Colored People* (Philadelphia: Geo. S. Ferguson Company, 1900), p. 26.

32. Ibid., p. 26.

33. Ibid., pp. 26-27.

34. *Richmond Times-Dispatch,* p. 5.

35. Ibid.

36. John M. Ellison, "Policies And Rationale Underlying The Support of Colleges Maintained By The Baptist Denomination," *The Journal of Negro Education.* Vol. XXIX, No. 3, Summer, 1960, published for The Bureau of Educational Research, Howard University, by the Howard University Press, 1960, p. 335.

37. Whitted, p. 150.

38. *Baptist Home Missions in North America,* p. 443.

39. Ibid.

40. J. A. Whitted, p. 153.

41. *Baptist Home Missions in North America,* p. 443.

42. *Journal and Guide,* Norfolk, Virginia, April 25, 1914.

43. *To Redress the Balance: Report of the President: The Shaw University 1966-1967* by Dr. James E. Cheek, p. 6.

44. Ibid.

45. Ibid.

46. *Baptist Home Missions in North America,* p. 417.

47. Ibid., p. 448.

48. Ibid., p. 460.

49. Ibid., p. 458.

50. Richings, p. 57.

51. *Baptist Home Missions in North America,* p. 456.

52. Ibid.

53. Ibid.

54. *Encyclopedia of Southern Baptists,* p. 2082.

55. *Proceedings of the Southern Baptist Convention,* 1872, p. 24.

56. *Bulletin of the American Baptist Theological Seminary and the National Baptist Missionary Training School,* Nashville, Tennessee, 1940-1941, p. 9.

57. The Fourth Annual Address of Dr. L. K. Williams, president of the National Baptist Convention, September 8-13, 1926, p. 11.

58. Ibid., pp. 13-14.

59. Ibid., p. 14.

60. Ibid.

61. *Bulletin of The American Baptist Theological Seminary* p. 9.

62. *Encyclopedia of Southern Baptists,* p. 2081.

63. Richings, pp. 47-48.

64. Ibid., p. 49.

65. *The Expected,* ed. M. C. Allen, September 1942, p. 12.

66. *Negro Population, 1790-1915,* p. 404.

67. Richings, p. 284.

68. Ibid., p. 343.

69. Booker T. Washington, *An Autobiography* (Atlanta: J. L. Nichols and Company, 1901), pp. 93-94.

70. Ibid.

71. Ibid., p. 70.

72. Ibid., pp. 138-39.

73. Ibid., p. 236.

74. Ibid., pp. 98-99.

75. John M. Ellison, "Policies and Rationale Underlying the Support Colleges Maintained by The Baptist Denomination," *The Journal of Negro Education,* Vol. XXIX, No. 3 (Summer 1960). Published for the Bureau of Educational Research, Howard University, Washington, DC, p. 337.

76. Ibid.

77. Ibid., p. 338.

## Chapter 5

1. *Report of the Joint Committee on Reconstruction at the First Session Thirty-Ninth Congress* (Washington, D.C.: Government Printing Office, 1866), p. 53.

2. Ibid.

3. Noah Davis, *Narratives of the Life of Reverend Noah Davis: A Colored Man* (Baltimore: Printed Solely for the Author's Benefit, 1859), p. 77.

4. *The Annual Cyclopedia and Register of Important Events of the Year 1861* (New York: D. Appleton and Company, 1862), pp. 128-29.

5. Charles S. Spivey, *A Tribute to the Negro Preacher and Other Sermons and Addresses* (Wilberforce, Ohio: Eckerle Printing Company, 1942), p. 5.

6. Ibid., p. 11.

7. Ibid., p. 10.

8. *The American Annual Cyclopedia and Register of Important Events of the Year 1868*, Vol. VIII (New York: D. Appleton and Company, 1869), p. 125.

9. *Report of the Joint Committee on Reconstruction at the First Session Thirty-Ninth Congress* (Washington, DC: Government Printing Office, 1866), preface page vii.

10. Ibid., p. 134.

11. Ibid., p. 138.

12. Ibid., pp. 28-29.

13. Ibid., p. 16.

14. Ibid., p. 62.

15. Ibid., pp. 148-49.

16. Ibid., p. 56.

17. Ibid., p. 60.

18. *Report of the Triennial Meeting and the Thirty-seventh Annual Meeting of the Consolidated American Baptist Convention* (Brooklyn: Consolidated Convention, 1877), pp. 19-20.

19. *Report of the Twenty-Ninth Annual Meeting of the Consolidated American Baptist Missionary Convention*, 22 Sept. 1869, p. 3.

20. *Report of the Thirty-Second Annual Meeting of the Consolidated American Baptist Missionary Convention*, 1872, pp. 27-28.

21. Charles H. Otken, *The Ills of the South or Related Causes Hostile to the General Prosperity of the Southern People* (New York: G. P. Putnam's Sons, 1894), pp. 6-7.

22. Harvey Johnson, "A Plea for Our Work as Colored Baptists, Apart from Whites," 14 Sept. 1897 (Baltimore: The Afro-American Printers, 1897), pp. 11-12.

23. Harvey Johnson, "The Hamite—The Only Historical Nation," *The*

*Expected,* ed. by M. C. Allen (Baltimore, July 1943), Vol. 13, No. 7, pp. 12-13.

24. Garland I. Penn, *The United Negro: His Problems and His Progress* (Atlanta: The Lutheran Publishing Company, 1902), pp. 522-23.

25. William B. Reed, "Echoes of the Emancipation Proclamation" (Published by W. B. Reed, Madison, N.J., December 13, 1908), pp. 21-23.

26. William B. Reed, "State of Country Address" delivered before the New England Baptist Convention, Forty-Second Session at Second Baptist Church, Philadelphia, Pennsylvania, 1916, pp. 22-24.

27. Ibid., p. 12.

28. L. B. Brooks, "State of Country," New England Baptist Convention, 1922, p. 16.

29. Ibid.

30. Ibid., p. 10.

31. Ibid., p. 11.

32. Ibid., p. 21.

33. Robert H. Brisbane, *The Black Vanguard, Origins of the Negro Social Revolution 1900-1960* (Valley Forge: Judson Press, 1970), p. 61.

34. Ibid.

35. *Minutes of The National Baptist Convention, U.S.A., Inc.,* 1924, pp. 97-98.

36. *Minutes of the New England Baptist Missionary Convention,* 1936, p. 17.

37. *Minutes of The National Baptist Convention, U.S.A., Inc.,* 1924.

38. Ibid., p. 301.

39. W. J. Winston, "Disfranchisement Makes Subject Citizens Targets for the Mob and Disarms Them in the Court of Justice" (Baltimore: Varsity Press, undated manuscript), pp. 4-10.

40. *Minutes of The National Baptist Convention, U.S.A., Inc.,* 1924, p. 293.

41. L. K. Williams, "Annual Address to the National Baptist Convention, U.S.A., Inc.," 1923, p. 17.

42. *Minutes of The National Baptist Convention, U.S.A., Inc.,* 1922, p. 52.

43. Ibid., pp. 63-64.

44. W. B. Reed, "The 1919 State Of Country," New England Baptist Convention (Newport, RI: Mercury Publishing Company, 1919), pp. 5-7.

45. *Minutes of The National Baptist Convention, U.S.A., Inc.,* 1938, p. 100.

46. *Minutes of The New England Baptist Missionary Convention,* 1942, p. 31.

47. *Minutes of The National Baptist Convention, U.S.A., Inc.,* 1941, p. 52.

48. Ibid.

49. *Minutes of The National Baptist Convention, U.S.A., Inc.,* 1944, pp. 267-68.

50. Fred C. Shapiro and James W. Sullivan, *Race Riots New York 1964* (New York: Thomas Y. Crowell Company, 1964), pp. 17 *ff.*

51. David M. Alpern, "The Black Revolution's Adam," *Newsweek,* Vol. 79, 17 April 1972, p. 32.

52. Roy Wilkins, "Adam Powell: A Black Appraisal," *New York Times,* 28 April 1972, p. 41.

53. *Congressional Record,* Vol. 109, Part 2, 88th Congress, 1st Session, 1963, p. 20519.

54. Ibid.

55. Ibid., p. 20520.

56. Ibid., p. 20521.

57. Ibid.

58. Ibid., p. 20519.

59. Ibid., p. 20526.

60. Ibid., p. 20519.

61. Ibid., p. 20524.

62. Ibid., p. 20519.

63. Ibid.

64. Ibid., p. 20520.

65. Ibid.

66. Ibid., p. 20522.

67. Ibid., p. 20523.

68. Ibid.

69. Ibid., p. 20524.

70. Ibid., p. 20525.

71. Ibid.

72. Ibid., p. 20526.

73. Ibid.

74. Ibid., p. 14293.

75. Richard Harwood, "Harlem's Rep. Adam Clayton Powell: There Is Nothing Ordinary About Him," *Washington Post,* April 1972, p. 1.

76. Edward Guinan, *Peace and Nonviolence* (New York: Paulist Press, 1973), pp. 122-23.

77. William Brink and Louis Harris, *The Negro Revolution In America* (New York: Simon and Schuster, 1963), p. 80.

78. Ibid., p. 104.

79. Ibid., p. 105.

80. Martin Luther King, Jr., *Stride Toward Freedom: The Montgomery Story* (New York: Harper and Brothers, 1958), p. 95.

81. Coretta Scott King, *My Life with Martin Luther King, Jr.* (New York: Holt, Rinehart and Winston, 1969), p. 57.

82. Ibid., p. 243.

83. Lucius J. Baker and Twiley W. Baker, Jr., *Freedom, Courts, Politics: Studies in Civil Liberties* (Englewood Cliffs, N.J.: Prentice-Hall, Inc., 1972), p. 238.

84. *U.S. News and World Report,* 1969, p. 60.

85. *Journal and Guide,* Dec. 15, 1982, p. 8.

86. *Chocolate Singles,* Vol. 3, No. 5, March 1984, p. 12.

87. Ibid.

### Chapter 6

1. Annual of the Northern Baptist Convention, Washington, D.C., 1926, p. 215.

2. Ibid., p. 174.

3. *Baptist Progress,* Progressive National Baptist Convention, Vol. 12, No. 1, Fall Issue 1977, p. 2.

4. W. T. Moore, *His Heart Is Black* (Atlanta: The Home Mission Board, Southern Baptist Convention, 1978), pp. 72-73.

5. *Ebonicity,* Vol. 1, No. 1, Summer, 1982, quarterly publication of the Ethnic Liaison Unit of the Baptist Sunday School Board, SBC, Nashville, TN, p. 6.

6. *95 Shocking Facts* (Atlanta: The Home Mission Board, Southern Baptist Convention).

7. *Ebonicity,* p. 6.

8. Ibid.

9. See ibid. for the names of some of these black Baptist employees.

10. *Removing Barriers Through Cooperative Ministries With National Baptists* (Atlanta: The Home Mission Board, Southern Baptist Convention, 1975), p. 7.

11. Quoted in Dan Martin, *A Road to Reco: The Human Touch in Cooperative Ministries with National Baptists* (Atlanta: The Home Mission Board, Southern Baptist Convention, 1979), pp. 7-8.

12. *African-American News And World Report,* Baltimore, Maryland, 8 July 1979, Vol. 1., No. 21, p. 8.

13. *Journal and Guide,* Norfolk, Virginia, Wednesday, August 12, 1981, p. 11.

14. Annual Address of President J. H. Jackson Delivered at the One

Hundredth Annual Session of the National Baptist Convention, U.S.A., Inc. September 11, 1980, p. 24.

15. William A. Jones, Jr., *God in the Ghetto* (Elgin, Ill.: Progressive Baptist Publishing Board, 1979), p. 13.

16. James W. English, *The Prophet of Wheat Street* (Elgin, Ill.: David C. Cook Publishing Co., 1973), pp. 79-80,85,106-109,122-24.

17. Souvenir Journal of the National Baptist Convention, U.S.A., Inc. 1971, p. 71.

18. The Official Program of the 93rd Annual Session of the National Baptist Convention, U.S.A., Inc., 1973.

19. Fourteenth Annual Session Progressive National Baptist Convention, Inc., 1975 (pages not numbered).

20. *Baptist Progress,* PNBC, Vol. 8, No. 2, Winter Issue 1974, p. 4.

21. *Baptist Progress,* PNBC, Vol. 8, No. 1, Fall Issue 1973, p. 8.

22. *Baptist Progress,* PNBC, Vol. 12, No. 4, 1978, p. 7.

23. *Baptist Progress,* PNBC, Vol. 13, No., 3, Jan., Feb. 1979, p. 7.

24. Reprint from the *Saint Louis American,* Thursday, 12 Aug. 1976.

25. Annual Report, Ebenezer Baptist Church, Atlanta, Ga., 4 Dec. 1981, pp. 9-18.

26. Fifth Founder's Day Observance, Temple Baptist Church, Nashville, Tenn., 1 Aug. 1982.

27. Jerry Falwell, "They Have Labeled Moral Majority the Extreme Right Because We Speak Out Against Extreme Wrong!" *News and Observer,* Raleigh, NC, 26 April 1981, p. 18.

28. Ibid.

29. Ibid.

# Bibliography

Adams, C. C. and Talley, Marshall A. *Negro Baptists and Foreign Missions.* Philadelphia: The Foreign Mission Board of the National Baptist Convention, U.S.A., Inc., 1952.

Alpern, David M. "The Black Revolution's Adam," *Newsweek,* Vol. 79, April 17, 1972.

*Baptist Home Missions in North America: Including a Full Report of the Proceedings and Addresses of the Jubilee Meeting, and a Historical Sketch of the American Baptist Home Mission Society 1832-1882.* New York: The American Baptist Home Mission Society, 1883.

*Baptist Progress.* Progressive National Baptist Convention.

Boone, Theodore S. *Negro Baptist Chief Executives in National Places.* Detroit: A. P. Publishing Company, 1948.

Boothe, Charles Octavis. *The Cyclopedia of Colored Baptists of Alabama.* Birmingham: Alabama Publishing Company, 1895.

Boyd, Jesse Laney. *A Popular History of the Baptists of Mississippi.* Jackson: The Baptist Press, 1930.

Brackett, Jeffrey R. *The Negro in Maryland: A Study of the Institution of Slavery.* Baltimore: Johns Hopkins University, 1889.

Brinks, William and Harris, Louis. *The Negro Revolution in America.* New York: Simon and Schuster, 1963.

Brisbane, Robert H. *The Black Vanguard: Origins of the Negro Social Revolution 1900-1960.* Valley Forge: Judson Press, 1970.

Brockway, Maude J. *Manual for Women's Missionary Societies.* Nashville: The Sunday School Publishing Board, 1947.

Brooks, Charles H. *Official History of the First African Baptist Church Philadelphia, Pa.* Philadelphia: Charles H. Brooks, 1923.

Brooks, L. B. "State of Country." New England Baptist Convention, 1922.

Chapman, Abraham. *Steal Away: Stories of the Runaway Slaves.* New York: Praeger Publishers, 1971.

Cone, James H. *Black Theology and Black Power.* New York: The Seabury Press, 1969.

*Congressional Record,* 88th Cong., 1st sess., 1963, 109, pt. 2.

Davis, Noah. *Narratives of the Life of Reverend Noah Davis, A Colored Man.* Baltimore: Printed Solely for the Author's Benefit, 1859.

Detweiler, Frederick G. *The Negro Press in the United States.* Chicago: The University of Chicago Press, 1922.

East, James E. "Report of the Foreign Mission Board of the National Baptist Convention, U.S.A., Inc.," 1925, 1926.

*Ebonicity.* Vol. 1, No. 1, 1982. Quarterly publication of the Ethnic Liaison Unit, Sunday School Board of the Southern Baptist Convention.

*Encyclopedia of Southern Baptists.* 4 volumes. Nashville: Broadman Press, 1958, 1971, 1982.

English, James W. *The Prophet of Wheat Street.* Elgin, Ill.: David C. Cook Publishing Co., 1973.

Fisher, Miles Mark. *A Short History of the Baptist Denomination.* Nashville: Sunday School Publishing Board, 1933.

Frazier, E. Franklin. *The Negro in the United States.* New York: New York: The Macmillan Company, 1957.

Freeman, Edward A. *The Epoch of Negro Baptists and the Foreign Mission Board, National Baptist Convention, U.S.A., Inc.* Kansas City, Kans.: The Central University Press, 1953.

Fuller, T. O. *History of the Negro Baptists of Tennessee.* Memphis: Haskins Print, Roger Williams College, 1936.

Garrett, James L., ed. *Baptist Relations with Other Christians.* Valley Forge: Judson Press, 1974.

Harwood, Richard. "Harlem's Rep. Adam Clayton Powell: There Is Nothing Ordinary About Him." *Washington Post,* April 1972.

Hesseltine, William B. *The South in American History.* New York: Prentice-Hall, Inc., 1943.

*Inventory of the Church Archives of Virginia.* "The Negro Baptist Church in Richmond." Richmond: The Historical Records Survey of Virginia, June 1940.

Jackson, J. H. *A Story of Christian Activism: The History of the National Baptist Convention, U.S.A., Inc.* Nashville: Townsend Press, 1980.

_____. *Unholy Shadows and Freedom's Holy Lights.* Nashville: Nashville: Townsend Press, 1967.

Johnson, Harvey. "A Plea for Our Work as Colored Baptists, Apart from Whites." Baltimore: The Afro-American Printers, 1897.

_____. "The Hamite—The Only Historical Nation." *The Expected,* ed. by M. C. Allen. Baltimore: n.p., 1943.

Jones, William A., Jr. *God in the Ghetto.* Elgin, Ill.: Progressive Baptist Publishing House, 1979.

Jordan, L. G. *Negro Baptist History, U.S.A.* Nashville: The Sunday School Publishing Board, 1930.

_____. *The Eighth Annual Report of the Historical National Baptist Convention, U.S.A., Inc.,* 1933.

_____. *The Ninth Annual Report of the Historical National Baptist Convention, U.S.A., Inc.,* 1934.

July, Robert W. *A History of the African People.* New York: Charles Scribner's Sons, 1974.

Kletzing, H.F. and Crogman, W. H. *Progress of a Race or the Remarkable Advancement of the Afro-American Negro.* Atlanta: J. L. Nichols and Co., 1898.

Lewis, James K. *Religious Life of Fugitive Slaves and Rise of Colored Baptist Churches, 1820-1865, in What Is Now Known as Ontario.* New York: Arno Press, 1980.

McCall, Emmanuel L. *The Black Christian Experience.* Nashville: Broadman Press, 1972.

*Minutes of the Consolidated American Baptist Convention,* September 1869, 1871, 1872, 1877.

*Minutes of the National Baptist Convention, U.S.A., Inc.,* 1922, 1924, 1933, 1938, 1941, 1944, 1956.

*Minutes of the Progressive National Baptist Convention, 1975.*

*Minutes of the New England Baptist Convention, 1924, 1936, 1942.*

Moore, W. T. *His Heart Is Black.* Atlanta: Home Mission Board of the Southern Baptist Convention, 1978.

Moyd, Olin P. *Redemption in Black Theology.* Valley Forge: Judson Press, 1979.

*Negro Population 1790-1915.* Department of Commerce Bureau of the Census. Washington: Government Printing Office, 1918.

Otken, Charles H. *The Ills of the South or Related Causes Hostile to the General Propserity of the Southern People.* New York: G. P. Putnam's Sons, 1894.

Pegues, A. W. *Our Ministers and Schools.* Springfield, Mass.: Willey and Company, 1892.

Penn, Garland I., *The United Negro: His Problems and His Progress.* Atlanta: The Lutheran Publishing Company, 1902.

_____. *The Afro-American Press and Its Editors.* Springfield, Mass.: Willey and Company, 1891.

Pius, N. H. *An Outline of Baptist History.* (Nashville: National Baptist Publishing Board, 1911.

Reed, William B. "Echoes of The Emancipation Proclamation." Madison, N.J.: W. B. Reed, 1908.

_____. "State of Country Address." Philadelphia: New England Baptist Convention, 1916.

*Report of the Joint Committee on Reconstruction at the First Session Thirty-Ninth Congress.* Washington: Government Printing Office, 1866.

*Review and Expositor.* Vol. LXX, No. 3. Louisville: The Southern Baptist Theological Seminary, Summer 1973. Theme of this issue: "The Black Experience and the Church."

Richings, G. F. *Evidences of Progress Among Colored People.* Philadelphia: Geo. S. Ferguson Co., 1896.

Rupp, I. Daniel. *An Original History of the Religious Denominations at Present Existing in the United States.* Philadelphia: N.Y.: Humphreys, 1844.

Shepperson, George and Price, Thomas. *Independent Africa: John Chilembwe and the Origins, Setting and Significance of the Nyasaland Native Rising of 1915.* Edinburgh: The University Press, 1958.

Simms, James M. *The First Colored Baptist Church in North America.* Philadelphia: J. B. Lippincott Company, 1888.

Smith, J. Alfred, ed. *The Church in Bold Mission; A Guidebook on Black Church Development.* Atlanta: Home Mission Board of the Southern Baptist Convention, 1977.

*Social Science Quarterly.* Vol. 49, No. 3, December 1968. "The Baptists and Slavery: An Examination of the Origin and Benefits of Segregation."

Souvenir Program of the 50th or the Golden Anniversary Celebration of the First African Baptist Church, Richmond, Virginia. Sunday, April 29, 1928.

Spivey, Charles A. *A Tribute to the Negro Preacher and Other Sermons and Addresses.* Wilberforce, Ohio: Eckerle Printing Company, 1942.

*The Annual Cyclopedia and Register of Important Events of the Year 1861.* New York: D. Appleton and Company, 1862.

*The Expected.* M. C. Allen, ed. 1942.

*The Mission Herald,* 1907, 1910, 1919, 1934, 1970.

*The Negro Church in New Jersey.* Compiled by James A. Pawley and Staff. Supervisor of Social Problem Unit, Negro Adult Education, 1938.

*U.S. News and World Report,* 1969.

Washington, Joseph R., Jr. *Black Religion: The Negro and Christianity in the United States.* Boston: Beacon Press, 1964.

Watson, Francis B. *The Native Liberian Missionary Field.* Washington: Courant Press, Inc., 1956.

Weatherford, W. D. *American Churches and the Negro: An Historical Study from Early Slave Days to the Present.* Boston: The Christopher Publishing House, N.D.

Weishampel, J. F. *A History of Baptist Churches in Maryland Connected with the Maryland Baptist Union Association.* Baltimore: Printed and Published by J. F. Weishampel, Jr., 1885.

Whitted, J. A. *A History of the Negro Baptists of North Carolina.* Raleigh: Presses of Edward and Broughton Printing Co., 1908.

Wilkins, Roy. "Adam Powell: A Black Appraisal." *New York Times,* April 28, 1972.

Williams, L. K. "Annual Address to the National Baptist Convention, U.S.A., Inc., 1923.

Winks, Robin W. *The Blacks in Canada: A History.* New Haven: Yale University Press, 1971.

Winston, W. J. "Disfranchisement Makes Subject Citizens Targets for the Mob and Disarms Them in the Courts of Justice." Baltimore: Varsity Press, undated manuscript.

Wittig, Glenn R., ed. *Radical Theology: Phase Two Essays on the Current Debate.* New York: J. B. Lippincott Company, 1967.

Woodson, Carter G. *The History of the Negro Church.* Washington: The Associated Publishers, 1921.

Woolley, Davis C. and others. *Baptist Advance.* Nashville: Broadman Press, 1964.

# Historical Documents

*[This material is from "Report of the Joint Committee on Reconstruction" at the first session of the Thirty-Ninth Congress (Washington: Government Printing Office, 1866).]*

WASHINGTON, *February* 3, 1866.

Madison Newby (colored) sworn and examined.

By MR. HOWARD:

Question. Have you any white blood in you?

Answer. No, sir.

Question. Where were you born?

Answer. In Surrey county, Virginia.

Question. How old are you?

Answer. Thirty-three.

Question. Can you read and write?

Answer. I cannot write; I can read a little.

Question. Can you read the Testament?

Answer. A little.

Question. Have you a family?

Answer. Yes, sir.

Question. Have you been a slave before the war?

Answer. No, sir; I never was a slave.

Question. How do the rebel white people treat you since the war?

Answer. They do not allow me to go where I came from, except I steal in there.

Question. Why not?

Answer. They say I am a Yankee. I have been there, but was driven away twice; they said I would not be allowed to stay there, and I had better get away as quick as possible. I had gone down to look after my land.

Question. Do you own land there?

Answer. Yes.

Question. How much?

Answer. One hundred and fifty acres.

Question. Did you pay for it?

Answer. Yes.

Question. Do you stand in fear of the rebel white men?

Answer. Yes, sir, I do. If all the Union men that are down there would protect us we would not be so much afraid. I went down there to pay my taxes upon my land, but I could not see any person to pay them to; I didn't want to pay any but the United States government; and finally, they told me at the court-house that I had better let it alone until I could see further about it.

Question. What is your land worth?

Answer. I gave $700 for it.

Question. Is there a house on it?

Answer. Yes.

Question. Do the colored people down there love to work?

Answer. They work if they can get anything for it; but the rebel people down there who have got lands will not let the colored people work unless they work for their prices, and they drive them away. They expect colored people down there to work for ten or eighteen cents a day. Six or eight dollars a month is the highest a colored man can get; of course he gets his board, but he may have a family of six to support on these wages, and of course he cannot do it.

Question. How do you get your living?

Answer. I am living in Norfolk at present. I piloted the Union forces there when they first came to Surrey; and afterwards the rebels would not let me go back.

Question. Were you impressed by the Union forces, or did you voluntarily act as a guide?

Answer. I was impressed. I told the Union forces when they came that unless they were willing to protect me I did not want them to take me away, because my living was there; and they promised they would see to me.

Question. Did they pay you for your services?

Answer. No, sir.

Question. They gave you enough to eat and drink?

Answer. They gave me plenty to eat when I was travelling, but nothing to drink except water.

Question. Now that the blacks are made free, will they not, if left to themselves without the protection of the whites, become strollers and rovers about the country and live in idleness, and pilfer and misbehave generally?

Answer. No, sir.

Question. Why not?

Answer. Because they have all been used to work, and will work if they can get anything to do.

Question. Do they not want to go away from the old places where they have been accustomed to live and go off west somewhere?

Answer. No, sir; we want to stay in our old neighborhoods, but those of us who have gone away are not allowed to go back. In Surrey county they are taking the colored people and tying them up by the thumbs if they do not agree to work for six dollars a month; they tie them up until they agree to work for that price, and then they make them put their mark to a contract.

Question. Did you ever see a case of that kind?

Answer. Yes, sir, I did.

Question. How many cases of that kind have you ever seen?

Answer. Only one; I have heard of several such, but I have only seen one.

Question. What is the mode of tying up by the thumbs?

Answer. They have a string tied around the thumbs just strong enough to hold a man's weight, so that his toes just touch the ground; and they keep the man in that position until he agrees to do what they say. A man cannot endure it long.

Question. What other bad treatment do they practice on the blacks? do they whip them?

Answer. Yes, sir; just as they did before the war; I see no difference.

Question. Have you seen them whipped since the war?

Answer. Several times.

Question. By their old masters?

Answer. By the old people around the neighborhood; the old masters get other people to do it.

Question. Do they whip them just as much as they did before the war?

Answer. Just the same; I do not see any alteration in that. There are no colored schools down in Surrey county; they would kill any one who would go down there and establish colored schools. There have been no meetings or anything of that kind. They patrol our houses just as formerly.

Question. What do you mean by patrolling your houses?

Answer. A party of twelve or fifteen men go around at night searching the houses of colored people, turning them out and beating them. I was sent here as a delegate to find out whether the colored people down there cannot have protection. They are willing to work for a living; all they want is some protection and to know what their rights are; they do not know their rights; they do not know whether they are free or not, there are so many different stories told them.

Question. Where did you learn to read?

Answer. I first picked up a word from one and then from another.

Question. Have you ever been at school?

Answer. Never in my life.

Question. Are the black people there anxious for education and to go to school?

Answer. Generally they are; but down in my neighborhood they are afraid to be caught with a book.

WASHINGTON, *February* 3, 1866.

Richard R. Hill (colored) sworn and examined.

By Mr. HOWARD:

Question. Where do you live?

Answer. Hampton, Virginia.

Question. That is where President Tyler used to live?

Answer. Yes, sir.

Question. Did you know him?

Answer. Yes, I knew him pretty well.

Question. Can you read and write?

Answer. Yes, sir.

Question. How old are you?

Answer. About thirty-four years.

Question. Were you ever a slave?

Answer. Yes, sir.

Question. When did you become free?

Answer. When the proclamation was issued. I left Richmond in 1863.

Question. Did you serve in the rebel army?

Answer. No, sir.

Question. Or in the Union Army?

Answer. No, sir.

Question. How do the rebels down there, about Hampton, treat the colored people?

Answer. The returned rebels express a desire to get along in peace if they can. There have been a few outrages out upon the roadside there. One of the returned Union colored soldiers was met out there and beaten very much.

Question. By whom was he beaten?

Answer. It was said they were rebels; they had on Union overcoats, but they were not United States soldiers. Occasionally we hear of an outrage of that kind, but there are none in the little village where I live.

Question. What appears to be the feeling generally of the returned rebels towards the freedmen; is it kind or unkind?

Answer. Well, the feeling that they manifest as a general thing is kind, so far as I have heard.

Question. Are they willing to pay the freedmen fair wages for their work?

Answer. No, sir; they are not willing to pay the freedmen more than from five to eight dollars a month.

Question. Do you think that their labor is worth more than that generally?

Answer. I do, sir; because, just at this time, everything is very dear, and I do not see how people can live and support their families on those wages.

Question. State whether the black people down there are anxious to go to school?

Answer. Yes, sir; they are anxious to go to school; we have schools there every day that are very well filled; and we have night schools that are very well attended, both by children and aged people; they manifest a great desire for education.

Question. Who are the teachers; white or black?

Answer. White, sir.

Question. How are the white teachers treated by the rebels down there?

Answer. I guess they are not treated very well, because they have very little communication between each other. I have not heard of any threatening expression in regard to them.

Question. Did you ever hear any threats among the whites to reduce your race to slavery again?

Answer. They have said, and it seems to be a prevalent idea, that if their representatives were received in Congress the condition of the freedmen would be very little better than that of the slaves, and that their old laws would still exist by which they would reduce them to something like bondage. That has been expressed by a great many of them.

Question. What has become of your former master?

Answer. He is in Williamsburg.

Question. Have you seen him since the proclamation?

Answer. Yes, sir.

Question. Did he want you to go back and live with him?

Answer. No, sir; he did not ask me to go back, but he was inquiring of me about another of his slaves, who was with him at the evacuation of Williamsburg by the rebels.

Question. How do you feel about leaving the State of Virginia and going off and residing as a community somewhere else?

Answer. They do not wish to leave and go anywhere else unless they are certain that the locality where they are going is healthy and that they can get along.

Question. Are they not willing to be sent back to Africa?

Answer. No, sir.

Question. Why not?

Answer. They say that they have lived here all their days, and there were stringent laws made to keep them here; and that if they could live here contented as slaves, they can live here when free.

Question. Do you not think that to be a very absurd notion?

Answer. No, sir; if we can get lands here and can work and support ourselves, I do not see why we should go to any place that we do not want to go to.

Question. If you should stay here, is there not danger that the whites and blacks would intermarry and amalgamate?

Answer. I do not think there is any more danger now than there was when slavery existed. At that time there was a good deal of amalgamation.

Question. Amalgamation in Virginia?

Answer. There was no actual marrying, but there was an intermixture to a great extent. We see it very plainly. I do not think that that troubles the colored race at all.

Question. But you do not think that a Virginia white man would have connexion with a black woman?

357

Answer. I do, sir; I not only think so, but I know it from past experience. It was nothing but the stringent laws of the south that kept many a white man from marrying a black woman.

Question. It would be looked upon as a very wicked state of things, would it not, for a white man to marry a black woman?

Answer. I will state to you as a white lady stated to a gentleman down in Hampton, that if she felt disposed to fall in love with or marry a black man, it was nobody's business but hers; and so I suppose that if the colored race get all their rights, and particularly their equal rights before the law, it would not hurt the nation or trouble the nation.

Question. In such a case do you think the blacks would have a strong inclination to unite with the whites in marriage?

Answer. No, sir; I do not. I do not think that the blacks would have so strong an inclination to unite with the whites as the whites would have to unite with the blacks.


WASHINGTON, D. C., *February 3, 1866.*

Alexander Dunlop (colored) sworn and examined.

By MR. HOWARD:

Question. How old are you?

Answer. Forty-eight years.

Question. Where do you reside?

Answer. In Williamsburg, Virginia. I was born there.

Question. Have you ever been a slave?

Answer. Never, sir.

Question. Are you able to read and write?

Answer. No, sir; I can read some. That was not allowed me there.

Question. Can you read the Bible?

Answer. Yes, sir.

Question. Do you belong to a church?

Answer. Yes; I belong to the First Baptist church of Williamsburg. I am one of the leading men and trustees.

Question. About how many are included in the church?

Answer. Our minutes show seven hundred and thirty-six.

Question. Do you own the church building?

Answer. We do.

Question. Are you a delegate to the President of the United States?

Answer. Yes, sir; I was sent by my people convened at a large mass meeting.

Question. For what purpose?

Answer. My purpose was to let the government know our situation, and what we desire the government to do for us if it can do it. We feel down there without any protection.

Question. Do you feel any danger?

Answer. We do.

Question. Danger of what?

Answer. We feel in danger of our lives, of our property, and of everything else.

Question. Why do you feel so?

Answer. From the spirit which we see existing there every day toward us as freedmen.

Question. On the part of whom?

Answer. On the part of the rebels. I have a great chance to find out these people. I have been with them before the war. They used to look upon me as one of the leading men there. I have suffered in this war; I was driven away from my place by Wise's raid; and so far as I, myself, am concerned, I do not feel safe; and if the military were removed from there I would not stay in Williamsburg one hour, although what little property I possess is there.

Question. In case of the removal of the military, what would you anticipate?

Answer. Nothing shorter than death; that has been promised to me by the rebels.

Question. Do they entertain a similar feeling toward all the freedmen there?

Answer. I believe, sir, that that is a general feeling. I ask them, sometimes, "Why is it? we have done you no harm." "Well," they say, "the Yankees freed you, and now let the Yankees take care of you: we want to have nothing to do with you." I say to them, "You have always been making laws to keep us here, and now you want to drive us away—for what?" They say, "We want to bring foreign immigration here, and drive every scoundrel of you away from here." I tell them that I was born in Virginia, and that I am going to die in Virginia. "There is but one thing that will make me leave Virginia," I say, "and that is, for the government to withdraw the military and leave me in your hands; when it does that, I will go."

Question. Has your property been destroyed by the rebels?

Answer. I had not much, except my blacksmith's shop. I carried on a large business there. The rebels and the northern men destroyed everything I had; what the one did not take, the other did; they did not leave me even a hammer.

Question. Have you a family?

Answer. Yes, sir; a wife, but no children; I bought my wife.

Question. How much did you give for her?

Answer. I gave four hundred and fifty dollars for my wife, and seven hundred dollars for my wife's sister. After I bought my wife, they would not let me set her free. I paid the money, and got the bill of sale.

Question. What hindered her being free?

Answer. It was the law, they said. She had to stand as my slave.

Question. How extensive is this feeling of danger on the part of colored people there?

Answer. I believe, sincerely, that it is the general feeling.

Question. Did you ever see a black rebel, or hear of one?

Answer. I must be honest about that. I believe that we have had some as big rebel black men as ever were white.

Question. Many?

Answer. No, sir; they are "few and far between;" but I believe that any man who, through this great trouble that we have had, would do anything to stop the progress of the Union army, was a rebel. When Wise made his raid into Williamsburg, I just had time to leave my house and make my escape. They broke up everything I had; they took their bayonets and tore my beds all to pieces. All they wanted was Aleck Dunlop; they wanted to hang him before his own door. One day, since the fall of Richmond, I met General Henry A. Wise at Norfolk. He spoke to me, and asked me how I was. I said, "I am doing a little better than could be expected." Said he, "Why?" Said I, "Them devils of yours did not catch me; I was too smart for them that morning." "Do you think," said he, "they would have hurt you?" "No," said I, "I don't think so, but I know it; they had orders to hang me."

Question. Did Wise admit it?

Answer. He did not say so; but he turned and went off. The day that Wise's men were there, my wife asked them what had I done that they wanted to hang me in preference to anybody else? They said it was because I was a Union man. I had worked for the rebels from the time the war broke out until General McClellan moved up; and then they concocted a scheme to get me to Richmond; but when I saw the wagon coming for me, I went off in the opposite direction. When General Hooker and General Kearney came there, they sent for me, within three hours of their arrival, and asked me about the country, and what I knew. I gave them all the information I could; that, through a colored friend, got to the secessionists and imbittered them against me. The next Union officer who came there was Colonel Campbell, of the 5th Pennsylvania cavalry; and I believe he was as great a rebel as Jeff. Davis. He was governor there for a long time. They captured him, and carried him to Richmond.

Question. The rebels never caught you?

Answer. They have never caught me yet.

Question. How do the black people down there feel about education?

Answer. They want it, and they have a desire to get it; but the rebels use every exertion to keep teachers from them. We have got two white teachers in Williamsburg, and have got to put them in a room over a colored family.

Question. Do the black people contribute liberally to the support of their own schools?

Answer. They are not able, sir. The rebels made many raids there, and destroyed everything they could get their hands on belonging to colored people—beds and clothing.

Thomas Bain (colored) sworn and examined.
  By MR. HOWARD:
Question. Where do you reside?
Answer. Norfolk, Virginia.
Question. How old are you?
Answer. I think about forty.
Question. Have you ever been a slave?
Answer. Yes.
Question. When were you made free?
Answer. When emancipation came, I was in Massachusetts; I had got there on the underground railroad. I went back to Virginia after the proclamation, and sent my child away to Massachusetts; I have been down there ever since.
Question. Can you read and write?
Answer. Yes, sir.
Question. Can you write a letter on business?
Answer. Yes, sir.
Question. Can you read the Bible?
Answer. Yes, sir.
Question. And newspapers?
Answer. Yes, sir; I subscribe to newspapers.
Question. What is your business?
Answer. Dentist.
Question. Did you ever start to be a dentist?
Answer. Yes, sir; I was raised in the business.
Question. Where?
Answer. In Norfolk. I spent ten years at it in Norfolk, and ten years in Massachusetts.
Question. Have you a family?
Answer. My wife died some time after I was married; I have one child—a daughter.
Question. Are you here as a delegate from the colored people of Norfolk?
Answer. Yes, sir.
Question. To make representations to the President?
Answer. Yes, sir.
Question. Have you had an interview with him?
Answer. No, sir.

361

Question. What is the feeling on the part of white rebels at Norfolk towards the colored people?

Answer. Their feelings are very hard—terrible. I have had a chance to travel around some, preaching.

Question. Do you preach?

Answer. Yes, sir; I am a volunteer missionary—a self-sustaining one. The church, under whose auspices I act, is not taxed for my services; neither are the people; I make my practice as I go along; just enough to support me; I can reach most of them in that way; I have a permanent office; and then I travel about the State and preach.

Question. To what denomination do you belong?

Answer. The Wesleyan Methodist.

Question. You preach to the colored people?

Answer. Yes; I have had occasion, of course, to visit a great many.

Question. How are the black people treated in Virginia by the whites since the close of hostilities?

Answer. The only hope the colored people have is in Uncle Sam's bayonets; without them, they would not feel any security; and what is true of the colored people in that respect, is also true of the Union men; the secessionists do not seem to discriminate between them; they do not seem to care whether a northern man is with us or not with us; if he is a Yankee, that is enough; they hardly wait to examine what his views are; it is not uncommon to hear such threats as this: "We will kill one negro, at least, for every rebel soldier killed by them."

Question. Did you, yourself, ever hear such a threat as that made?

Answer. I have heard it at night, in the streets of Norfolk. (Witness related some incidents going to show how much afraid the colored people there are of ill treatment from the whites.) Last June there was a threat by a white citizen of Norfolk to get up a riot.

Question. Did he get one up?

Answer. Yes; they got one up.

Question. What did it result in?

Answer. It resulted in three colored men being shot. One white man got shot through the shoulder; had his arm amputated, and died. It was got up to attack the colored people, and clear all the negroes out of the city.

Question. Are the colored people whipped now as they used to be?

Answer. Not in my vicinity; I only hear reports of that.

Question. Have you heard of cases of whipping by white men?

Answer. Yes, sir.

Question. During the summer?

Answer. Yes, sir.

Question. Many cases?

Answer. Yes, sir; and it is not so much that the colored people are afraid of the white people, as it is that they are a law-abiding people.

Question. Do they submit to be whipped?

Answer. They do, in places near where there are military men. They fool the colored people into believing that the military ordered them to be whipped; they do not want to resist the government.

Question. Are the black people down there fond of education?

Answer. I think that they are excelled by no people in an eagerness to learn.

WASHINGTON, *February* 3, 1866.

Edmund Parsons (colored) sworn and examined.

By MR. HOWARD:

Question. How old are you?

Answer. A little over fifty.

Question. Where do you reside?

Answer. In Williamsburg, Virginia.

Question. Can you read and write?

Answer. I can read a little. I have been a regular house-servant, and I had a chance to turn my attention to it.

Question. Have you ever been a slave?

Answer. Yes, sir. I have been a slave from my childhood up to the time I was set free by the emancipation proclamation.

Question. How do the black people in your neighborhood feel toward the rebels?

Answer. I did think myself always secure with the whites; but it is very different now sir, very different.

Question. Do you stand in fear of them?

Answer. Yes, sir.

Question. What have you to be afraid of?

Answer. When the Union forces came there first a good many officers became attached to me and my wife, and we felt perfectly secure; but now the rebels use the officers that are there "to pull the chestnuts out of the fire."

Question. Have you heard threats of violence by white rebels against the blacks?

Answer. Yes.

Question. What do they threaten to do?

Answer. They threaten to do everything they can. My wife died about a year ago. I had a house, where I had been living for twenty years. A lawyer there went and got the provost marshal to send a guard and put me out of my house. They broke my things up, and pitched them out, and stole a part of them.

Question. The Union guard?

Answer. Yes, sir; it is a positive fact. They put me out of my own house. That was January, 1865.

363

Question. What was the pretext for putting you out?

Answer. My wife had been left free. She had a half-sister and a half-brother; and they pretended to be owners of the property where I had been living all my lifetime.

Question. Who was the provost marshal?

Answer. Reynolds.

Question. Do the returned rebels threaten to commit violence on the colored people there?

Answer. I can hear people complaining of that; but I have really been so mortified at the bad treatment I received, that I have not paid much attention.

Question. How do the colored people feel in regard to education?

Answer. They are very anxious to get education, and feel grateful for it.

Question. Are you a member of a church?

Answer. Yes, sir. I have been deacon of the Baptist church for years. It is pretty much my living.

Question. Are you willing to go away and leave old Virginia?

Answer. No, sir.

Question. Why not?

Answer. I would rather stay in Virginia.

# Index

368